ADOPTING BIOMETRIC TECHNOLOGY

Challenges and Solutions

ADOPTING BIOMETRIC TECHNOLOGY

Challenges and Solutions

Ravindra Das

CRC Press
Taylor & Francis Group
Boca Raton London New York

CRC Press is an imprint of the
Taylor & Francis Group, an **informa** business

CRC Press
Taylor & Francis Group
6000 Broken Sound Parkway NW, Suite 300
Boca Raton, FL 33487-2742

First issued in paperback 2020

ISBN-13: 978-1-4987-1744-1 (hbk)
ISBN-13: 978-0-367-59702-3 (pbk)

Visit the Taylor & Francis Web site at
http://www.taylorandfrancis.com

and the CRC Press Web site at
http://www.crcpress.com

*This book is dedicated to the loving memory of Dr. Morgan Deters.
Your spirit has been a guiding influence in my
life, and will be so in the coming future.*

Contents

SECTION II   TWO WORLDWIDE IMPLEMENTATIONS OF BIOMETRIC TECHNOLOGY

Preface

This book, *Adopting Biometric Technology: Challenges and Solutions,* was specifically written about how to increase the adoption rate of biometric technologies. There are many security technologies out there, but biometrics is one of the latest and cutting-edge technologies to come out onto the marketplace.

This type of technology is often viewed with awe, mystique, curiosity, hesitancy, as well as a poor understanding. It is even viewed more as a "black box" type of security technology. Compared to the other security technologies on a spectrum, biometric technology is more prone to social implications. For example, if you were to examine a router or a firewall, you would not give too much thought to it. It would simply be installed at the place of business or organization, and assumed as well that it will do its job to filter out the bad data packets and keep out the cyber attackers. However, if you were to look at or further examine a biometric technology (such as a fingerprint recognition device or a facial recognition camera), there would be many more questions asked about them.

This is because a snapshot of our physiological/biological or behavioral selves is being captured in order to confirm our identity. No other security technology does this, except biometrics. That is why its adoption rate and its usage vary greatly around the world.

For example, in developing nations (such as those in Asia, Africa, and Eastern Europe), biometric technology is a popular tool. The primary reason for this is that each and every individual can be counted as a citizen by his or her own government. Thus, he or she is now able to receive the entitlements and the benefits to which he or she is entitled to, which he or she received before. Now, an audit trail can be created to help ensure that every individual receives his or her fair share.

However, the adoption rate of biometric technology is very poor in developed nations, such as the United States. The primary reason for this is that we are guaranteed (at least in theory) that we will be recognized by our own Federal Government and have assurances that we will receive our entitlements and benefits.

We have the luxury of taking our freedoms and liberties for granted because of this, and we can contest the mandated usage of biometric technology by claiming that it is a sheer violation of both our privacy rights and civil liberties.

Thus, it is the goal of this book to further examine why the adoption rate of biometric technologies is so great in some parts of the world and so poor in others. This will be examined through the use of various case studies as well as ascertaining both deployment and social methods that have worked and those that have not worked. In particular, the e-passport, the national identification card, as well as the e-voting infrastructures will be examined and reviewed.

Finally, conclusions will be drawn and recommendations will be made as to how the adoption rate of biometrics can be greatly improved upon. This is ultimately the bigger aim of this book—to improve the implementation rate of biometric technologies in geographic areas of the world where it has been least accepted, especially the United States.

STRUCTURE OF THIS BOOK

This book is divided into the following sections and chapters:

- Section I—*The Social Barriers Affecting the Adoption Rate of Biometric Technology*: This section discusses the key lessons learned and provides a general overview of the concepts that are fundamental to understanding the issues surrounding the adoption of biometric technology, from both a technical and a social perspective. It also reviews the specific reasons why the adoption rate of biometric technology is so low in the United States in comparison to the rest of the world. It consists of the following chapters:
  - Chapter 1: *Introduction*
    It is important to note many of the concepts I will review in this chapter, which serve as a backdrop for what will be covered in later chapters, were drawn from my first book, *Biometric Technology: Authentication, Biocryptography, and Cloud-Based Architecture*,* which examined and reviewed the foundation, science, and technologies behind biometrics. A more comprehensive list of what was covered in my first book can be found in "Further Reading" at the end of this book.
  - Chapter 2: *The Social Barriers Affecting the Adoption Rate of Biometric Technology in the United States*

---

* R. Das. *Biometric Technology: Authentication, Biocryptography, and Cloud-Based Architecture*, CRC Press, Boca Raton, FL, pp. 329–354, 2014.

- Section II—*Two Worldwide Implementations of Biometric Technology*
Case Studies and Real Life Implementations of Actual Biometric Implementations: This section examines the actual case studies of various biometric applications that have been implemented worldwide and how a higher adoption rate can be achieved in the regions where the usage is low, such as the United States. It consists of the following chapters:
  - Chapter 3: *Biometrics and the e-Passport*
  - Chapter 4: *Biometrics and e-Voting*
- Section III—*How the Adoption and Usage Rates Can Be Increased in the United States*: This section pitches the potential end user of biometric technology (especially the C-level executive) how and why it is important to utilize biometric technology. For example, why should biometric technology be applied when it is so controversial in comparison to other noncontroversial security technologies that exist in the marketplace? In other words, a more clear picture of the value and practicality of what biometric technology actually has to offer to both the C-level executive and the place of business or organization, and the specific ways in which it can be realistically applied are also examined. This section consists of the following chapter:
  - Chapter 5: *Strategies for Increasing the Adoption Rate of Biometrics in the United States*

Ravindra Das
BiometricNews.Net, Inc.

Acknowledgments

First and foremost, I thank Jennifer Abbott for her help in the completion of this book. I also acknowledge the work of Anita Das, Mary Hanlon Bhalla, Dennis Johnting, Willy Miranda and his family, the First United Methodist Church of Bensenville (Bensenville, IL), the members at the Rev3 Innovation Center, the members and staff at the Naperville Community Career Center (Naperville, IL), Erskine Fred, and Nasser Ghazi.

Author

Ravindra Das, MS, MBA, is the owner of BiometricNews.Net, Inc., a technical communications and biometrics consultancy firm based out of Chicago, Illinois. He has been a technical writer for more than 15 years, and has published worldwide. His first book (*Biometric Technology: Authentication, Biocryptography, and Cloud-Based Architecture*, 2014) was also published by CRC Press. He is currently working on his third book (*Biometric Software Development, Customization, and Application: Security Technology In Practice*, CRC Press, forthcoming).

The Social Barriers Affecting the Adoption Rate of Biometric Technology

section 1

The Social Barriers Affecting the Adoption Rate of Biometric Technology

CHAPTER **1**

Introduction

I'd like to begin with an overview of some of the key concepts of biometric technology, specifically the key social and technical implications of its use. Just a quick disclaimer, much of what I will cover in this chapter is derived from my first book, *Biometric Technology: Authentication, Biocryptography, and Cloud-Based Architecture,*[*] as it presents very important lessons to be learned and applied about biometric technology. (For more information about *Biometric Technology*, please see the "Further Reading" section at the end of this book.)

THE SOCIAL AND TECHNICAL IMPLICATIONS OF BIOMETRIC TECHNOLOGY

Probably, one of the most fundamental issues surrounding the creation, development, and deployment of biometric technology is its societal impacts on citizens of each and every country. For instance, when biometric technology is viewed on a spectrum in comparison with other security-related technologies, it is often viewed with awe, surprise, wonderment, confusion, fear, bewilderment, and probably most of all, a total lack of understanding as to what the technology can do.

Why is this the case? Well, unlike other security-related technologies, a piece of our biological/physiological or behavioral self is captured and analyzed via a series of mathematical algorithms, and from there, our identity is either confirmed or rejected.

However, this is not the case with security-related technologies, such as firewalls, routers, encryption devices, network intrusion devices, and anti-spyware/malware/adware software. In all of these cases, the only input that is needed is simply the monitoring of network traffic and data packets.

Therefore, as one can see, with biometric technology, not only computerized information and data are needed, but also the human input. This is what gives it both its anonymous and dark side. For instance,

---

[*] R. Das. *Biometric Technology: Authentication, Biocryptography, and Cloud-Based Architecture*, CRC Press, Boca Raton, FL, pp. 329–354, 2014.

3

when installing a router or a firewall into a network topology, the network administrator does not think twice as to what the impacts of it will be to the end user.

All he or she needs to think of is how best that particular security device can protect the information technology (IT) assets of the business or organization.

However, the situation of a biometric system administrator is a totally different issue. First, not only does he or she have to actually install the particular device, but he or she also needs to make sure that it is compatible to both the IT and the network environment of the particular place of business or organization. Second, from a technical perspective, there are a lot of other issues to be addressed. For instance, where will the biometric templates be stored at? Will they require their own dedicated database server, or can they just simply be stored in a particular instance of that database server (i.e., can the biometric templates reside with other types of information and data)?

Also, as the biometric system is finally installed, will it be able to share the same network medium with other IT assets as well? Or will specialized networking be required?

Other technical considerations include where the actual verification and/or identification of the individual will take place. For example, will this occur within the actual biometric device itself (also known as "local authentication") or at the server level (also known as "client–server-based authentication")?

Also, because there is no such thing as two identical biometric templates, at what particular level will the security threshold be set at? For example, if the threshold is set too high, there will be a high probability that there could be a high percentage in the false acceptance rate (also known as the "FAR" metric). This simply means that a legitimate employee will not be granted access to the place of business or organization.

Or, if the security threshold is set too low, there is also a distinct possibility that a high percentage in the false rejection rate (also known as the "FRR" metric) could occur. This is the total opposite of the FAR, in that an unauthorized person could gain access to the place of business or organization.

However, it is important to keep in mind that over time, and with proper planning, most of the technical issues surrounding the procurement and deployment of a biometric system can be resolved. As alluded to in earlier discussion, unlike other security technologies, biometrics has a very strong social impact as well. These also need to be taken into consideration by the biometric system administrator, as the system is being installed and implemented. These social issues surrounding biometric technology are much harder to resolve than the technical issues.

For example, how will the employees of the business or organization be trained into using the newly implemented biometric system? After all, if a chief executive officer (CEO) expects to get the full cooperation of their employees, they will need to be thoroughly trained in how to properly use it. After all, there is a strong correlation between in-depth training and increased acceptance of a biometric system by end users.

Also, another strong social issue to be taken into account is what if the employees at the place of business or organization simply object to having a snapshot of their biological/physiological or behavioral self from being taken? Will another backup system be put into place so that their identities can be confirmed?

Other serious social issues include end users objecting to use a biometric system based upon religious beliefs. How would a CEO deal with this? It would be a very difficult as well as very touchy issue if this were to happen at their business or organization. Of course, he or she would have to do everything in their power to respect the wishes of their employees in question, unless they wanted to be faced with a major lawsuit. Interestingly enough, these kinds of social issues transpire for the most part in those geographic regions of the world, which are developed in terms of economic growth and conservative in cultural beliefs, such as in the United States.

These are just some of the general issues which biometric technology and the biometrics industry face as a whole. Some of these are both technical and social in nature, but at this point, it is important to review them. They will lay down the foundation for the rest of other chapters in this book.

There are two types of biometric technologies (also known as "modalities") which are available today: physical and behavioral. The former refers to examining the unique features of our biological or physiological selves, and the latter refers to extracting our unique behavioral mannerisms. From this, the physical biometrics is the most prone to public scrutinization and lack of acceptance, especially facial recognition.

For example, this particular modality can be used very covertly, without public knowledge or awareness. It can also be used in conjunction with closed-circuit television (CCTV) camera technology. One of the most controversial applications of facial recognition came at a time when it was used to track suspects and wanted felons at major music venues in the United States, with the most recent occurrence in Boston, Massachusetts.

Other countries have followed suit in this regard, with Brazil using facial recognition to further enhance security at the World Cup and Australia using the modality at its major sporting events, and its usage is even further supported by the Football Federation Australia.

In terms of another technical aspect, there are serious issues being raised if biometric technology can truly confirm the identity of a particular individual at a 100% confidence level. Biometric technology is not perfect—it has its fair share of flaws just like any other security technology. In this regard, it is fingerprint recognition which has received probably some of the harshest reviews and criticisms for its true effectiveness.

For instance, depending upon the durability of the optic sensor and how "oily" the end user's fingerprints are, a latent residue of the actual fingerprint can actually be left behind. From this, it is quite possible that a fingerprint image can be reconstructed again. In theory, the entire fingerprint image does not need to be reconstructed, but just some of the unique features so that it can literally "spoof" a fingerprint recognition system.

The biometric vendors claim that a fingerprint recognition system cannot be spoofed, because a live sample (i.e., a fingerprint image is presented to the sensor from a living human being) is required. However, research conducted from leading institutions has proven that the opposite can actually happen.

For example, faculty from the department of computer science at Michigan State University released a paper called "From Template to Image: Reconstructing Fingerprints from Minutiae Points,"[*] as to how theoretically, a fingerprint recognition system can be tricked into accepting a spoofed fingerprint image.

At the present time, there is a lot of research and development going on for various biometric technologies that could potentially be used in the future. Some of the technologies of potential biometric modalities include the following:

- *Earlobe recognition*: This is essentially in many ways similar to that of hand geometry recognition, in that it is the unique shape and geometry of the earlobe which is being examined. Studies have shown preliminary results that each and every individual possesses some sort of unique earlobe structure.
- *Gait recognition*: This potential biometric technology examines the way in which an individual walks. Rather than looking at the entire, aggregate walking stride, only several elements are studied. For instance, only movements of the knee may be examined, or certain lengths and distances might be looked at (this would include the distance between the knee and the ankle region, the distance between the buttocks and the knee,

---

[*] A.A. Ross, J. Shah, and A.K. Jain. Toward reconstructing fingerprints from minutiae points. In *Proc. SPIE 5779, Biometric Technology for Human Identification II*, SPIE, Orlando, FL, pp. 68–80, April 5, 2005.

etc.). The unique features that are extracted include the lengths (as just described), the angles, and the speeds our strides possess.

- *Deoxyribonucleic acid (DNA) recognition*: This futuristic biometric modality, if it ever becomes feasible, will be considered the most reliable ever, even more so than that of iris recognition or retinal recognition. This is so because the DNA structure possesses the most unique biological and physiological characteristics of the human body. The DNA strand consists of the following four nucleotides:
  - Guanine
  - Thymine
  - Adenine
  - Cytosine

With regard to these three potential biometric modalities, there is a lot of controversy on both the technical side and the social impacts side. For example, from within the biometrics industry itself, there are many leaders who feel that there is no need to spend critical research and development funds on developing these futuristic biometric technologies if there is not much potential for them to ever become viable in large-scale applications.

With regard to these three potential modalities, gait recognition has held the most promise thus far. If DNA recognition ever proves to be a viable biometric technology, this would be the most prone to social issues. This is so because the testing process involved for DNA samples is a very intrusive process to the individual, and very often it has a very negative connotation with both forensics and law enforcement (in a manner very similar to that of facial recognition).

Very often, a blood or saliva sample is required, thus escalating the public negativity of it even more. Also, at the present time, DNA analysis can take days or even weeks to complete. This time frame has to come down to just 1 or 2 seconds in order to confirm the identity of an individual in any type of application setting.

Biometric templates are merely nothing but mathematical representations of the biological/physiological or behavioral samples that are extracted from us. Therefore, for example, an image of the unique features of either our hand or our finger would be represented as a binary mathematical file, which is nothing but a long string of zeroes and ones: 00010101010000111111101010. Other biometric technologies, such as iris recognition, rely upon more complex mathematics, such as vector spaces and Gabor wavelets. The behavioral-based biometric technologies often rely upon the creation of statistical-based profiles to represent a newly created biometric template. For example, the distinct mannerism of how we type on a computer keyboard is often represented with a technique known as "hidden Markov models."

However, despite the fact that not the actual biological/physiological or behavioral image is stored in the database of a biometric system but only the mathematical representation is, there is still a greatly heightened fear among the public that if a particular template is hijacked or tampered with, it would lead to identity theft.

The primary reason why this fear is prevalent is that the public is simply not educated enough to understand what a biometric template is truly composed of. There is a high probability of identity theft occurring with a stolen credit card number than with a stolen biometric template.

We also reviewed in some detail various best practices and key performance indicators (KPIs) as set forth by the U.S. federal government. Some of these include the "Biometric Data Interchange Formats," the "Common Biometric Exchange Formats Framework" (also known as "CBEFF"), the Biometric Technical Interface Standards (in particular, the BioAPI specification was closely examined), as well as various testing standards.

Although it is quite advantageous and beneficial to have these sets of biometric standards and best practices, people in the biometrics industry and other biometrics-based consultants feel that many of these established policies are too confusing, complex, laborious to understand, and just too theoretical to be implemented in any type of real-world security applications.

Also, another serious issue is that many of the other industrialized nations (particularly those in Europe) have also created their own set of biometrics-based best practices and KPIs, which simply do not match up with what the United States has. There have been many calls for creating a universally common set of best practices, standards, and KPIs, which could be used by all of the biometric vendors worldwide for many different biometric products and solutions.

However, so far, this has not existed, and any efforts taken to create have culminated in very long time lags and delays. In many of the traditional biometric modalities, including both the physiological- and behavioral-based ones, direct contact with the technology is required. For instance, if fingerprint recognition were being used, direct contact of the fingertip is required on top of the optical-based sensor.

The only exceptions to this direct contact are facial recognition and iris recognition, where a specialized camera takes the picture, and from there, the unique features are then extracted. Voice recognition is also included in this particular mix, as the end user merely has to recite a passage or a phrase into an audio receiver.

The main issue with direct contact is that of hygiene. To date, there has been no known medical cases where an end user has actually contracted a disease or an ailment from contact to a sensor. However, still this issue pervades the public in general. To help alleviate this situation, biometric vendors suggest specific guidelines and recommendations as to how to best maintain the biometric sensor in this regard. Despite all of these, the emerging trend now in the biometrics industry is to develop and create technology that does not require any direct contact. The best example of this is vein pattern recognition, one of the newest modalities available.

With this, all an end user has to do is to merely position his or her finger or palm on top of a specialized sensor. From there, an infrared beam of light is shot, and the vein pattern structure is thus illuminated. The sensor then captures this structure, and the unique features are subsequently captured.

This contactless technology is now starting to gain popularity, in terms of both geographic regions (especially that of the Pacific Rim, such as Japan) and market applications (the health-care sector). At one time in the last decade, iris recognition was even deemed to be too user invasive to be utilized in mass market applications.

However, because of this change now toward no contact with the sensor, the public is accepting it more and, in fact, it is becoming much more appealing. Probably, the biggest social issue and concern that remains about biometric technology is that its whole concept is a total violation of privacy rights and civil liberties. Although this is an issue that is worldwide, its magnitude as well as its depth greatly depend upon the geographic region which is being examined. Interestingly enough, there is a correlation that exists here.

Consider the United States as an example. The citizens of this country are endowed with certain, inalienable rights guaranteed to them by their very own Constitution. For example, we have the rights to privacy and to pursue and conduct activities in any manner we choose to, as long as it does not impede upon the rights of others or does not violate the law.

Since biometric technology does indeed take a snapshot of our biological/physiological and behavioral selves, the American public often views this as personal violation. Many times, we do not have much of a choice whether to use a biometric system, especially if an employer or the government mandates its use.

As a result, this further fuels the public stigma and negativity toward the use and adoption of biometric technology. Also, as citizens of the United States, we are guaranteed of being, for the most part, recognized as individuals in the eyes of our own federal government. On account of this, we do have some guarantees and assurances that we will receive any entitlements and any types/kinds of benefits (such as social security) that we are allowed to receive.

Now let us transit over to a country where the citizens are not so lucky and which is underdeveloped. An example of this kind of geographic region is found in Africa, Asia, and some parts of the Middle East. The citizens of these nations are not even recognized by their own governments. Whatever entitlements and benefits they are deserved to receive, they often do not; the money often goes back into the crooked hands of their respective governments.

This is where biometric technology has literally become a "savior" for them. By being enrolled into a biometric system, there is now a much higher probability that these citizens will finally be recognized as individuals, because there is now an electronic audit trail that is associated with their particular biometric template, not a paper one that can be very easily destroyed and forgotten by a government official. This template gives the citizens of these underdeveloped and corrupt nations the chance to vote, receive medical insurance, ensure their proper ration of food supplies, and so on.

Another gargantuan social issue faced by the American public with regard to biometric technology is its covert nature. Obviously, the contactless modalities cannot be covert, but the non-contactless ones such as facial recognition and iris recognition can become very covert. For instance, these two technologies are very often used in mass applications, such as sporting events, music concerts, and international airports. The cameras that are installed based on these two technologies can be very covertly placed at very strategic locations without the slightest knowledge of the public. This is best exemplified with facial recognition.

This modality can now be used in conjunction with CCTV camera technology, to add an extra level of sophistication. For example, not only can the traditional image or video of a particular individual be captured, but they can now be transmitted to the facial recognition component in real time in order to ascertain the true identity of the individual. Before this, a security official or system administrator would have to make this determination based upon his or her own level of experience and the records as well as databases that are available to him or her by law enforcement agencies.

One of the best examples of this modality is the vast and complex system of CCTV cameras that are dispersed throughout the streets of London. At just about every corner and traffic light intersection, there is a CCTV camera using facial recognition technology to keep tabs on the people there. Even here, there have been many outcries by the U.K. population that these cameras are, once again, a sheer violation of privacy rights and civil liberties.

However now, here comes the flip side of the equation. With this enormous network of sophisticated CCTV cameras, Scotland Yard can now capture and apprehend any known criminals or terror suspects they are after, literally within a few days. This is best exemplified by the July 7, 2005, bombings, which transpired in the London Underground train system.

Four British Islamic extremists were blamed for this, and after a few days of examining the video footage, many arrests were made in connection with these bombings. Therefore, this brings up one of the most fundamental social issues surrounding the use of biometric technology.

The trade-off between the violation of privacy rights and the civil liberties and security advantages it brings helps in apprehending terror suspects, such as the ones associated with train bombings in London. Another social issue related to privacy rights and civil liberties is that of the fear of the federal government itself, and what they can and will do with the biometric templates of the American citizens it possesses.

Currently, not only is the federal government currently the biggest customer of the biometrics industry, but it also houses some of the world's largest biometric template databases in the world. A prime example of this is the "next-generation identification," which is currently managed by the Federal Bureau of Investigation (FBI).

The primary objective of this new database is to replace its aging one, known as the "Integrated Automated Fingerprint Identification System." This database consists of iris recognition-, fingerprint recognition-, as well as palm recognition-based biometric templates. It also stores latent fingerprint biometric templates as well as mug shots of individuals and their associated tattoo images. These bits of information and data are stored very covertly, and truthfully speaking, nobody really understands how the federal government uses these biometric templates, except for the personnel that manage them. On account of the lack of these facts, the American public is often fearful that the federal government is watching them behind their backs, thus giving more credence to Orwellian concept that "Big Brother Is Watching You."

One of the major obstacles in the adoption rate of biometric technology, at least in the United States, has been the sheer lack of training to the end user on how to properly use a modality. This, of course, depends upon both the type and the magnitude of the biometrics application that is being deployed. For instance, a Fortune 500 company with a high enough budget could probably afford to hire a biometrics vendor to do literally everything from the beginning to the end.

This would include conducting a feasibility study of the existing security environment, deciding which biometric modality would work best based upon the requirements of the place of business or organization, actually installing and implementing the system, and finally conducting end user training. Now, of course, the budget of a small to medium-sized business (SMB) is much smaller, and all they could probably budget out is just the procurement and deployment of the biometric technology.

The business owner(s), or the upper level management, will be left to their own guises to conduct this much needed training to their employees. Since the level of training will not be of high caliber as that by a biometric vendor, frustration could arise with employees after they start using the biometric system. For example, the employees may not know or fully understand how to properly place their fingerprint onto an optical sensor in order to get a correct read.

This process may have to be repeated many times until it is done properly, thus increasing the aggravation of the employee. Eventually, the word would get around through gossip and rumors that the newly implemented biometric system does not work properly, and the business owner(s) will be forced to implement a new, manual-based security system in order to fully confirm the identity of that particular employee.

This is simply another capital expenditure that could have been avoided if proper training would have been provided to the employees of the business or organization. There is movement in the biometrics industry, at least in the United States, to incorporate end user training as part of the total biometrics implementation package, and not just as a separate component.

However, unfortunately, in the United States, the good which biometrics brings out is very often not relayed to the public via the American Press, which just happens to be the main conduit for relaying such type of news and information. Very often, just the negative news about biometrics is reported, with the prime tactic being, of course, to increase the readership of both the online and print versions of the major newspapers.

Some typical market applications in which biometric technology has been used successfully are as follows:

- *The current war on terrorism*: Ever since the tragic events of 9/11, biometric technology has played a very crucial role in this theater of operation. For instance, the major biometric modalities of facial recognition, iris recognition, fingerprint recognition, hand geometry recognition, and even vein pattern recognition have all been used either separately or in some sort of combination with each other in order to help positively identify terror suspects and bring them to some sort of defined level of justice.

  Unfortunately, there has been quite a bit of controversy surrounding the use of biometric technology at Guantanamo Bay, located in Cuba. Many civil liberty groups feel that the covert use of biometrics should be to keep tabs on suspects after they are released to their home countries.

  Just as it was described previously, the federal government also maintains its own secret biometrics database on these terror suspects, with DNA being one of the primary biometrics that is being stored.

Apart from this, especially in the geographic regions in and around Afghanistan and Iraq, biometric technology is also being used to identify displaced refugees and to give them any type or kind of assistance which is available.

- *Time and attendance applications*: With this, many businesses, especially the SMBs, still use the traditional methods of keeping track of time worked with the traditional punching in and punching out with the time card. Of course, this has many disadvantages with it, especially the following:
  - Inaccurate time reporting.
  - The problem of "buddy punching" (this is where one employee clocks in for another employee, although he or she is absent for his or her scheduled work period, and as a result, he or she still gets paid).
  - Greatly increased administrative costs due to the extra time it takes to process the time cards and human resources-related paperwork.
  - The use of biometric technology greatly simplifies and automates the entire time recording and payroll process. For example, with a simple scan of the hand, fingerprint, iris, face, or even the vein pattern, an employee can very easily clock in and clock out.

    For the administrative personnel, calculating payroll is just as easy as clicking the mouse a few times, because everything, including the biometric templates, is stored electronically.

    This drastically reduces the amount of paperwork needed and the number of people needed to keep track of the time worked and to calculate the payroll. Using biometric technology in this regard also provides an irrefutable audit trail, in case an employee disputes the time he or she has actually worked.

- *Single sign-on solutions*: The combination of both the username and the password has always been the traditional means of security when logging in to secure websites or online portals. The problem with this nowadays is that everyday passwords are being hacked into and hijacked for the purposes of identity theft.

As a result, many of the businesses and organizations are now requiring their employees and even customers to create long and complicated passwords that are very difficult to remember. For example, to create a password, there has to be both uppercase and lowercase letters, punctuation marks, spaces, numbers, and so on.

On account of the complexity involved in creating and remembering these long and complex passwords, both employees and customers are now resorting to writing them down on various types of post-it notes and attaching to their computer monitor. This has been endowed as the "post-it syndrome," thus defeating the initial purpose of the newly created password all together.

Biometric technology has made significant inroads in being the ultimate replacement for passwords. For example, with a scan of your fingerprint or iris, within 2 seconds or less, you can automatically be logged in to your tablet, smartphone, workstation, or even corporate network. As of now, fingerprint recognition is the primary single sign-on solution, and quite surprisingly, the issue of direct contact with the optical sensor is not very much of an issue.

This is probably due to the fact that humans 100% want to eliminate the password is starting now to escalate.

- *Law enforcement*: Biometric technology has always had a long association with law enforcement applications at the federal government level, but it is until recently that it has now started to be used with law enforcement agencies at the local and the county level. Given that the recent advances in biometric technology has now allowed for the modalities to become very small and portable, law enforcement officers can now carry with them portable fingerprint, iris, facial, as well as vein pattern recognition devices.

  For example,

  > Some mobile devices also are capable of obtaining latent fingerprints from crime scenes and of utilizing various card-reading technologies. These devices can transmit biometric data to databases via personal area networks such as Bluetooth, local area networks such as Wi-Fi, wide area networks such as cellular networks, and mobile satellite communication systems .... If a person is identified through mobile biometrics and is known to have a record, an officer may choose a different tactic, technique, or procedure to preclude a physical altercation. Some mobile biometric devices also allow for full bookings in the field and thereby save time and keep officers where they are needed most: in the field.[*]

  However, despite these obvious advantages of using mobile-based biometrics in the field, this is another sore point with both civil liberties groups and law enforcement agencies. This is especially the case with the latter. All an apprehended suspect needs is a good attorney to claim that his or her judicial rights were infringed by the intrusive use of a mobile-based biometric modality.

---

[*] P. Wolfhope. Mobile biometric devices: What the future holds. *The Police Chief*, LXXVIII, no. 9, September 2011. http://www.policechiefmagazine.org/magazine/index.cfm?fuseaction=display_arch&article_id=2476&issue_id=92011.

Another key issue is in the actual definition of what biometrics is really all about. There are two ways in which it can be looked at:

- *The medical definition*: Here, biometrics can be referred to the actual physiological or biological measurements of a particular individual, such as heartbeat, pulse rate, blood pressure level, glucose level, and perspiration level.
- *The technological* (or *computer science-based*) *definition*: The verification or identification of a particular individual based upon either his or her unique biological/physiological characteristics or unique behavioral mannerisms.

On account of these two ways in which biometrics can be looked upon, there is very often fear in the public that a biometric template that has been captured in a totally different application (such as physical access entry) will be automatically tied to their medical data. This is of course totally false.

The only way the biometric template can be associated with an individual's medical records is if they actually were enrolled by a biometric device which was specifically designed to associate that particular template with medical information and data.

There are numerous biometric technologies that are available on the marketplace today. These include the physical biometrics, the behavioral biometrics, and the biometric technologies of the future (the specific modalities that fall under these three categories can be seen at the beginning of this chapter).

There are a lot of major differences between the physical and behavioral biometrics, as well as major factors that need to be taken into consideration when deciding upon whether to use a physical or a behavioral-based biometric technology.

Of course, a lot depends upon the security requirements of the place of business or organization, the environment upon which it will operate in, and whether that particular modality will be used for verification or identification applications.

Also, both the social and technical issues of each biometric technology were reviewed, and they are summarized briefly in the sections that follow.

Physical Biometrics

Fingerprint Recognition

Although it has been claimed throughout the centuries that no two people have the same fingerprints, and that each fingerprint contains distinct enough features, amazingly, there has been no actual scientific proof that this is actually the case. Thus, the uniqueness of fingerprints is in theory only; perhaps that is why there is the distinct possibility that latent fingerprints left on a silicon sensor can perhaps be replicated (at least according to the studies cited earlier in this chapter).

Fingerprint recognition can be considered as one of those "external" types of biometric modalities, that is, the unique features which it possesses are prone to the harshness of the external environment. Thus, over time, the fingerprint can degrade in quality over time, and even perhaps change in appearance. As a result, fingerprint recognition would not work well at all in construction types of settings and applications, or for that matter, in any type of environment where people are exposed to the outdoors for long periods of time in their job functions.

There can be serious, technical issues with taking the snapshot of a fingerprint image and extracting the unique features. For instance, any oils, dirt, or moisture on the fingerprint can impact the extraction process. Also if the end user applies too much pressure on the sensor, or too much rotational pressure (this is where the end user moves his or her finger side to side on the optical sensor rather than just directly placing his or her finger directly onto the optical sensor), a proper fingerprint image may not be collected. This is where end user training serves of great importance, as the employee of the place or business will then learn how to properly place his or her fingerprint onto the optical sensor.

Also, for the longest time, the fingerprint has also been associated with law enforcement agencies, across all levels, including the local, state, and federal branches. Really, if you think about it, the fingerprint is the logo that is most widely used to represent the various law enforcement agencies. On account of this, there is often a correlation with law enforcement agencies, and that law enforcement officials may totally misuse fingerprint recognition technology if they step out of the bounds they are given.

Hand Geometry Recognition

This particular biometric modality, although widely used in warehouse and commercial applications, also suffers from the same types and kinds of technical issues as fingerprint recognition, with regard to the availability of stable, unique features. However, hand geometry recognition has even less unique features than that of the fingerprint. In reality though, no true unique features are actually captured from the hand. Only the unique distances (such as from the knuckles to the palm or from the knuckles to the fingerprints) are captured and utilized.

Just like fingerprint recognition, hand geometry is also considered to be an "external" type of biometric modality. Thus, the actual physical structure of the hand can change greatly over time, thus rendering them totally useless for use by a hand geometry scanner.

Unlike the other full contact biometric modalities, the scanning area of a hand geometry scanner is quite large, in order to fully accommodate the shape of the entire hand. On account of this, there is even a greater chance that more germs, dirt, and so on could be contained onto the scanning area. As a result, there is a greatly heightened fear among the public of contracting a disease or an ailment from the direct contact of a hand geometry scanner (in fact this level of fear is even greater than that of fingerprint recognition).

Vein Pattern Recognition

This type of biometric modality has raised a lot of promises of increased rate of end user adoption and usage. This is because it is a non-contactless type of technology and has a very high rate of perceived ease of use; all that an end user has to do is merely place his or her palm (or even finger) directly over the sensor at a predetermined height, and the image of the vein pattern is captured. Although this non-contactless nature of vein pattern recognition provides its distinct advantages, there are serious concerns raised by professionals in the biometrics industry and even outside of it if an accurate image of the structure of the vein pattern is truly captured.

There is also no hard-core scientific proof yet if there is enough uniqueness in the structure of the vein pattern strong enough to be used in identification types of applications. However, it works well for verification types of scenarios, where not much processing power is required for the mathematical algorithms or database to verify an end user.

Compared to the other biometric technologies, there are hardly any issues associated with privacy rights or civil liberties violations (this is primarily due to both, once again, its non-contactless nature and high level of ease of use).

Palm Print Recognition

This biometric modality, compared to the others, is hardly used or even heard of by the American public. This type of technology can be considered as a subcomponent of hand geometry recognition, in that the surface of the palm can also be considered as a part of the hand. However, for some reason or another, there is a strong association by the public of palm print recognition with certain types of diseases such as Downs syndrome, Aarskog syndrome, and Cohen syndrome. There needs to be more social science research conducted as to why there is a public association with these types of diseases. Perhaps once this is accomplished, the barriers to palm print recognition can be further broken down, and as a result, its wider public acceptance as well as its deployment will occur.

Facial Recognition

Of all the biometric technologies that are available today, it is facial recognition which is the most susceptible to privacy rights and civil liberties issues. Its rate has actually diminished over time, but back in the last decade, it was at all-time highs. After the incidents of 9/11 occurred, facial recognition received all of the hype and attention that it would be the ultimate security solution. Just like the dot-com boom of the late 1990s, the biometrics industry, with facial recognition at the forefront, was experiencing the same type of trend. Venture capitalists were pouring money into the industry, and there emerged a plethora of new biometric vendors. But just like the dot-com boom, the biometrics industry also faced its huge and climactic downturn. For instance, facial recognition simply could not live up to the hype it received. The modality simply did not live up to the performance metrics as it was promised by the biometric vendors. It could neither verify nor identify end users without large FAR as well as FRR. As a result, the media greatly criticized the viability and sustainability of facial recognition as a viable means to track down and capture terror suspects. On account of this, the American public started to have enormous misgivings and a lack of trust about facial recognition, thus triggering its association with privacy rights and civil liberties violations.

With regard to technical issues, facial recognition, compared to other biometric modalities, really does not possess a lot of uniqueness. For example, even members of the same family, even identical twins, can share the same type and kind of facial structure, and features, based upon the DNA which is handed down to the subsequent generations.

The features of the face can change rapidly and drastically over time. For example, an individual can experience rapid weight gain or weight loss, or assume voluntary changes to their facial structure, or the aging process can also affect certain facial features over time. As a result, the face is not really a stable source of unique information and data.

To a much more extreme degree than either fingerprint recognition or hand geometry recognition, the face is very much prone to the harshness and the extremities of the external environment. This can include many factors and variables, such as the weather, or even changes in the lighting conditions, physical ailments caused by being exposed to external sources, and even the wearing of prescription-based eyeglasses and/or contact lenses.

On a social issue note, the use of facial recognition technology is even strictly tabooed in certain cultures. In this regard, the Islamic culture forbids women to have the pictures of their face captured or even looked at. They are often required to wear head scarves, in order to conceal their face. As a result, facial recognition would obviously not work well in this type of environment.

Iris Recognition

Compared to all of the other biometric modalities available, iris recognition, although complex in terms of the technology and the mathematical algorithms incorporated into it, is very easy to use and deploy in both small- and large-scale applications. It is very rich in terms of possessing unique information and data, is stable throughout the lifetime of an individual (i.e., the physiological structure of the iris hardly ever changes), and is not prone to the ruggedness of the external environment; the iris is considered to be an "internal" type of organ. However, in terms of social issues, iris recognition, in the past decade, has suffered its fair share of setbacks. For example, it is just human nature to be very squeamish and even frightened at the thought of this biometric modality capturing an image of one's iris at a very close distance. However, now this fear has greatly dissipated due to the fact that the image of a particular individual's iris can be now captured at a much greater distance. In fact, an end user does not have to be stationary; they can be on the move (such as walking in an airport setting) and still have the image of their iris captured. Although it has the potential to be a social issue, iris recognition can also be used very covertly (in a manner very similar to facial recognition), without the knowledge of the end user.

Retinal Recognition

This particular biometric technology is deemed to be the "ultimate" modality of all. This is because the retina possesses the most unique information and data (except for DNA, as described earlier) on any individual. For instance, scientific studies have proven that even identical twins have different retinal structures. Just like the iris, the retina hardly ever changes during the lifetime of an individual (unless that particular individual suffers from such physical ailments as glaucoma or diabetes), and is also considered to be an "internal" type of biometrics. Retinal recognition suffers from a number of issues, from both the technical and social perspectives. For example, the technology developed for retinal recognition demands that the end user sit at a very close distance to the camera. In fact, the particular individual has to take special efforts in order to place his or her eye into a specially built receptacle. From this point, an infrared beam of light is then flashed toward the eye in order to fully illuminate the retina. This is done in a circular fashion and can take up to 2 minutes to complete. With regard to the social impacts for the individual, that particular person must be extremely cooperative and not move during this scanning time. As a result, the individual feels very constrained in this type of environment, with a high probability that within a minute or so, he or she will become uncooperative. Probably, the most negative social impact retinal recognition possesses is that it is just deemed to be too user invasive to be used in market applications on a large scale. On account of these factors, retinal recognition is only deployed in those conditions where it is absolutely needed—mainly for those areas where extremely high levels of security are required, such as entering a nuclear facility, or even a highly classified military installation point.

Voice Recognition

Compared to other biometric technologies, voice recognition is one of the easiest technologies to not only deploy but also to train an end user on. For example, the only equipment that is really needed in order to capture the unique features is just a receiver, such as that on a landline phone, or even a smartphone. Voice recognition is not at all language dependent; therefore, anybody who has a clear voice should be able to enroll very quickly and easily into a voice recognition system. However, in terms of issues, voice recognition suffers more of them on the technical side than the social aspects. First, the voice does not possess many unique features, such as in comparison with those of the iris or the retina. Second, in a manner similar to that of facial recognition, the quality of the voice can degrade over the lifetime of the individual (any number of factors can affect this aspect, such as medications, any sicknesses or physical ailments, fatigue, or even the emotional state of the end user). Third, the same medium must be used again in order to fully verify the identity of the end user. In other words, if a landline phone receiver is used to extract the unique features of an end user's voice, then the same phone system needs to be used again. Voice recognition does not allow for the interchangeability of the collection medium, a smartphone cannot be used to create the enrollment template, and subsequently a landline phone receiver cannot be used to create the verification template, in order to verify the identity of a particular individual. Fourth, given the dynamic nature of the vocal cords and how it can greatly change, voice recognition is best suited for applications that are verification based, where a large number of end users are involved.

With regard to any social issues surrounding the use of voice recognition, quite surprisingly it is widely accepted by end users in those market applications where it is deployed at.

Behavioral Biometrics

Keystroke Recognition

This particular biometric modality, even more so than voice recognition, is easier to deploy. This is because all that is needed is just a specialized software in order to create the enrollment and verification templates, and also to confirm the identity of a particular individual. The medium to collect the unique features of an end user is any standard computer keyboard, which even includes those found on wireless devices, tablets, netbooks, iPads, and even smartphones. As a result, this key advantage to using keystroke recognition allows it to have a very strong level of end user acceptance. In fact, this modality can even be deemed to be the most accepted compared to all of the biometric technologies, whether it is physical or behavioral based.

However, despite this very strong level of social acceptance, keystroke recognition does suffer from a number of technical issues. First, this modality can only be used for small-scale verification applications, such as verifying the identity of employees in a small business. Second, just like all of the other physical-based biometric technologies, the mannerisms in the way an individual types on a computer keyboard can change greatly over time. These can be based on both physical ailments and mental issues an end user may have. Fourth, although an individual can be theoretically verified using different keyboards, it is highly recommended by the biometrics industry that the exact same keyboard be used in order to minimize any errors (such as a high FAR) in verifying the identity of the end user. Fifth, even though sophisticated statistical profile models are used to create both the enrollment and verification templates, compared to the other biometric modalities, keystroke recognition templates can be very easily spoofed. This is where high levels of encryption are required (this is where the new and emerging field of biocryptography will play a substantial role).

Signature Recognition

It should be noted that signature recognition does not actually examine the signature itself. Rather, it analyzes the unique mannerism in the way the signature is composed. Some of these variables include the downward pressure that is applied from the pen onto the writing tablet (this is considered to be the "sensor" for signature recognition), the level of grip pressure applied by the end user onto the pen, the angle at which the pen is used when the end user signs his or her name, and the total amount of time it takes to complete the entire signature. Other variables can be taken into consideration as well, such as speed, acceleration, any sudden stops or starts when the actual signature is being composed, and any other changes in pressure or speed. However, just like keystroke recognition, signature recognition suffers more technical issues rather than social issues. For instance, signature recognition hardly suffers from any privacy rights or civil liberties violation concerns from the public. It is also a very easy biometric modality to install and deploy, and is deemed to be extremely noninvasive to the end user. Compared to all of the biometric modalities reviewed so far in this chapter, signature recognition does not require any type of end user training, which thus greatly enhances its level of both adoption and acceptance rates by end users. As long as an individual can adequately compose his or her own signature, he or she should be able to use a signature recognition system without any problems whatsoever.

In terms of the technical issues, an end user's signature can vary greatly over time. However, compared to the other biometric modalities (both physical and behavioral), this time span can be very short, within just a few minutes. The same factors that affect keystroke recognition are at play here with signature recognition, such as any physical ailments the end user may be suffering from, or even any mental issues as well. For example, the ability of the end user to properly grip the pen and apply enough downward pressure to create robust enrollment and verification templates could be greatly compromised. Signature recognition templates are also prone to being hijacked and/or even being spoofed, just like the case with keystroke recognition templates. The only way to protect these particular biometric templates is when they are 100% encrypted.

Biometric Technologies in the Future

As mentioned previously, a lot of resources and critical funding are being spent on the research and development of newer biometric technologies. Many industry experts have raised serious concerns about this spending, even if it is worth the effort to conduct all of these research and development activities.

There are many new biometric modalities that are being examined, and they range the extremities that include odor recognition (in other words, confirming the identity of an individual based upon the unique features of his or her particular odor) all the way to brain mapping (this involves taking a snapshot of an individual's brain, mapping the fissures in both the cerebrum and the cerebellum, and from there extracting the unique features to create the respective enrollment and verification templates).

However, there are three main potential modalities that are being examined most closely, and both their technical and social issues will be examined.

DNA Recognition

At the present time, the DNA possesses the richest and most unique information about any individual. For instance, the use of DNA can literally be the "make-or-break" decision in a legal case, and the latent DNA can even be used as evidence in a court of law years later. The integrity and binding structure of DNA is very strong. In fact, if it is proven to be a viable biometric modality, it would then be considered as the "ultimate biometric of all," taking this title now currently held by retinal recognition. However, even if DNA recognition makes its ranks with the other existing biometric modalities, there are a number of both serious technical and social issues it will face.

With regard to the social issues, DNA recognition, in comparison with the other biometric technologies, will be the most susceptible and prone to both privacy rights and civil liberties violation issues. In fact, DNA recognition would even far surpass facial recognition on this point. There has been no social science research conducted into these fears by the public, but a large part of the angst on using DNA recognition stems from two primary areas: (1) Its strong, very negative association with law enforcement and forensics (in a manner very similar to that of fingerprint recognition, as reviewed earlier in this chapter), and (2) an actual blood sample or saliva swab must be used to collect the DNA, even when it is a viable biometric technology. This is totally unlike the other biometric technologies, where only a snapshot of the physiological/biological self is captured. In this regard, DNA recognition can be considered to be an intrusive type of potential biometric technology, whereas the other, existing biometric modalities can be considered to be extrusive in nature.

In terms of technical issues, at the present time, it can take up to 4–5 hours (or even longer, such as days or weeks, if the DNA analysis is complex) to fully break down, analyze, and obtain the results of a DNA test. If DNA recognition is going to be a viable biometric technology, the result of any test has to come down to a matter of just 1 or 2 seconds. This is because the verification and identification times of the other biometric modalities are actually even less than that. In practical market application settings, no business or organization is going to wait for 4–5 hours in order to confirm the identity of just one individual. Also given the extremely, sensitive nature of DNA recognition, very special security protocols will have to be developed in order to protect the DNA recognition templates as they are stored in a database. This could prove to be very costly as well as time consuming.

Gait Recognition

Although this future biometric modality is still under heavy research and development, it promises to hold strong potential as a viable technology. Preliminary research even indicates that if this is truly the case, it would even have very strong levels of end user acceptance, due to its noninvasive nature. However, once it is proven as a viable biometric, it can also be used very covertly in mass application settings, such as those of the international airports, in order to track down known terror suspects.

In terms of technical issues, it is widely anticipated that the quality of the gait recognition templates could degrade over time (but at a rate much slower than the other physical and behavioral modalities) due to physical ailments. Also, the true amount of unique features that can be garnered from gait recognition has not been ascertained yet, and this potential technology prohibits the use of any type or kind of walking aids.

Earlobe Recognition

Compared to both the research and development studies currently being done on DNA recognition and gait recognition, earlobe recognition still lags far behind. The interest of the earlobe possessing unique features dates all the way back to the 1960s. However, if ever proven to be a viable biometric technology, earlobe recognition holds some great potential. For instance, the methodology behind it would be very similar to that of hand geometry recognition, in that the predetermined distance in the actual earlobe would be captured, and from there, the unique features would then be extracted.

In terms of social issues associated with earlobe recognition, at this time, it is highly anticipated that there will not be much of them. This is because no direct contact with the ear will be required; thus, there should be no concerns with regard to privacy rights or civil liberties rights violations.

Although it is exposed to external environment, the earlobe is a physiological structure, which is deemed to be very stable throughout the lifetime of an individual. This simply means that the basic structure of the earlobe does not change significantly. At this point in the research and development, studies show that the only technical issues earlobe recognition faces are degradation to the biometric templates if there are any changes in lighting in the environment from which the image of the earlobe is captured, or if the end user is wearing any jewelry, or wireless components (such as a Bluetooth device) in his or her earlobe subsequently when the verification templates are composed.

Conclusions Drawn from Comparing the Physical and Behavioral Biometrics

As some of the major technical and social issues of all of the biometric modalities available today, as well as those that are planned well into the future, have been summarized and reviewed, a number of key conclusions can be formulated, which are as follows:

1. The physical biometrics seem to be the most widely deployed, and accepted by the public, despite the high level of social controversies they have brought up about.
2. The behavioral biometrics, though not as widely deployed, seem to hold the most potential for end user acceptance and adoption, with very little impact with regard to claims of privacy rights or civil liberties violations.
3. Compared to one another, the physical biometrics pose more technical issues than the behavioral biometrics if they were to be procured and deployed at a place of business or organization.

4. In terms of a cost and capital expenditure standpoint, the behavioral biometrics are much cheaper as well as much less cost prohibitive to deploy than the physical biometrics.

5. Since the physical biometrics are at the forefront of deployment today, this has contributed heavily to the extremely slow adoption rate of biometric technology in the United States and other industrialized parts of the world, given all the social issues it has experienced (especially that of facial recognition).

6. The biometrics industry, at least in the United States, should promote much heavier deployment and usage of the behavioral biometrics. This is because the behavioral biometrics seem to have the much higher rate of end user acceptance, despite its limited market availability. If this were to ever happen, the end result could be that the adoption rate of biometrics in general could greatly increase by the American public.

7. With regard to the social impacts of biometric technology, and as pointed out earlier in this chapter, there is a remarkable difference between the acceptance rates of the developed nations and the developing nations. This is primarily due to the fact that in the United States, the citizens have certain inalienable rights guaranteed to them by their Constitution, which they can use to defend themselves from everything by embracing the use of biometric modalities. However, the citizens of the developing nations do not have such rights endowed onto them by their governments; thus, they heavily embrace the use of biometrics.

8. It is quite possible that as newer biometric modalities are being investigated, the biometrics industry, in the United States, will take into strong consideration the social implications the existing biometric technologies have brought on and design systems that are much more user friendly and will lead to a higher rate of adoption. This is best illustrated by the research and development, which is currently being conducted on gait recognition as well as earlobe recognition. As reviewed, it is highly anticipated that both of these potential technologies will have higher levels of end user acceptance, because they both are noninvasive in nature.

9. The physical biometrics, especially that of fingerprint recognition, hand geometry recognition, vein pattern recognition, and facial recognition, all require higher levels of end user training. If this is not administered properly, the business or organization will experience a much lower rate of adoption among its end users. By sharp contrast, the behavioral biometrics (keystroke recognition and signature recognition) require the least amount of end user training, because typing on a computer keyboard

and signing one's own signature are already inherited traits that have been learned over time.

10. The behavioral biometrics possess a stronger level in terms of ease of use for the individuals utilizing these systems compared to the end users who have to use a physical-based biometric technology.

There are also various key aspects that a C-level executive (such as a chief information officer or a CEO) needs to take into consideration when procuring and deploying a biometric modality at his or her place of business or organization. Some of these crucial factors reviewed include the actual biometric system architecture, the analysis and design process, and the various networking topologies in which a biometric modality can fit into.

Some Key Lessons to Be Learned from Both Technical and Social Perspectives

Most businesses, especially the SMBs, often rely upon just one means of a security defense in order to protect their IT assets. Although this is all that they may be able to truly to afford, having just one means of security of any type (no matter what type of security technology is being employed) is clearly not enough; once that defense perimeter is broken through, all of that entity's IT assets are at great risk. However, with multiple layers of defense, that perimeter is not so easily broken through.

In fact, many people feel that by just using biometrics as their sole means of protection, they will be safe. However, this is far from the truth. In my more than 20 years of professional biometric experience, I never recommend using just biometrics as the sole means to fortify your place of business or organization.

Once again, multiple layers of biometric defenses are needed, and they can be of two basic types:

1. *Synchronous biometric systems:* Under this scenario, two or more biometric devices are used in conjunction with another in order to confirm the identity of an individual. For instance, this particular individual may be attempting to gain access to the business or organization, or to the network resources. For example, a fingerprint recognition reader can be used at the same time as an iris scanner in order to confirm the identity of an individual.

2. *Asynchronous biometric systems:* Under this particular scenario, two or more biometric devices are used to confirm the identity of an individual. Again, the same examples of fingerprint recognition and iris recognition can be used. However, rather than devices being used exactly at the same time, these two biometric devices are used in a sequential fashion, with one device being used first, then the other device being used second.

Therefore, in this particular situation, first the iris recognition device could be used to verify the particular individual at the main premises of the business, and subsequently, the fingerprint recognition device could be used to provide a further means of security (assuming, for example, that the particular individual needs to gain access to a more secure area at the place of business or organization).

With today's advances in biometric technology, implementing a multimodal solution is actually a fairly inexpensive and headache-free process. However, using this approach does bring up some technical issues, and perhaps even some social ones as well. First, typically with a multimodal biometric system, different biometric templates will obviously be used.

The biometric devices in this type of setup will not be operating by themselves, rather they will be working in conjunction with other devices. Therefore, one has to ensure that the two biometric systems are capable of "talking" with each other. This is not an issue when the same types of biometrics-based modalities are being used in a homogenous environment, but it can become a serious issue if different biometric modalities are attempting to communicate with each other in a heterogenous type of environment.

For example, if a fingerprint recognition device successfully confirms the identity of an individual, this same type of information has to not only be transmitted to the iris recognition device, but it must also be able to understand and decipher it. Second, proper end user training is a must here. Keep in mind that it is not just one system being used but at least two or more. These are also differing systems, which can be very confusing for the end user.

Therefore, the training provided by the place of business or organization must be at 100% optimum levels, in order to help not to just ensure a much more streamlined security process, but to also increase its user acceptance. Keep in mind that when most end users are faced to use one biometric system, there could often be resistance to it.

However, now when faced with two or more biometric systems, initial fear and opposition could greatly increase. In this manner, it is extremely imperative to train the end user on how to properly place his or her finger onto the silicon template, or where to stand in order to have a good quality image of the iris taken.

Another key technical issue is that the system administrator of the multimodal biometric system has to remember that enrollment templates have to be created in all of the biometric modalities that comprise the entire multimodal system. For instance, if a fingerprint enrollment template is successfully created, the same process also has to be done for the iris recognition device component, in order to make both systems work to help confirm the identity of the same individual.

Finally, the last technical issue concerning multimodal biometric systems is that the system administrator has to establish the right threshold for the optimum number of attempts needed to create both the enrollment and verification templates for all of the modalities that are involved. For example, allowing far too many attempts by the end user will greatly increase the FAR.

Whenever a biometric system is implemented for the first time, many people, especially those on the IT administration side of the place of business or organization, often fail to forget the fact that a biometric system is much more than just a piece of hardware, which is merely collecting biological/physiological or behavioral samples from an end user.

There is a lot more that goes into it, especially from the standpoint of the software applications and application program interfaces, as well as the databases that are needed to fully support the entire biometric system. A particular technical issues with regard to this are as follows.

In the biometrics industry, and by clients who maintain large-scale biometrics databases (such as the FBI and its Next Generation Identification System database as reviewed earlier in this chapter), the concept of "winnowing" is utilized. This involves the specialized filtering and indexing of the biometric templates and their associated information and data, and optimization of search results, especially when identifying a particular individual. However, this winnowing technique can also damage the structural integrity of the biometrics database and can lead to major search and retrieval errors.

As we have addressed in multimodal biometric systems, biometric templates from very different modalities are collected and are often stored into one database (and it if is large enough, the database will have to be partitioned in order to optimize the search results).

On account of this massive heterogenous environment, the search times for finding the right biometric template and its associated information and data need to be very quick. To help further enhance the search times, special image processing algorithms have been created to help fuse these multiple and varying biometric templates together.

However, these algorithms are still also considered to be in the research and development stage, and therefore, are not truly effective yet in helping to speed up biometric database search and retrieval techniques.

Also, another issue with storing massive amounts of biometric templates and their associated information and data into just one database is that it can put much burden on the processing power of the database, thus greatly impeding search and retrieval times as well.

The biometric database technology has even evolved to the point that if a particular biometric image that is collected (such as that of a finger, face, or even iris), that particular image can be further enlarged as needed in order to create a much better quality biometric template. Although this is a good thing in terms of a quality control standpoint, this too can also put a large constraint on the processing power of the database, thus also slowing down search and retrieval times.

Remember that it is not just one person or entity who is accessing this particular database, but it could be hundreds of individuals from across all over the world who are trying to access this particular biometrics database as well.

Therefore, keeping a biometrics database optimized for very quick search and retrieval times for the end user is always a constant battle that is being fought, but unfortunately, it is often one of the most overlooked items on the IT administrator's "to-do list."

After a particular biometric modality has been installed and fully deployed, and all of the end users at the place of business or organization have been fully trained, one of the next key factors to be decided upon, and which often brings up serious technical issues and concerns, is a particular level of the security thresholds, which should be established for the biometric system. Unlike most other security technologies, establishing thresholds for a biometric modality can be a very tricky and complex process. Let us take for example that of a firewall or router.

Once it is actually installed onto the network perimeter, certain rules have to be established into its access control list as to what kind of data packets it can permit into the network perimeter of the place of business or organization. Though these rules can become more complex over time, essentially, the crux of them is not to allow data packets into the network perimeter, which are deemed to be "malicious" and can cause serious damage.

However, with a biometric modality, this is a far different story. For instance, the system administrator has to decide what level is optimal so that the legitimate employees will be allowed to enter into the place of business or organization (as well as any other types or kinds of corporate resources they might be seeking as well) and keep the impostors out.

This is of course dependent on a lot of varying factors, which include the specific security requirements that have been mandated, the size of the business or organization, the nature of the IT assets that need to be protected, and so on. The optimal security threshold setting for a biometrics modality is known as the "equal error rate" (ERR).

On a graph, this simply means that all legitimate employees are being accepted by the biometric system and that all illegitimate employees are being denied by the biometric system. However, this setting is just theoretical; it is truly a rare case if it actually ever does occur in the real world. Most likely, there will be some employees who will be falsely rejected by the biometric modality (this is also known as the "false rejection rate"), and some other nonemployees (such as contractors) who could be accepted by the biometric system, when they shouldn't be (this is also known as the "false acceptance rate").

In these situations, it is always best to err on the side of caution and have a higher FRR metric, and thus a correspondingly lower FAR metric. In other words, it is much better a situation if more legitimate employees were randomly being rejected by the biometric modality rather than having more unauthorized people being allowed to enter into the place of business or organization.

This is one of the greatest technical issues an IT staff has to face, which can also trigger an even greater social issue. For example, legitimate employees who are randomly denied entry or access could grow to harbor even stronger resentment toward the biometric modality, and not even use it at all. This would then force the C-level management at the place of business or organization to consider implementing a manual security system in these types of situations.

In some organizations, especially the large Fortune 500 entities, establishing a security threshold for a biometric modality can even become a politically motivated one. For example, a C-level executive may place a higher value on the convenience of his or her shareholders and users, rather than placing a higher value on the level of security at the place of business or organization with which they are charged to lead.

In this manner, this can be referred to as a "liberal security" threshold setting. However, if the C-level executive places a higher value on security at his or her place of business or organization, this is known as a "conservative security" threshold setting. In the end, most biometric modalities lie in between these two extremes, with more favor being given to the scale of a higher level of security.

Biometric templates are just basically the mathematical snapshots of the actual physiological/biological or the behavioral samples that are taken from us. There are basically two types of biometric templates that are created: enrollment template and verification template. The former is first created when an end user first enrolls into a particular biometric modality and stays permanently in the database of the biometric system. The latter is created when the end user enrolls into the biometric modality again for the second time (or who knows how many times), and he or she wishes to gain access to the place of business or organization, or requires access to certain network resources.

In order for the particular person to gain access to whatever he or she wants, both the enrollment and verification templates need to be compared with each other to see if they indeed have come from the same individual. Generally speaking, if they have, the end user is granted access, and if not, he or she is not granted access. However, keep in mind that there are no two biometric templates that are ever 100% alike, even if they come from the same person.

Even if the same person submits 100 brand new verification templates, all of these templates will be structurally different from one another. Therefore, when comparing the enrollment and verification templates to each other, the biometric system examines the degree of statistical closeness between these two templates in order to make a decision as to whether or not to confirm the identification of a particular individual.

This involves, just like in the above example, the establishment of a certain threshold by the biometrics system administrator. Therefore, for example, at a certain threshold, if both the enrollment and verification templates display enough statistical likeness or closeness to one another, the person will be verified by the biometric system, but if the closeness or the likeness is out of the range of the particular threshold, then of course, that particular will not be verified.

Determining at what level to set the particular biometric template comparison threshold setting involves the same iterative process as described in the previous example. Once again, the ideal metric to have here would be the ERR, but this is not realistic when comparing the enrollment and verification templates together. Thus, the optimal threshold setting is where there is a higher level of FRRs, which would in turn correspond to lower FARs. Just like the setting of the security threshold for a particular biometric modality, the same technical and social issues also abound for when comparing the enrollment and verification templates.

For instance, it is much more of an art than a science in order to determine the biometric template matching threshold "sweet spot" that will meet the particular security needs of the particular application and thus, can take many numerous iterative efforts to find it. As a result, on the technical side of things, this can put an extra processing overload on the biometric modality, as more experimentation is being done to find the exact, optimal biometric template comparison point.

However, once again, the social impacts that are felt can be even greater. For example, if a legitimate employee at the place of business or organization is constantly being rejected by the biometric system for access to certain resources which he or she requires for his or her everyday job duties, impatience, and even frustration and total resentment toward the particular biometric modality could also set in.

Also, the financial costs associated with having to resort to the traditional means of allowing employee access to certain privileged network resources could rise as well for the business or organization. After all, wasn't the biometric technology that was procured in the first place designed to prevent this from happening, which is automating the process by which employees can gain access to protected resources?

This example also illustrates that although the biometric technologies are a great tool to confirm the identity of an individual, it does have its serious limitations as well.

One of the key social lessons is that the end user acceptance is ultimately the "make-or-break" factor for many biometric technologies today. For instance, a biometrics vendor may come out with the latest security features in his or her device, with the best performance metrics and key performance indicators possible, but if the end user or the public is not going to accept it, what is the point then of having all of this fancy technology?

This is where the concept of creating a biometric device that is ergonomically appealing to the end user is now starting to garner some serious attention. For instance, back in the last decade, many biometric vendors would just create products and solutions based strictly upon the end user requirements. Although of course this is a good thing, many biometric vendors did not take into account the end user, and how this new device would fit both a esthetically and pleasingly into their environment.

The thought at the time was simple: the device would be accepted and adopted if it met security needs. However, today's reality is far different than this. In today's biometrics systems analysis and design phases, special ergonomic consultants are even consulted upon by the biometric vendors in order to help create a biometric device, which looks pleasing to the end user and can even meet their own differing requirements.

Creating a biometric device that can fit and be used very easily into the end user's environment will go a long way in terms of acceptance and usage of the biometric system. However, these can be just considered "cosmetic" enhancements to the biometric modality in order to further enhance both its look and appeal.

There is a certain percentage of the end user population who also may possess certain physical ailments, which may severely limit their access in adequately using a biometric modality. Therefore, in these cases, the biometrics vendor has to accommodate all of physical needs of the end user.

Some of these key considerations include the following:

- The various height variances as well as differences between the end user population.
- The actual frequency of usage of the particular biometric modality. For example, if a device is not used very frequently, and if the end user population is small enough (perhaps less than 10 employees), then it might make more sense to offer special assistance to the end users who are physically challenged.
- Perhaps even, the biometric modality can be contained in a semi-private area and cordoned off to give the end user a sense of privacy, although he or she completes the enrollment and verification processes. This factor could also greatly increase the chance of end user acceptance of a newly implemented biometric device.

Although many biometric systems and modalities of today operate in a stand alone mode (i.e., each biometric device houses its own processing units and databases for the purposes of enrollment and verification template comparison and storage), all of the devices will be networked with each other. In these types of scenarios, the client–server network topology is utilized.

For instance, the primary biometrics database will be held in a central server (which will of course be also interconnected with other redundant servers), and from this point, all of the biometric devices located within the place of business or organization will also be interconnected to these servers.

Although this topology does serve its many benefits to the place of business or organization, it does provide its fair share of technical issues. The first issue is the network processing load. With a stand alone approach, there is not much of a load placed on the biometric device because all of the authentication is done locally.

However, with a biometrics-based client–server network topology, there is a much greater bottleneck on network performance, because now the respective biometric templates that have been created by the biometric devices have to make their way across the appropriate network media to reach the database at the central server.

Now, if there are just a few devices that are trying to accomplish this task, network performance will probably not be so much of an issue. However, if hundreds of biometric devices are trying to connect with this server (or servers), then the network performance will become a much graver issue, which has to be taken into consideration in the biometric systems analysis and design phase.

Any type of network bottlenecks that cut back drastically on the network load times will in turn lead to much slower enrollment and verification template comparison times, which will of course only lead to frustration to the end user. Probably, some of the best examples of very large-scale biometrics applications which are based upon a client–server network topology are that of the FBI's gargantuan biometrics database (as discussed earlier in this chapter) and large international airports (such as those of Heathrow in London and O'Hare International in Chicago).

Any bottleneck in the biometrics network would of course cause substantial backlog in background and security checks for the passengers. A second major technical issue faced with biometric templates in a client–server network topology (or for that matter in any other network topology, such as that of a peer-to-peer network or hybrid network [which is just a combination of the peer-to-peer network and the client–server network]) is the exposure of the biometric templates themselves as they traverse across the network medium.

Although a biometric template is (as described previously) just a mathematical representation of the actual biological/physiological or behavioral sample, it is still exposed to cyber-based threats and hacks. These biometric templates very often need to be further protected themselves, which is the objective of the brand new field of biocryptography.

Third, another major technical issue faced with biometrics-based client–server network topologies is that of network traffic collisions. If a biometrics-based network topology is complex and large scale enough, very often, routers will be used to help direct the traffic of the biometric templates and to optimize the network flow. This is very often done by making use of what is known as a "routing table."

This is merely a map located in the router itself that directs the traffic of the incoming biometric templates and also calculates the shortest route they need to take in order to reach their destination server.

If the incoming traffic coming into the ports of the router is large enough, the biometric templates can literally get backed up against one another, thus further exacerbating the verification as well as identification times of individuals and end users.

The science as well as the technology behind cryptography can be used to help further protect the biometric templates, in a new and emerging field known as "biocryptography."

Biometric templates are nothing but mere mathematical representations of the actual biological/physiological or behavioral traits of a particular individual. Traditionally, the physical-based biometrics use binary mathematics, Gabor wavelet mathematics, or Eigen-based mathematical theories. The behavioral-based biometrics utilize statistical-based profiling in order to create their own set of biometric templates; most of the time, the concepts of hidden Markov models are used.

Although biometric templates can be hacked into and tampered with, there is not a lot a hacker can do with it. For instance, the American public equates this type of hacking to that of stealing credit card information, and in reality, the two are totally different.

For instance, credit card information and data can be very easily reverse engineered, but it is much more difficult to do that with a biometric template (though the possibility does exist that it can happen). As a result, there is continuous research and development going on how to further protect these biometric templates, especially as they are used in a client–server network topology and have a much further distance to travel across the network medium.

Cryptography simply involves the scrambling and descrambling of information and data. With regard to its usage with biometric templates, the principles of cryptography would be used to help scramble and descramble the biometric templates.

For example, once an enrollment template is created at the point of origin, it would be rendered into a scrambled state, and from there transmitted across the network and into the server. At this level, the biometric template would then be descrambled so that the identification of the particular individual can then occur.

However, in terms of technical issues, this is still in theory. Not all biometric modalities possess this cryptographic functionality, implementing it by the biometrics industry, would render the biometric devices to be much more expensive than they are now. This increased expense would then thus further drive down the demand of biometric products and solutions.

If the principles of cryptography could be implemented into biometric modalities and the networks in which they are in, this would simply add to the network load and lead to a greatly increased chance that more network bottlenecks (especially at the server level) could occur as alluded to in the last section. Greater bottlenecks would then translate into more network administrative issues, thus crippling a biometric-based client–server network topology even more.

At the present time, leading biometrics industry standards dictate that all types and kinds of biometric modalities have verification processing times which are no more than just 1 or 2 seconds long. If the principles of cryptography were to be implemented into a biometric device, these verification processing times could very well be greatly increased, thus increasing the amount of time it takes to confirm the identity of a particular individual.

Of course, greater wait times translate into more frustration for the end user and decrease acceptance and usage of the biometric system in general. If crpytography can be technically implemented not only into the biometric devices themselves but also into a biometrics-based client–server network topology, there are two types of methodologies that can be used: symmetric cryptography and asymmetric cryptography. However, they both have their own sets of technical issues.

Symmetric cryptography makes use of just one set of keys—both of which are known as "private keys." The transmission and sharing of these keys imply implicit trust on all parties involved with a particular biometric transaction, because the private keys are not secure themselves. As a result, secure communications channels will have to be created and implemented into a biometrics-based client–server network topology, thus adding more to its complexity.

With symmetric cryptography, the private keys that will be used to secure the biometric templates need to be securely stored in a separate database themselves, either at the level of the biometric device itself or at the server level. The technical issue with this aspect is that given the insecure structure of the private keys, either the server or the biometric device itself will become the source of greater hacks and cyber-based security attacks.

Given the inherent security weaknesses of symmetric cryptography (especially the private keys), this type of cryptographic methodology will work best in a biometrics-based environment in which there are not many end users. This is also referred to as a "closed" or "sterile" security environment.

The other alternative to using symmetric cryptography in a biometrics-based client–server network topology is that of another cryptographic methodology known as "asymmetric cryptography." The main advantage of using this approach is that two different pairs of keys are being used: the private key and the public key. Thus, this offers greater levels of security to a biometrics-based network, but this too has its technical limitations.

Its major technical issue is that because two different types of keys are being utilized, the processing power that is required to help fortify the biometric templates is much greater. For instance, it is, on average, at least two to three times slower than that of symmetric cryptography. If this were to be implemented into a biometrics-based client–server network topology, the time it would take to confirm the identity of an individual would take not just a matter of seconds, but a matter of minutes, given how much is involved with using asymmetric cryptography in securing the biometric templates.

Asymmetric cryptography in this regard would not scale well at all for large-scale, commercial applications. Rather, it would be better suited for large-scale law enforcement-based identification searches.

Another feature of cryptography that can be used to help secure the biometric templates is using mathematical-based hashing algorithms. These types of algorithms do not actually scramble the state of the biometric template, rather they are used to help ensure that the integrity of the biometric template stays intact although it is in transmission across the network medium in a client–server network topology.

These mathematical hashing algorithms are the "fingerprint" of the biometric template. However, the use of these algorithms also possesses a very serious technical issue, which may even defeat its use in helping to secure a biometric template.

These too can be the point of a cyber-based attack, in which the attacker can physically alter the state of the hashing algorithm and, from there, even create a spoofed hashing algorithm in order to give the appearance that a biometric template has indeed remained intact while in transit across the network medium.

An alternative to using either symmetric-based or asymmetric-based cryptography is the virtual private network (VPN). This is essentially a hidden network from the public network and can afford the biometric templates and possibly even greater levels of security. Essentially, the biometric template would be enveloped further into another data packet, making it virtually invisible to the outside world.

However, there is one serious technical issue with implementing a VPN, especially that for the SMB. The cost that is involved is very expensive, and implementing a VPN for just a biometric-based client–server network topology would be much too complex. This would take much greater levels of technology, which only the largest of businesses could possibly afford.

If a VPN were to be implemented for a biometrics system, there are also three types of technical risks that are posed to it, which are as follows:

1. *Integrity risks*: The biometric templates that are in transit across the medium in a VPN are also at risk of having the mathematical representations of the biological/physiological or behavioral self being compromised, which means that the "internal content" of the biometric template can be altered.
2. *Confidentiality risks*: As mentioned, the employees of a business or an organization could become very apprehensive if they know that their biometric templates are not stored locally, but rather are being transmitted across a very large network medium. Fear of the thought of identity theft could spike even further, thus decreasing the usage and acceptance of the biometric system.
3. *Availability risks*: Since the biometric-based client–server network topology will be located literally with the VPN (or in other words, be a direct function of it), any downtime experienced by the VPN will also have a direct impact upon the biometric system. Thus, if there are any network outages or shortages within the VPN, all enrollment, verification, authorization, and identification transactions will suffer greatly as a result.

Although in theory it is possible to implement a biometric-based client–server network topology within a VPN, there are many other technical considerations that need to be carefully examined as well, as this could have a great impact on biometric processing times. Some of these ramifications that need careful study include the following:

- Impacts on the web server
- Impacts on the application server
- Impacts on the database server (this is probably one of the most important facets to be considered, as the biometric templates will be stored here and biometric template transactions will also occur at this level)
- Impacts on the firewall and router infrastructures

There are four main areas in which a biometrics-based client–server network topology is vulnerable inside a VPN (in other words, the points at which the process of the data packet surrounding the biometric template will commence):

1. Just after the biometric template creation (this applies to both the enrollment and verification templates)
2. When the biometric templates are stored in the database of the central server
3. When the biometric templates are in actual transmission across the network medium between the various biometric devices and the central servers (or, in fact, even between the backup servers as well, as the biometrics databases will need to be replicated and stored)
4. In a hosted environment, especially when the place of business or organization utilizes an outsourced third party for a VPN infrastructure

When trying to install and configure a VPN in a biometrics-based client–server network topology, there are some final technical issues that need to be considered as well. For instance, making use of a virtual memory-based system in this fashion may not be the best alternative when the time comes to actually conduct biometrics-based transactions.

It is probably better to utilize some sort of physical-based memory in the central server for conducting these types of biometric transactions. If it is decided that if either symmetric cryptography or asymmetric cryptography is used, it is totally imperative that every method possible is utilized in order to strengthen both the private keys and the public keys, in order to protect them against any cyber-based attack.

It is also equally important to conduct what are known as "penetration tests" into the VPN that houses the biometrics-based client–server network topology. This simply involves conducting simulation tests that try to break down the security defenses of the virtual private server, and from there, trying to discover the security weaknesses and vulnerabilities, so that it can be repaired and no longer pose a threat to the place of business or organization.

Equally just as more important than the technical side of a VPN, biometrics-based client–server network topology is the human side of managing such a system. Probably, the biggest threat in this area will include that of social engineering and being trustworthy of the system administrators who will manage and operate this biometric system.

Strict security policies will need to be formulated, created, and implemented, as well as to assign the minimum amount of privileges needed in order to fulfill and execute the job requirements as required by the biometric system. Although it is important to establish some sort of trust model with the employees at the place of business or organization, you can never assume a 100% level of trust.

It is important to maintain high levels of fault recovery from within your place of business or organization. This concept simply describes the ability of your VPN, biometrics-based client–server network topology to still maintain high levels of security despite the fact that there could be other types or kinds of components or other IT asset breakdown within your IT infrastructure.

Although the costs associated with many biometrics-based products and solutions have come down greatly in price, it can still be quite cost prohibitive for an SMB to actually procure, deploy, and implement the needed hardware and software. Therefore, a new type of service is being very seriously looked at by the biometrics industry. This is also known as "biometrics as a service," or "BaaS" for short.

With the advent of the cloud, there are many types and kinds of IT assets which are now available "as a service." For instance, probably the most popular service in this aspect is the "software as a service."

In other words, software applications that were once considered to be expensive of a proposition to be procured by an SMB are now available at the enterprise-grade level for just a fraction of the retail price of the actual software product.

The basic premises behind these cloud-based offerings are as follows:

- There are no licensing fees associated with purchasing software applications from an Internet service provider.
- There are no other types or kinds of hardware or software upgrades that are required to be done by the end user; everything is accomplished in this regard by the Internet service provider.

- The cost of procuring a software application from an Internet service provider will be made available to the end user at a fixed and predictable price (whether it is monthly or annual).
- The end user does not have to worry about any types or kinds of security issues; it is primarily assumed that the Internet service provider will assume this responsibility.
- The software application that is made available to the end user by the Internet service provider will be scalable and can be sized quickly and easily to fit the dynamic needs of the end user.

There are also many other benefits of cloud-based applications that are available to the end user. Thus, the basic idea behind a BaaS offering is that the entire biometrics infrastructure will be outsourced to an independent third party such as the Internet service provider.

All that a place of business or organization needs to do then is to acquire the needed biometric devices, install them, and then select a BaaS plan from the Internet service provider. Everything will be made available—from the databases to conducting all of the biometrics-based transactions.

All that the end user has to do is to merely keep up with the maintenance of the actual biometric hardware.

As mentioned, cloud-based services, especially if it were able to be offered as a BaaS offering, would offer many benefits, especially to that of the SMB owner. However, there are also other advantages to using the cloud, and some of them are described as follows:

- *The IT resources and the IT assets*: These are made available through the cloud are always available on demand and can be very quickly provisioned.
- *On premise*: Since the cloud is so very easily accessed via an Internet connection, it gives the feeling that all of the software and hardware resources are right on the premises of the place of business or organization, right at our fingertips, when in fact these applications are actually stored many hundreds of miles away.
- *IT asset scalability*: As it is dictated by the needs of the SMB owner (or even a larger corporation or organization for that matter), the IT assets (which include both the hardware and the software) can either be scaled up or scaled down. Take for example that of a database application. Starting out, an SMB owner probably will not need that much of database server space. However, as time continues, there could be a very strong need for extra space. As a result, with just a few simple clicks of the mouse, all the SMB owner has to do is just to increase

the memory size of the database, to whatever the specific needs of the application are. Both horizontal and vertical scaling are involved in this aspect. This will also prove to be quite advantageous to a biometrics system. For example, if the business or organization is growing, there will be more physical or logical-based assets, which need to be protected. In this fashion, all the SMB owner needs to do is to simply procure and install the devices that are needed, and merely select a larger BaaS plan with the Internet service provider.

- *Proportional costs*: One of the biggest benefits of using the cloud is predictable and fixed pricing. This is primarily inherent in the fact that the costs of using a cloud-based infrastructure are actually proportional. The cloud resources that are utilized are on what is known as a "pay-as-you-go basis." In other words, you pay only for those IT assets and resources that are being used, nothing more and nothing less. For example, if you downgrade your services, you pay less; if you upgrade your existing services, you pay more. This is also true if you require specialized software services. For instance, if there is a unique type of software application, and the Internet service provider has to custom configure it and install it, there will be of course a much higher cost associated with that. This concept will prove to be of great benefit for the SMB owner, especially when the time comes to deploy a biometrics system. Except for the price of the hardware, the entire biometrics infrastructure and software-related costs will be controlled and mitigated.

- *24 × 7 × 365 Availability and reliability*: One of the biggest benefits of using a cloud-based infrastructure is its constant availability and reliability. This stands in total contrast to your IT infrastructure being onsite at your place of business or organization. There would be total dependence upon the IT staff to make sure everything is up and running all the time. This would also come of course at a great expense to the business or organization. This constant uptime will also prove to be of great benefit to a biometrics-based client–server network topology, which is housed within a VPN. In this regard, there will be at least 99.999% uptime and reliability.

However, despite these obvious advantages of using a cloud-based infrastructure for a BaaS application, there are a number of technical issues that are associated with it. First, there is a huge leap of faith required on part of the Internet service provider in order for the place of business or organization to entrust them with the biometric information and data which they currently possess. After all, all of this now will be in the hands of a third party, the Internet service provider.

The Internet service providers are probably the most prone victims to cyber-based attacks and threats. As a corresponding result, any BaaS applications that reside will also fall prey. Therefore, more security defenses need to be especially established for this, which could thus translate into higher expenses for the Internet service provider.

In the eyes of the American public, biometrics has enough a hard time being accepted by the people. This is the case where the actual biometric system will reside at a place of business or organization, and also where the end user will have some say so about the control over their biometric templates and their associated information and data.

However, when all of this is placed into the hands of the Internet service provider, there will be much more mistrust and misgivings about biometrics in general, thus potentially leading to a much drastic rate in acceptance of the technology. This is because there is now a third party involved in the biometrics-based transactions, and the end user has much less control in this regard.

One of the primary reasons why the cloud is so much cheaper rather than having an on-premise IT infrastructure is that the resources at the Internet service provider are "shared." Suppose you have a virtual private server. Although you may get the look and feel of actually thinking it is your own server, the resources that are associated with it are actually shared among other virtual private servers on the same physical server.

Thus, there is also a growing fear among the American public that another customer who shares the same cloud-based resources for a BaaS infrastructure could also launch an attack or a threat, because of the very close proximity between the two parties on the physical server.

Since Internet service providers pretty much let their customers install and do anything they want with their cloud-based services, there is very little governance on part of the Internet service provider in order to make sure that the cloud-based services are not used for malicious purposes by the end user.

This simply means that the place of business or organization will have to adopt and enforce much stricter security policies for the system administrators who will be managing and operating the biometrics as a cloud infrastructure for their place of business or organization.

Unfortunately, every Internet service provider has its own sets of best practices and standards for offering cloud-based services not only to its end users but also to the hardware and software applications that reside in them. Therefore, for example, suppose an SMB owner moves his or her customer database to one Internet service provider, but then decides to move it over to another Internet service provider for a myriad of reasons.

However, because of the lack of common standards and best practices, the data may not all transfer over easily and quickly to the cloud-based servers of the new Internet service provider. This will hold especially true for those Internet service providers who could potentially offer the BaaS application.

In theory, the biometric templates and their associated information and data could be moved easily from one Internet service provider to another, but reality dictates quite the opposite. This is further compounded by the fact that there is also a lack of a standard set of best practices and standards within the biometrics industry itself.

An Internet service provider can be very large and span many countries and even continents. As a result, the data and the information that reside on their servers are prone to the legal issues and constraints upon the country in which these servers are located. For example, financial data that reside on servers with an Internet service provider in the United States will be subject to the different laws for the same type and kind of data that reside on the servers of a different country, say, for example, that of Sweden.

For another example, an end user can select a software as a service application on a server that is based in Russia, but the physical premises of the Internet service provider exist in the United States. Although it is not too common with the governments of these countries to be intrusive of the information and data which resides with an Internet service provider, this could become much more magnified as biometric templates will be stored within their services.

For example, because of federal legislations and mandates set forth by the U.S. government, in particular, the USA PATRIOT Act, this very well could be a catalyst in examining what is being stored on the servers of the Internet service providers, with regard to the biometric templates and their associated information and data.

Knowing that this could be made available to the U.S. federal government, the chances will be very high that there will be a huge American public backlash over this, with claims being made that "Big Brother Is Watching You." The reason for this is that the American public feels that their biometric templates contain much more personal information than what their credit cards hold and contain.

It may not be logical, but this is the public perception at the current time and will probably remain so for a very long period of time to come yet. There will also be huge cries of privacy rights and civil liberties violations. Perhaps one way that an Internet service provider could quell some of these social impacts of a BaaS offering if a private cloud deployment model was utilized.

There are also other types and kinds of security risks posed to a biometrics as a cloud service offering, which are as follows:

- *Anonymous attacker*: This type of attacker has no cloud-based resource permissions and can launch attacks on a cloud-based infrastructure via the public networks.
- *Malicious service agent*: This type of threat or risk actually exists and comes from the cloud-based infrastructure itself and possesses the ability to not only intercept but also capture the data packets that house the biometric templates within a VPN.
- *Malicious insider or malicious intermediary*: This type of attacker is normally an ex-employee (such as that of the Internet service provider), who still retains his or her specific login credentials. These types of threats pose grave risk to a BaaS application.
- *Traffic eavesdropping*: This type of cyber-based attack occurs primarily when biometric templates are in the transitory stage and are making their way across the network medium between the biometric devices and the central (as well as the secondary) servers. The biometric templates are covertly hijacked (most likely with a network sniffer) and attempted to conduct identity theft attacks.
- *Distributed denial of service (DDoS) attack*: With this type of security threat, the goal is to primarily bombard and flood the central servers with malformed data packets in order to entirely cripple the servers, rendering them absolutely useless. Of course, as described previously, if this happened to a VPN that housed a biometric-based client–server network topology, all biometric transactions would cease as well, because it is a direct of the VPN.
- *Virtualization attack*: There is little operational governance conducted by an Internet service provider once it makes its hardware and software available to the end user, business, or organization. Therefore, the system administrator could pose to be the biggest threat and launch their own brand of insider attacks to the BaaS applications that reside within the Internet service provider.
- *Overlapping trust boundaries*: Also, as described previously, any type or kind of cloud-based services (such as the software as a service) are all housed on the same physical server. As a result, SMBs often have their own "cloud boundaries" in order to help draw their clear lines of cloud-based IT asset ownership. These are technically known as "trust boundaries." However, at times, these specific boundaries can overlap, and as a result, this can pose a very serious threat and risk, as the owner of one cloud server could overstep the boundaries into another cloud server, especially if it houses a BaaS application.

Finally, there are also other key technical and social issues with regard to a biometrics-based client–server network that resides in a VPN. For given how slow the adoption rate for biometrics here is in the United States in general, the idea of putting all of those products and solutions into the cloud as a BaaS application will receive even much more luke warm reception, for reasons outlined in the earlier subsections.

Actually, there are already some small-scale versions of BaaS applications already deployed by some of the larger biometric vendors, but they have not been deployed on a large scale. Not each and every Internet service provider will be offering the BaaS application. By nature, at the present time, the main revenue generator for Internet service providers are all cloud-based offerings, which relate to software applications and other collaborative and communications tools.

As a result, it could take a very long time for the Internet service providers (whether large or small) to warm up to the idea of even offering a BaaS application offering. This is because not only will it take a long time to implement, but it will also require a much greater capital expenditure in the technology that is required to support a BaaS application infrastructure.

Implementing this type of needed technology will also mean a drastic change in the current business processes of the Internet service providers, which could also greatly slow down the offering rate of this service. A BaaS application offering needs to be scalable. As described earlier in this chapter, one of the prime benefits of cloud-based offerings is that they can be scalable to demand.

This simply means that as the size of the business or organization grows or contracts, the cloud-based services required can also correspondingly either contract or grow in size very quickly as well (literally at just a few clicks of the mouse), depending upon the need of the business or organization.

However, at least in the beginning and the intermediate stages, it is widely anticipated that the BaaS will not be a scalable application service. The reason for this is that not only will it take time for the Internet service providers to implement this type of application service, but the initial demand for it could also very well be extremely slow. Therefore, it will be very difficult to forecast the demand scalability on part of the businesses and organizations who are considering the use of a BaaS application offering.

However, it is also anticipated that once this service offering finally takes root, and the American public (as well as Corporate America) becomes more receptive to it, its scalability will also start to increase.

The BaaS application offering will be very narrow in scope in the beginning stage: Largely due to the costs associated with the technology that will be needed on part of the Internet service provider, as well as the highly anticipated slow adoption rate, any BaaS application offering will be very limited, and will thus be best suited for small-scale security applications, which are required by the SMB businesses.

In this regard, it is quite likely that the initial biometrics applications to use a cloud-based application offering will be that of physical access entry and time and attendance scenarios.

TWO MAIN APPLICATIONS OF BIOMETRIC TECHNOLOGY

So far, in this chapter, both the key social and technical implications surrounding the use of biometrics technology have been examined in detail. I'd now like to change gears and use the remainder of this chapter to examine in further detail the main applications of biometric technology and why it is important to discuss primarily these three market applications (physical access entry, single sign on, and time and attendance), versus all of the other biometric applications (which are primarily those of physical access entry, logical access entry, and time and attendance).

e-Passport Infrastructure

The primary purpose of the e-passport infrastructure is to do away with the traditional paper passport. The primary idea behind this technology is to use biometrics as the main vehicle in which to confirm the identity of a particular traveler. The e-passport is primarily composed of a microprocessor chip, as well as a miniature antennae. The chip actually stores the biometric templates of the traveler. At the present time, the primary biometric technologies that are being used for the e-passport infrastructure are fingerprint recognition, facial recognition, and iris recognition. The microprocessor chip can hold and contain just one type of biometric template, or it can contain a combination of all three of the biometric templates. For instance, when a traveler disembarks at the country of their destination, all he or she has to do is merely "flash" the e-passport in front of the radio-frequency identification reader (which is the primary purpose of the antennae; this then transmits the biometric templates and the associated information and data to the reader). If the identity of the particular individual is positively confirmed, he or she is then allowed to the country of their destination.

At the present time, it is primarily the European countries that have adopted the e-passport infrastructure. However, despite its obvious advantages, the e-passport infrastructure still has tremendous barriers to face before full-scale adoption can be realized, especially in the

United States. The following reasons can be cited, from both a technical and a social standpoint:

1. *Data leakage threats*: This is the point at which the e-passport has to be read by the radio-frequency identification scanner. This is a very short distance, even as short as 3 feet. Although one may get the notion that no particular security threat can exist from this very short distance, this is far from the truth. A threat known as "skimming" is very prevalent here. For example, anybody with a covert network sniffer could easily scan the contents of the smart chip contained within the e-passport (in particular, the biometric templates) and use such data to conduct security breaches like that of identity theft.

2. *Covert tracking and hotlisting*: Although one cannot glean a lot of information and data from just a few movements of a particular individual at an international airport setting, but as they enter into their country of destination, the covert tracking of a particular traveler (such as that of a frequent business traveler) could very likely occur. As a result, this same traveler could very well become "hotlisted," and subsequently, he or she could become a victim of serious racial profiling by the respective government in that particular country.

3. *Too much reliance upon automation*: Given the use of biometric technology in this fashion, and especially with the advent of "e-gate" technology, there is a strong fear of the "relaxation of the human oversight factor." This simply means that there will be so much reliance upon the automated use of biometric technology, and that airport security officials will become even more lax in their particular roles and jobs. As a result, real potential terrorists could actually slip through the cracks of the existing international airport security systems.

4. *Spillover of technology*: As the use of specific biometric modalities becomes the *de facto* standard in the e-passport infrastructure, there is fear that the technology of one biometric modality could very easily spill into another, legacy security technology infrastructure. For example, if there is a specific and targeted threat to just the biometric technology infrastructure, there is a strong fear that this could create a "ripple security risk" to the structural integrity of the other security technologies that are present (and which are also non-biometric in nature).

5. *The fear of global identity theft*: There is a strong fear in the United States that as people travel abroad, the biometric templates that are stored in the memory chip of the e-passport could

very well be intercepted and used maliciously by the respective government of the country of destination.

6. *Large biometric databases will have to be used*: If the e-passport infrastructure ever becomes the primary identity document protocol in the United States, the biometric templates (taken by a factor of 3, for the three biometric modalities that will be used) of all of the e-passport enrollees will have to be stored in huge, widely dispersed databases, which will reside in the hands of the federal government. Because no clear guidelines probably will not be issued as these biometric templates will actually be secured, there is strong fear among the American public that the federal government will misuse these biometric templates for the covert surveillance of particular individuals.

7. *Lack of standards and best practices for adopting an e-passport infrastructure*: Although International Civil Aviation Organization standards have been developed, at least in the United States, there are no set of guidelines on how to best handle the biometric templates that are stored in the e-passport, thus further stoking more fears and misgivings with regard to privacy rights and civil liberties violations.

Even though other countries have adopted their own version of the e-passport infrastructure, there is still much more work to be done from both the technological and social aspects until it garners the full rate of acceptance in the United States.

e-Voting Infrastructure

Electronic voting, also known more simply as "e-voting," is merely the process by which a voter can easily cast his or her particular ballot. Rather than having to actually physically appear at a polling station and casting a vote manually at the booth, the individual can now cast his or her ballot via the telephone, the Internet, or even a VPN. Although the primary intention of e-voting is to make the voting process an easy and enjoyable experience for the particular voter, this so far has not been the case in the developed nations, such as the United States. Under the traditional method of voting, a voter had to show a form identification, such as a state ID or even a driver's license in order to prove and confirm his or her identity. However, with the newer methods of e-voting, there is no need to show such types of documentation anymore. Rather, the use of biometric technology is being called upon to replace these traditional vehicles of identification.

Primarily, fingerprint recognition has been called upon for use in the e-voting process. The fingerprint template serves as the primary means of confirming the identity of the voter and allowing him or her to vote electronically from a remote location. Although fingerprint recognition is the *de facto* standard technology in biometric applications, it starts to receive opposition in the United States for the e-voting process for the following reasons:

1. The fingerprint recognition biometric template, although secure in its own right, can be spoofed, as reviewed earlier in this chapter. Thus, there are fears from voters that their fingerprints could be lifted covertly from an optical-based sensor and used subsequently for malicious purposes.
2. Although there have been no known cases of anybody contracting a serious ailment from using an optical fingerprint sensor, hygiene issues are now starting to come into play and literally "spook" the voter. Fingerprint recognition requires a direct contact with the optical sensor. Therefore, rather than using a "full contact" technology, voters are much more interested in using a "non-contactless" biometric modality, such as facial recognition, which requires no direct contact with the actual camera.

Although facial recognition is a step-up from fingerprint recognition, it too possesses a strict set of limitations, which can impede the adoption of e-voting in the United States. Again, the reasons are both technological and social:

1. From a technical standpoint, suppose that an e-voter is registered to confirm to vote in a presidential election. Four years later, assume that this same person has gained a massive amount of weight during those 4 years, and in the next presidential election, he or she wishes to vote again. This time, the facial recognition system will not be able to confirm the identity of this person, because of the drastic changes in appearance.
2. From a social perspective, facial recognition is the most prone to claims of both privacy rights and civil liberties violations. Therefore, although the technology in theory may work in an e-voting system, the voter's attention to his or her rights will almost impede its use in an e-voting system.
3. Also, facial recognition can be used very covertly without the voter's knowledge and literally be embedded into a CCTV camera (as discussed earlier in this chapter). If this were to be used for surveillance at a national election, and word leaked out that it is being used, nobody would submit their biometric template in order to confirm their eligibility to vote.

a. It has also been proposed that in order to resolve the above issues of using a single biometric modality in the e-voting process, a multimodal approach be utilized. In this regard, more than one biometric modality will be utilized, such as both facial recognition and fingerprint recognition. However, implementing this type of system nationwide at each and every polling station in the United States would be just too cost prohibitive to implement. Therefore, as it has been suggested, a balance needs to be struck between the cost-effectiveness of such a multimodal biometric solution versus the enhancement it will bring to the e-voting process. This is something that has been ignored in the United States, in the face of other countries (such as the developing ones) implementing successful e-voting infrastructures.

b. Here in the United States, the fears of very sophisticated Internet attacks are becoming very pronounced. One such threat is that of the DDoS attacks. Although this particular threat has been around for a long time, it is still quite prevalent. For example, in an e-voting scenario, a DDoS attack can be launched, thus slowing the verification and/or identification of the biometric templates before the voter can be allowed to cast his or her ballot. As a result, this could even drastically change the predicted outcome of a close presidential election.

c. On account of the above issues, the United States is quickly phasing out the use of e-voting mechanisms. For example, in the 2012 presidential elections, 56% of the polling places used the traditional paper ballots which were optically scanned in, and only 39% of the polling stations utilized the e-voting system in some fashion.

d. Diebold, the main provider of the e-voting machines during the presidential elections, itself had many security-related flaws and serious trust issues with the voters. These incidents with Diebold have thus steered away the United States from full-scale e-voting across all of the 50 states.

The above issues are illustrations of case studies that will be used in this book to specifically illustrate how biometrics are being used more in the developing nations than in the developed ones like the United States. However, more and varied case studies will also be provided in this book in order to illustrate why the United States is so slow to adopt and implement biometric technologies, whereas the rest of the world is quickly jumping on board.

Finally, in Chapter 5 of this book, recommendations and specific strategies will be provided to the C-level executive as to how the acceptance rate of biometric technology can be increased, which will thus lead to an increased level of the demand of other biometrics-based products and solutions. These recommendations and strategies will be formulated from the case studies that will be reviewed in this book.

CHAPTER 2

The Social Barriers Affecting the Adoption Rate of Biometric Technology in the United States

Chapter 1 provided a summary of the major lessons learned from the first book, *Biometric Technology: Authentication, Biocrpytography, and Cloud-Based Architecture.*[*] The implications for using biometric technology was closely examined, from both a technical and a social perspective. In this chapter, these particular implications are examined in more detail.

The goal of this chapter is not to review every single implication once again, but rather to focus more on the social reasons why biometric technology is poorly adopted in the United States and why the adoption rate is so high in other parts of the world, such as the developing nations of Africa, Asia, and the Pacific Rim.

It is important to keep in mind that although the adoption rate of biometric technology in the United States is very slow (this is also true in other developed nations around the world, which include especially those in Europe), there are other market segments utilizing biometrics that are actually taking off.

Unfortunately, the American public never hears about these "good news stories" of biometrics, because all that is portrayed about biometrics is its negativity and how the federal government will misuse the biometric templates in order to keep tabs on the American public. If the American public were much more aware of these booming market applications, perhaps its adoption rate will also greatly increase. Therefore,

---

[*] R. Das. *Biometric Technology: Authentication, Biocryptography, and Cloud-Based Architecture,* CRC Press, Boca Raton, FL, pp. 329–354, 2014.

it is also the goal of this chapter to bring out these good news stories, in order to further educate the American public.

By reviewing these "golden" market opportunities for biometrics, this content will also offer a counter mechanism to all of the negativity that surrounds it. This will show that yes, although biometric technology does have its certain issues, it can still be a widely accepted and used tool as well.

The major issues that are slowing down the growth rate of biometric technology in the United States are discussed in the sections that follow.

PRIVACY RIGHTS ISSUES

As alluded to in Chapter 1, privacy rights issues are right now the biggest "negative," which is associated with biometric technology. The primary reason for this is that it is a snapshot of our physiological and behavioral selves, which is being captured by either an optical sensor or a camera (such as the case in facial recognition or iris recognition). It is only human nature to be shy away from the use of such technologies, as we never have to provide any of these types or kinds of snapshots in any other part of our lives (except for when we see our primary care physician, of course).

The issue of privacy rights is a rather large and nebulous topic, and has no clear-cut definitions associated with it. This is probably due to the fact that the violation of privacy rights carries different meanings as well as connotations to not only each and every individual, but also each and every type and kind of business or organization. However, based upon research, the issue of privacy rights violations can be broken down into three categories:

1. Anonymity
2. Tracking/surveillance
3. Profiling

With regard to anonymity, many privacy rights advocates (particularly those belonging to civil liberties groups and associations) claim that we lose our anonymity when it comes to the use of biometric technology. This is due to the fact that our biometric template (which was discussed in Chapter 1) is often associated with an ID number of sorts in the biometric database.

In other words, to a biometric system, we can never claim to be an anonymous person—it will recognize us based upon our template that is stored. This will be an exception only when considering extremely large-scale biometric applications, such as the law enforcement.

In these cases, if a suspect or a criminal is apprehended, his or her biometric template will be entered into the database to see if his or her identity can be confirmed. Of course, if this particular person has not been previously enrolled into a biometric database (such as that of the Federal Bureau of Investigation (FBI)'s Next Generation Identification System biometric database), obviously, his or her identity more than likely will not be confirmed.

It has been proven that the American citizens like to exercise their right to anonymity when it comes down to making electronics-based purchases as well as for voting (whether it is done by the ballot or by other electronic means).

This same group of privacy rights advocates firmly believe that if biometric technology were to gain widespread acceptance in the United States and proliferate itself into everyday life of the average American citizen, our right to anonymity would dissipate itself very quickly.

It is anticipated that as we conduct these transactions in other places, the right to anonymity will fade there as well. In other words, we will not lose our right to anonymity in just one place we exist at; it will occur in all of the places we exist.

In terms of tracking and surveillance, there is a very strong fear among the American public that "Big Brother" will be watching them. Its concept stems from George Orwell's book *1984*.* The primary catalyst of this fear comes from the federal government, in the sense that they could potentially misuse the biometric information and data that reside in their databases.

However now, this fear and mistrust have started to trickle down to the levels of the state and local governments as well. Again, the main negativity toward the adoption and use of biometric technology in this regard is primarily aimed toward the law enforcement branches. For example, a biometric template can literally serve as a universal identifier (because each template is unique to each and every individual) in a manner very similar to how the social security number is being used for this purpose today.

An example of this is having your fingerprint recognition template being stored in your driver's license. Rather than using your driver's license number being the main way to confirm your identity, your fingerprint template now serves this purpose. In fact, this is not just a hypothetical example, which has actually been put into practice. There are some states in the United States that now mandate the storage of biometric templates into your driver's license. The American public has been fearful of having their driver's license being replicated by a malicious party if it were to be ever lost or stolen. Now, with biometric templates being stored on it, the fear of using the driver's license as a primary means of identification is significantly increased.

With the example of law enforcement, there is also a very heightened apprehension by the American public if they were to be ever stopped by

---

* G. Orwell. *1984*. Signet Classics. July 1, 1950.

an officer. For instance, the fear stems from the fact that after a finger-print recognition template has been submitted, a particular individual could be subject to much harsher treatment by a law enforcement officer if it is found that he or she does indeed have a criminal history.

The use of biometric templates in this regard has far-reaching implications, because the technology can now connect to the massive biometric databases and produce a search result in just a matter of seconds. If just a driver's license number were to be used to check the criminal history of this individual, the search would just be limited to the state biometric databases. There is also a strong level of anxiety that the state and local governments could take the biometric templates of each and every citizen, and use that information and data to further extrapolate upon and intrude into their personal lives, without just cause.

Finally, in terms of profiling, biometric technology is often associated with criminal identification. As it was reviewed in some detail in Chapter 1, just by human nature, there is often a strong correlation of relating the image of a fingerprint and law enforcement, as this is often used as part of a broader logo scheme.

The fear of profiling when using biometric technology is also even great among the senior citizens in the United States. For this group of citizens, trying to claim the appropriate amount of welfare entitlements and benefits can be quite literally a nightmare when dealing with government officials at the local or state level. However, if biometric templates were to be used to confirm the identity of these senior citizens, there is angst that they could be just reduced down to a record in a database, and thus, receive even more unjust treatment from government officials.

Even religious groups fear the use of biometric technology. These individuals often cite the fear of the "mark of the beast," in which the American citizen has to give up his or her individual being, or at least part of it, to a much higher level symbol of authority (such as the federal government), which bears no religious significance whatsoever.

However, in the end, this area of profiling will be one of the major catalysts curtailing the adoption rate of biometric technology, especially when it comes to law enforcement applications and usage. This is because this area can be specifically extrapolated to racial profiling, which is very much a hot button topic these days, given the recent mishaps with officials and the American public.

In broad terms, the concept of privacy is actually a very nebulous one, upon which many definitions of this concept have been formulated. In it, the American public often correlates privacy with security. However, the two are very fundamentally different. The primary reason for this confusion is that protection of privacy also includes tenets for physical security. In other words, privacy actually becomes a subset of security, which means that if a layer of physical security is afforded, then privacy should come immediately along with that.

However, it is very interesting to note that this is not the case with biometrics. Yes, the technology does offer a strong level of security, but once again, privacy rights issues abound when it is offered to the American public. As stated in Chapter 1, a snapshot of our physical or behavioral selves is captured, which causes great unease among the American public. Compounded with this level of angst, the greater fear is that if the biometric template is hijacked or stolen, it cannot be reset again, like a password can be.

In very broad terms, privacy can be defined as: "[what] is left after one subtracts... the monitored, and the searchable, from the balance of social life."* The American public believes that privacy rights are actually guaranteed to them by the U.S. Constitution. However, this is far from the truth. It does not guarantee privacy in any shape or form.

However, although not directly stated, the U.S. Constitution does offer implied protections to privacy rights. These implications can be found as follows:

- *The Fourth Amendment*: This protects the American public from unreasonable search and seizure.
- *The Fifth Amendment*: This protects American citizens from self-incrimination.
- *The Fourteenth Amendment*: This allows any American citizen to exercise control and safeguard his or her personal information.

However, there is one key piece of legislation that does provide a broad framework for privacy rights protection.

The Privacy Act of 1974 guarantees the rights of privacy to American citizens whose information and data might be stored in federal databases. Much debate took place shortly after this legislation was passed if a similar bill should be introduced to the U.S. Congress to offer this level of protection to the private sector. However, in the end, this idea was rejected by the Privacy Protection Study Commission.

BIOMETRIC TECHNOLOGY

As alluded to in Chapter 1 very briefly, one of the major stumbling blocks or obstacles toward the adoption and use of biometric technology in the United States is the identity theft, also known as ID theft. Many people

---

* L. Lessing. The architecture of privacy. In *Taiwan Net '98 Conference*, Taipei, Taiwan, March 1988. http://www.jetlaw.org/wp-content/uploads/2014/01/08_1VandJEntLPrac 561999.pdf.

associate this with the digital era. However, truth to be told, ID theft goes much further back than before the dawn of the Internet. The first cases of ID theft occurred back in the early 1900s when it first evolved as a physical crime.

In these cases, the victim would often be murdered and disposed of, so that his or her wallet, which would contain his or her social security number and other types and kinds of personal information and data, could be easily and quickly stolen.

After this, ID thieves soon started to realize that they would have to be much more covert and secret in their efforts to assume somebody's identity. As a result, the telephone was the next logical choice. This has been deemed to be the first technological form of ID theft. In these particular cases, the ID thief, at random, would call his or her victims with promises of winning large sums of cash or similar prizes.

Using the tactics of social engineering, the ID thief would then proceed to ask the victim for his or her personal information, making the claims that this was needed to fully confirm his or her particular identity. Since the cases of ID theft were not disclosed to the public during this time frame (in between the 1960s and 1970s as the telephone was the tool used 100% of the time to conduct ID theft), victims were readily open in disclosing their private information and data to virtually anybody.

This would include such items as their bank account number, social security number, or even credit card number.

However, given the digital era of the twenty-first century, the use of the telephone now only accounts for a mere 7% of ID theft cases. Now, as we move forward to the 1980s and the mid-to-late 1990s, the next tool for conducting ID theft was using the ordinary garbage can.

This form of ID theft is known more technically as "dumpster diving." ID thieves would commonly and routinely scour the garbage cans of not only individuals but also those belonging to corporations, entities, and other business-related entities.

The ID theft victims never considered that their garbage would ever be the scene for the origination of a crime. Once cases of actual ID theft came out in the public (and also after it was determined by law enforcement officials that dumpster diving was the source of ID theft), the American public then resorted to purchasing shredders to make sure that their documents were rendered to be obsolete and irreparable.

It is very interesting to note that in the United States, there are no laws to protect against dumpster diving.

With the dawn of the Internet in the late 1990s up until today, this has now become the main venue for conducting of ID theft attacks and hacks. The first cases of cyber-based ID theft occurred with e-mail systems and packages. In these instances, the victim would receive an authentic looking e-mail message coming from a legitimate source.

Very often, the victim would be coaxed into a link, which would then take him or her to a website where then he or she would then be further coaxed to submit his or her personal information and data.

These forms of ID theft were and are still known as "Phishing" types of e-mail messages. However, as the Internet has further evolved and grown exponentially in terms of sophistication, ID theft has also, at the same time, become much more advanced. Today's cases of ID theft are very covert and stealthy, and can occur in just a matter of seconds.

Although the goal of ID theft when it first occurred was just to assume the actual identity of the victim, today's cases now involve stealing and hijacking personal information and data for monetary as well as financial gain. In fact, according to the Federal Trade Commission, Internet-based ID theft occurs for more than 62% of all cases in the United States.*

Since ID theft is so prevalent in this digital era, this has now translated into strong fear amongt the American public about cases of ID theft occurring with biometric templates. As it was discussed in detail in Chapter 1, biometric templates are nothing but a mere mathematical representation of either our physical or behavioral beings.

In other words, it represents the images that were taken by the biometric system. After a biometric template has been created (whether it is an enrollment or a verification template), the actual images that were taken are then discarded by the biometric system, and also deleted from the biometric database.

This then begs the question, if a biometric template is nothing but a mere mathematical formula (such as in the case with fingerprint recognition-based templates and hand geometry recognition-based templates), what can ID thief do with such information? Really, there is not much that they can do.

After all, it is not the same as stealing a credit card number. However, given the level of sophistication in which hackers can launch cyber-based attacks, there is also a heightened fear as well in the biometric industry that a biometric template could eventually, at some time, become a source of ID theft.

This is especially the case when latent residues are left behind on an optical sensor, especially with those biometric technologies that require direct contact. A prime example of this is actually within fingerprint recognition itself.

As it was reviewed in Chapter 1, studies have shown that latent fingerprints left on an optical sensor can actually be used to reconstruct an entirely brand new fingerprint and, as a result, even be used to spoof a fingerprint recognition system.

---

* Identity-Theft-Scenarios.com. Identity theft: Protect yourself with knowledge. 2015. http://www.identity-theft-scenarios.com/identity-theft-facts/history/.

Latent material left behind on sensors with those biometric technologies that require direct contact provide the source for legitimate fear of ID theft. However, what about those biometric technologies that do not require direct contact and only camera is used to capture a snapshot of our physiological selves?

There is no proof that ID theft can actually arise from here, it is quite possible that over time it could, once again, based primarily on how sophisticated cyber-based hackers and attackers are becoming. The following sections discuss the concerns and fears as to how ID theft can arise from the use of biometric technology.

Legal Aspects of Using Latent Information and Data Presented by a Biometric System

So far, at the present time, there has been no legal precedence, which exists in the United States to protect victims from cases of ID theft if it arises from the use of latent information and data left on the sensor of a biometric system. Thus, this only proliferates the motivation of both hackers and attackers to specifically hunt and target those particular biometric systems in such latent information that can be found readily and easily. There is only legal case that actually contested the use of latent fingerprints in order to bring to justice an ID thief. This case is known in the legal world as *United States v. Mitchell*,[*] and no conclusion could be drawn.

Biometric Templates (Both Physical and Behavioral Based) Are Greatly Impacted by Time

It should come to no surprise that through the aging process, this can greatly degrade and impact the quality of biometric templates that are taken. This is best exemplified through both fingerprint recognition and facial recognition. With the former, the image of the fingerprint can be extensively degraded from our youth into our older age. With the latter, our facial structure can also be impacted through time, whether intentional or nonintentional. The goal of any biometric technology is to possess the ability to confirm the identity of a particular individual using the same biometric template (both enrollment and verification) at different points in time. Obviously, there are many variables that do not make this possible. Apart from the aging process, this also includes any changes, alterations, or modifications made to the external environment, lighting, and any types or kinds of background "noises." The bottom line is that the accuracy of biometric systems do actually degrade over time.

---

[*] *United States v. Mitchell*, 463 U.S. 206, Supreme Court of the United States. 1983.

Thus, any previous biometric templates that were recorded need to be discarded or deleted from the database. Thus, these particular biometric templates could themselves be prone to a cyber-based attack, because there is no security protection offered as they have been deleted from the biometric database.

Only the Unique Features Are Extracted

In this regard, the biggest advantage of biometric technology could also prove to be its biggest Achilles heel. For instance, even though an entire image of our physiological self is taken, only the unique features are actually used to construct the biometric templates. This can be best illustrated with the example of the fingerprint. When an end user presents their fingerprint to an optical scanner, the entire image of the fingerprint is actually captured (this is known as the "raw image"). After this, the biometric system then looks for the unique features to be captured to construct the biometric template. In this case of fingerprint recognition, it would be the minutiae that are captured. However, to actually extract these particular unique features, the actual raw image has to be cropped many times further, and the parts of the raw image that are not utilized are quickly discarded by the biometric system. These components of the discarded raw image could also be a trigger point for an ID theft attack within a biometric system. For instance, given the sophistication level of a hacker, these discarded components from the raw image could actually be used to reconstruct the actual fingerprint image, and thus be used to spoof a fingerprint recognition system.

Introducing More Speed into a Biometric System Can Actually Introduce Errors

The speed by which the unique features from a raw image can be extracted and the resultant biometric templates can be created is a direct function (or correlation) of the type of mathematical algorithms, which are embedded into the particular biometric device. As a rule of thumb, the biometric vendors aim to do all of this in just a matter of a few seconds. However, of course, shrinking down this time can be a great marketing boon as well. As a result, there is often a lot of pressure placed on the biometric industry to keep increasing these processing times. Another variable to be taken into consideration is the actual population size of the end user base. With a small one, there could be more variance allowed in the processing times. However, with a much larger one, this window of variance thus greatly shrinks. In order to expedite the processing times of a large end user population, the concept of partitioning the biometric database comes into play (this is known specifically as "binning" and the partitions become known as "bins"). Many variables can be utilized to create the different partitions, such as gender or race, or even the internal characteristics of the biometric templates themselves (e.g., with fingerprint recognition, the partitions in the biometric database can be based on the whorls, loops, and arches that are collected in the raw image). However, if there is more pressure to increase the processing time of a biometric system, the chances are much greater that a biometric template can be wrongly binned (i.e., it goes into a different partition of the biometric database which it was not originally intended to go into) and never be found. These unfound biometric templates can also be the source from which a cyber-based attacker can launch ID theft attack, and again, given his or her level of sophistication, can also be used to trick a biometric system.

PERCEPTION ABOUT BIOMETRICS

One of the other biggest factors that are contributing to the decline of the adoption rate of biometrics in the United States (as well as some other parts of developed countries) is the perception which the American public holds about biometrics. As described previously, a biometric-based device or component is often viewed as a "black box" phenomenon, that is, the way the American public perceives it is literally "garbage in and garbage out."

The end user merely presents his or her fingerprint on top of the optical sensor, the enrollment and verification templates are created, and seconds later, that particular individual's identity is then confirmed (or not confirmed). On account of the lack of understanding of what is really taking place behind the scenes, the American public views biometric technology as "black magic."

A disclaimer needs to be made at this point. The American public does not need to understand all of the technical details of how a biometric system works; rather, all they really need or want to know is just the basics of what is happening. In particular, they are most concerned about how the raw images will be used and where especially the biometric templates will be stored at.

On this level, they will also want to know what safeguards have been taken to protect their biometric templates and who will have access to it. Of course, they will also want to know what backup and recovery steps will be taken in case the biometric database is hacked into or tampered with.

In the end, these questions for the most part are easy to answer, but the biometric industry (in the United States) has failed in this regard. The best time to have these questions addressed is when the training to the end users (such as the employees at the place of business or organization) takes place.

However, the concept of public perception about biometric technology extends into another realm of psychology, which is also known as "human factors." This area of study can be broadly defined as "... the scientific discipline concerned with the understanding of interactions among humans and other elements of a system, and the profession that applies theory, principles, data and methods to design in order to optimize human well-being and overall system performance. Ergonomists contribute to the design and evaluation of tasks, jobs, products, environments and systems in order to make them compatible with the needs, abilities and limitations of people."[*]

In the biometric industry, especially in the United States, there is enormous pressure on the vendors to create the fastest and most robust mathematical algorithms possible. Usually, much more emphasis is placed on speed, as this is a great advertising vehicle for the particular vendor in question.

Faster enrollment and verification times mean more of the end user population who can have his or her identity confirmed much quickly, which can be a great boon to the business or organization. After all, nobody really wants to wait in line for a long stretch of time to have his or her identity be confirmed by the biometric system. The vendors are very cognizant of this and realize that a delay caused by a biometric system will just lead to much more resentment by the American public.

In other words, the biometric vendors are much concerned about the theoretical aspects as to how a particular device will perform against certain other metrics and key performance indicators (KPIs) such as the equal error rate, the false acceptance rate, and the false rejection rate. Very little thought has actually been given to as to how the external factors in the outside environment or from the human factors standpoint could affect system performance as well.

It is important to keep in mind that achieving faster verification or enrollment times and surpassing the benchmarked metrics (as mentioned in the last paragraph) are just two individual components that need to be taken into consideration in the development and creation of new biometric devices. This concept can also be referred to as the "total system performance" (TSP). Specifically, the TSP can be thought of as "... the integration of biometrics in to broader processes and should be borne in mind when considering such applications."[†]

The human factors component plays a huge role in the impact of the levels of TSP, of which a biometrics vendor strives for. Although such variables as cuts, bruises, or even to a certain degree physical deformities are taken into account in the development of a biometric technology,

---

[*] Licht, D. M., Polzella, D. J., and Boff, K. *Human Factors, Ergonomics, and Human Factors Engineering: An Analysis of Definitions.* CSERIAC-89-01, Dayton, OH, 1989.
[†] Maghiros, I., Punie, Y., Delaitre, S., Lignos, E., Rodríguez, C., Ulbrich, M., Cabrera, M., Clements, B., Beslay, L., and van Bavel, R. *Biometrics at the Frontiers: Assessing the Impact on Society.* Study for the European Parliament Committee on Citizens' Freedoms and Rights, Justice and Home Affairs (LIBE), IPTS, Sevilla, Spain, February 2005. http://www.statewatch.org/news/2005/apr/jrc-biometrics-julian-ashbourn.pdf.

there are other physical-based human factors that need to be taken into further consideration by the biometric industry.

These include such variables as the aging process (especially crucial for facial recognition technologies), genders of various end user populations, ethnicity considerations, and the state of health of other end users of the biometric system (the issue of hygiene with a biometric device was discussed in Chapter 1 and still continues to be a major impediment against the adoption rate of biometrics).

To expand further into these variables, with regard to the aging process, this can lead to much more brittle skin forming, which could result in serious forms of arthritis. This can have a detrimental impact on the use of fingerprint recognition devices. Regarding ethnicity, scientific studies have shown that some serious inconsistencies have existed between the enrollment and verification templates even among the same end user population, with regard to the iris and the face. The gender factor has demonstrated that females have, in general, much smaller hands than males do. This, of course, can also have a negative impact on hand geometry scanners, as special accomodations will have to be made to fit both genders.

Even end users of biometric systems who possess other types or kinds of physical disabilities need to be taken into consideration as well. Prime examples of these include autism, dyslexia, other forms of learning disabilities, and even hearing- and vision-based ailments. All of these factors can greatly impede in how well an end user (if they are indeed afflicted with these ailments) can use a biometric system, especially in the way he or she learns how to use it.

However, all of the exact presence of these variables just reviewed depend on the magnitude of the end user base in question. For example, the statistical probability of all these factors being present in a small end user population will most likely be negligible. As the end user population increases to the point where a large-scale biometric system and relevant applications need to be implanted, the odds of these variables being present are, of course, much greater.

If the biometric devices that are in place do not address the concerns just described, then the probability of a certain percentage of end users in a large population could very well be discriminated. This fact of discrimination will not only create further resentment of the biometric system by the end users who actually possess these physical disabilities, but also resonate strongly with the entire end user population.

Finally, it is also important to keep in mind the technical limitation of the biometric industry. Although it has been stated that all of these variables just discussed need to be taken into consideration as a biometric device is created, the probability of such a device conforming to all of them is nearly impossible. The biometric vendors can only take into account the factors or variables that are most prevalent, or common within a large end user population. However, the biometric vendors at the very least need to be aware of all of these factors and variables as they abound, and make special accommodations to those end users who need it the most.

The bottom line is that the human factors equation in the design of a biometric system is of utmost importance: "... the variations in performance directly attributable to human and environmental factors are typically an order of magnitude greater than the variations in performance between capture devices and matching algorithms."[*]

Just as important as it is to examine the human factors psychology from the standpoint of large end user population, it is also equally just as crucial to examine this from the standpoint of an individual. It is important to note here that many of the large-scale applications of biometric technology (at least those that originate from the biometric industry in the United States) exist within the federal government, or are deployed in another country from a biometrics vendor based in the United States.

Examples of this include biometric technology being deployed in both Iraq and Afghanistan, and the massive biometrics database project in India, the biometric-based e-gates, which are found at the major international airports in the United States, as well as worldwide.

Many of the biometric applications are small scale in nature. Thus, the end user population is much smaller; therefore, the perceptions and views about the particular biometric technology from the standpoint of each individual carry much more weight. The views of a single end user from a small population can stem from a wide variety of variables. Some of these include their views on biometric technology, in general assuming that they have some baseline knowledge about the subject matter); what their specific views are on the processes that are utilized in the biometric system; and probably most importantly, how much of their personal information (i.e., the snapshots that will be taken of their physiological selves) they are willing to give up.

The reason why the latter is the most crucial is that this belief system held by the end user will of course have a strong impact between them and the entity who provides the biometric-based service. For the sake of simplicity, this could be the relationship between the employee and the employer. An employee who is staunch against using the biometric technology deployed by his or her employer could very well have a much more dampered relationship with his or her immediate supervisor than if the biometric system has not been deployed.

In the business world, just one negative view held by an employee is, of course, not enough justification to revamp the newly deployed

---

[*] Maghiros, I., Punie, Y., Delaitre, S., Lignos, E., Rodríguez, C., Ulbrich, M., Cabrera, M., Clements, B., Beslay, L., and van Bavel, R. *Biometrics at the Frontiers: Assessing the Impact on Society*. Study for the European Parliament Committee on Citizens' Freedoms and Rights, Justice and Home Affairs (LIBE), IPTS, Sevilla, Spain, February 2005. http://www.statewatch.org/news/2005/apr/jrc-biometrics-julian-ashbourn.pdf.

biometric system. However, if there are negative feelings about it among more individual employees, and the relationships between them and their immediate supervisors, then the place of business or organization will obviously have to find an alternative means of verification and/or identification for those affected employees. This does not necessarily mean that the newly deployed biometric system will be taken out. Rather, it will remain in place for those employees who don't have an issue with it; the alternative methods will be made available for those particular employees who have negative issues with it.

This example brings up another very important point with regard to the individual perception of biometric technology. Before any biometric system is deployed, such as in this case with a business or organization, it is very important that the end user population be introduced to it in phases. For example, this could involve first discussing with the employees that a biometric system is being given serious consideration as a means for further enhancing the current levels of security. It is important at this point that the employees start the learning, or the discovery process, as to how this particular biometric technology (which is being considered) will benefit them as well as the organization or business.

Then, as the biometric technology is being deployed, the employees should also be involved to a certain degree to see how the entire system will work and how they will be affected by it. All of these involvements will then have a very positive effect toward the climatic part of the biometric technology deployment: the end user training. If all of the employees have been involved with the major phases of the deployment, then there is a very strong likelihood that the employees will be perceptive as to what is being taught to them and, most importantly, will be engaged and cooperative when they have to start using the biometric system (going through both the enrollment and subsequent verification processes).

However, on the other end of the spectrum, if the employees have not been engaged by the management of the business or organization, then obviously a very negative attitude will develop toward the biometric system. The employees will not only feel left out but also very well feel "blindsided" as well with the sudden exposure they are receiving about the biometric system they will be required to use. As a result, this will have very negative repercussions on the employees when they are trained in how to properly use the biometric system. The chances are that when the employees are required to start the enrollment and verification processes, they could very well be uncooperative and unwilling to use the new biometric system.

The bottom line of this is that a phased-in approach when deploying a biometric system will lead to a much more positive rate of perception about the use of it as opposed to no approach or engagement offered at all to the end user population.

ERGONOMIC DESIGN OF BIOMETRIC DEVICES

Coupled along with the human factors, the third major constraint against the adoption rate of biometric technology in the United States is regarding the ergonomic design of biometric devices. For example, back in the last decade, many biometric-based technologies were designed in such a way that they were bulky, were difficult to use, and basically looked very "eerie" to the end user. Probably, the two best examples of this are the hand geometry scanner and the retinal/iris scanners. With the former, as the technology first evolved and became available in the marketplace, the devices were very bulky.

It was first difficult to install and very cumbersome to maintain, and worst of all, the end users found its use very difficult and intimidating. Over time, the vendor (Ingersoll Rand, Davidson, NC) improved the technology so that it would be much more user-friendly and easier to maintain as well. Although the internal technology changed, the outside of it has not changed much. As a result, end users have likened the hand geometry scanner compared to that of a "cappuccino maker" and are still, to a certain degree, intimidated by it upon first glance.

With regard to the retinal and iris scanners, they have received a much worse reception on part of the end user compared to the hand geometry scanner. In terms of the retinal scanner, this has been deemed as one of the most user-invasive biometric technologies ever created. This is because the device required the end user to sit in an extremely close proximity to the camera.

The end user could not move at all whatsoever and had to remain still in order for a good image of the retina to be captured. To make matters worse, an infrared beam of light was shone into the end user's eye, in order to fully illuminate the structure of the retina.

These factors totally diminished the cooperativeness required by the end user in order to create stable and robust enrollment and verification templates. On account of this, retinal recognition has not been widely adopted, nor has it captured the market traction perhaps once it had long time ago. Retinal recognition is now being used only in those types and kinds of applications where the highest level of security is required, such as those of nuclear facility installations or highly classified military bases.

Perhaps not to the same level as that of retinal recognition, iris recognition too has suffered from a poor reception due to its ergonomic design. It was not deemed to be as user invasive as retinal recognition, but still the technology was bulky and the end user was required to stand once again in very close proximity to the camera. With iris recognition, just an image of the iris is captured in order to create and configure the enrollment and verification templates; infrared light is not used. However, still the end user remained squeamish and resonated great fear about having to stand close to a camera in order to have an image of his or her iris captured.

What primarily triggered this great fear is that the end user could still see the image of his or her iris as it was being captured by the camera. Over time though, the biometric vendors listened to the fears and misgivings of iris recognition by the end user and developed the technology in such a way now that an image of the iris can be now captured at a much greater distance, and the capture mechanisms have also greatly reduced in size, thus making it very ergonomically friendly. On account of these changes in the design of way an iris recognition now looks, it has become widely accepted in many of the applications which it currently serves.

Thus, as one can see from the examples illustrated above, the way a biometric device looks to an end user upon first glance can have a great impact on its level of acceptance and subsequent usage. This is ergonomic design and creation plays a crucial role in the biometric technologies that are available today. Specifically, ergonomics can be defined as follows: "Ergonomics is about designing for people, wherever they interact with products, systems or processes. The emphasis within ergonomics is to ensure that designs complement the strengths and abilities of people and minimise the effects of their limitations, rather than forcing them to adapt. In achieving this aim, it becomes necessary to understand and design for the variability represented in the population, spanning such attributes as age, size, strength, cognitive ability, prior experience, cultural expectations and goals."[*]

It is important to keep in mind that the field of ergonomics, especially as it relates to biometric technology, is much more of an engineering type of concept than it is a psychological approach. In this regard, ergonomics consists of the engineering subcomponents discussed in the sections that follow when it comes to various biometric modalities.

The Data Acquisition Environment

The high-performance mathematical algorithms that are "housed" in the specific biometric device are actually a direct function of the quality of the biometric templates that are created (both the enrollment and the verification). This, in turn, is also heavily dependent on the ergonomic design of the biometric device in question. For example, with a fingerprint recognition device, if the optical-based sensor is large and is within easy reach of the end user, then it can be almost guaranteed that a good-quality raw image will be captured. This means that robust enrollment and verification templates being created.

---

[*] Licht, D. M., Polzella, D. J., & Boff, K. *Human Factors, Ergonomics, and Human Factors Engineering: An Analysis of Definitions.* CSERIAC-89-01. 1989.

Enhancing the End User Experience

A majority of the biometric technologies (including both physical and behavioral) and their associated mathematical algorithms work the best in controlled environments, or where the applications are small in scale. However, it is important to keep in mind as well that a bulk of the large-scale biometric applications do not operate in controlled environments; rather they perform their functions in very dynamic instances where the variables and external conditions are not known or uncontrollable. Thus, it is always a constant challenge for the biometric industry to improve both verification and identification performance in these unknown conditions.

In order to alleviate this issue and to provide a more ergonomic environment for the end user, serious research and development spending is going into creating biometric devices, which can be deployed "at-a-distance" or "on-the-move." With this type of technological advancement, the raw images of the end users can be captured while they are in large groups and on the move. In this regard, there is no direct cooperation that is required from them; these raw images can be collected in a very covert style.

As discussed earlier in this book, probably the best example of this is iris recognition. The technology has far advanced to the point now that the iris raw images of end users can be captured while they are on the go, and even without their knowledge of it. As a result, this on the move technology has found its unique feature at the major international airports worldwide. The other biometric technology in which on the move techniques are being examined on is that of facial recognition. However, there is still quite some time until this can be deployed in the same fashion as that of iris recognition.

This is because capturing the raw images of the facial structure is heavily dependent on the pose of the end user, the view reach of the facial recognition camera, and the illumination that is provided by the outside environment. Thus far, studies have shown that the accuracy of facial recognition systems falls well below 47% when it is deployed in an on the move fashion.[*] Although this technique will no doubt increase the ergonomic convenience to the end user, there will be a steep trade-off here: The issue of privacy rights and civil liberties violations.

The field of ergonomics and how it can be used to improve the acceptance rate as well as the perception level of biometric technology are also receiving a lot of attention in the academia world. Numerous studies have

---

[*] A.K. Jain and A. Kumar. Biometrics of next generation: An overview. In E. Mordini and D. Tzovaras (eds.), *Second Generation Biometrics*, Springer, 2010. http://citeseerx. ist.psu.edu/viewdoc/download?doi=10.1.1.389.7907&rep=rep1&type=pdf.

been conducted, especially at Purdue University. One of the pioneering studies in this field was "Implementing Ergonomic Principles in a Biometric System: A Look at the Human Biometric Sensor Interaction (HBSI)."[*]

In this specific scientific study, live subjects were asked to login into a laptop computer, utilizing a fingerprint sensor (which was actually installed into it). As the subjects tried to be enrolled and verified into this laptop computer, a testing administrator was also present to note any feedback provided by the end users. The software that was developed for this particular scientific study also provided feedback for the end users, in case they were having troubles aligning up their finger on the optical sensor. In this regard, the feedback offered to the end user included the following types of scenarios:

- Move right.
- Move left.
- Try again.
- Slow down.
- Align finger.
- Match failed: The end user did not complete the actual enrollment process first.
- Finger matched: This indicated to the end user who was able to login into the laptop; there was a close enough match between the enrollment and verification templates.

It should be noted that in this study, the end user was required to enroll all 10 fingers in order to have a robust sampling of fingerprint biometric templates. The end users were also given training on how to place all of his or her fingers to the optical scanner by way of a video; and they were also allowed to have four practice runs.

The end user population for this study was divided into two groups: those who use their right hand predominantly and those who use their left the most. In all, there were a total of 88 end users in the age range of 26–65. About 81% of the end users were Caucasian, and 92% of them were right-handed. The way in which the end users presented their fingers to the optical sensor was consistent: index finger first, followed by the middle finger, then the ring finger, little finger, and the thumb.

The primary performance metric for this study was the "failure to acquire" (FTA) rate. Specifically, it can be defined as the "... proportion of verification or identification attempts for which the system fails to capture or locate an image or signal of sufficient quality."[†]

---

[*] E.P. Kukula and S.J. Elliott. Implementing ergonomic principles in a biometric system: A look at the human biometric sensor interaction (HBSI). In *Carnahan Conferences Security Technology, Proceedings of the 40th Annual IEEE International*, IEEE, Lexington, KY, pp. 86–91, 2006. http://icbrpurdue.org/wp-content/uploads/2014/01/2006-Implementing-Ergonomic-Principles-in-a-Biometric-System-A-Look-at-the-Human-Biometric-Sensor-Interaction.pdf.
[†] Ibid.

The results of this study revealed some very interesting findings, especially on how it relates to the ergonomic design of various biometric modalities:

- There is an actual decrease in the FTA rate if the fingers of the right hand were swiped first onto the optical sensor.
- Much more research needs to be further conducted in the area of ergonomic design in biometric devices, especially in the way how human beings interact with various types and kinds of sensors.
- More training for the end user population would actually result in a much lower FTA rate.
- The way the optical sensor is designed onto the laptop can greatly affect the FTA rate.
- The most frequent feedback to the end user in this study was "try again."
- The way the optical sensor is oriented on the laptop can also have a considerable impact on the end user's perception of the fingerprint recognition system and the FTA rate.
- Further research is needed to determine the level of how finger dexterity can impact the FTA rate.

From this study, it is quite obvious that the optical sensor used in fingerprint recognition devices need to be large and comfortable enough so that the end user can properly place his or her finger, with the end resultant being that high-caliber enrollment and verification templates can be created and used. Also, the optical sensor on the computer (or for that matter any device) needs to be positioned in such a way that it can be easily seen and recognized by the end user, and needs to be designed in such a way that it emphasizes a more user-centric approach.

The same group of researchers as reviewed in the first scientific study also published another research work, "Human Biometric Sensor Interaction" (HBSI),[*] which was examined in much more detail by Kukula and colleagues in "The Effects of Human Interaction on Biometric System Performance."[†] The basic premise behind the HBSI model is that various biometric modalities that are available today are heavily dependent on the sensor (e.g., the optical sensor on a fingerprint recognition device) in order to acquire the appropriate raw images, and from there, to segment those data so that the unique features can be quickly and efficiently extracted. In other words, the HBSI model is concerned specifically with the data collection portion of a biometric system model. The specific trait being collected and subsequently measured (fingerprint, hand samples), for

---

[*] E.P. Kukula, S.J. Elliott, and V.G. Duffy. The effects of human interaction on biometric system performance. In V.G. Duffy (ed.), *Digital Human Modeling*, HCII 2007, LNCS 4561, Springer, Berlin/Heidelberg, Germany, pp. 904–914, 2007.
[†] Ibid.

example, needs to be presented in a consistent manner, providing unique samples for downstream modules of the biometric system to process.

However, this is just the technical component of the HBSI model. The other component is that the human interaction with various biometric sensors, which again lends itself to the importance of ergonomic design in the development of biometric systems. The model lays down the basic premise that several of the major ergonomic design issues could be easily resolved if some of the subfields of ergonomics were actually integrated into the design of biometric systems. These subfields include industrial and interactive design, as well as the perceived usability (on part of the end user) of a biometric system.

This research work also probes various reasons why end users perceive biometric devices that are difficult to use. The chief reason cited for this is that the biometric vendors (in the United States) are much more heavily focused on the technical design and deployment of the machine or system, rather than also focusing on how the end user will perceive its level of ease of use and overall ergonomic friendliness. The researchers cite that this trend in the biometric industry is largely due to the fact that the biometric sensors are not tested sufficiently on large numbers of differing end user populations, primarily due to financial reasons.

Another factor cited is that the biometric sensor–end user interaction can also pose serious cognitive-based interaction problem. This is because there is an extra burden of conscious thought, which is required by the end user on how to properly place his or her finger or hand onto the appropriate sensor. To help resolve these problems of thinking and perception, the HBSI model was created to alleviate the issues of complex ergonomic designs in biometric systems.

The HBSI model is actually a combination of various other social science methodologies, which include anthropometry, user-centered design studies, and perceived usability. The primary thrust of the HBSI model is to apply the principles of ergonomics in the design of a specific biometric modality. The resultant of this model is that a scientific framework can be established within the biometric industry, which helps to reduce or even exclude the stressors on the human bodies of the end user populations.

One of these stressors includes the mental model of the end user. The goal here is to create a biometric device, which is so ergonomically comfortable and easy to use that the actual act of placing a finger on the optical sensor of a fingerprint recognition device becomes literally a subconscious movement for the end user.

The second major stressor that is addressed by the HBSI model is to appropriately place the biometric device in a repeatable environment so that the end user can feel free to a submit his or her biometric sample in the most optimal conditions possible. With these two major stressors eliminated, it is also expected that the HBSI model will help to lead to a huge increase of overall biometric system performance, newer and intuitive end user interfaces to the biometric system, and above all, a greater interaction between the end user and the biometric sensor.

The HBSI model, in this research study, also addresses the five key ergonomic principles, which are crucial to the design of a diometric system. The model states that if these five topics are addressed, then the end user perception and acceptance of the biometric system should also increase. These five principles are as follows:

1. *Universality*: The biometric modalities of today can be used by all of the end user population. This simply means taking into account the physiological and behavioral differences, which are prevalent in societies all over the world.
2. *Invariance*: The unique features that are extracted from the raw images do not change over time (of course, this is only in theory; reality dictates quite the opposite).
3. *High levels of intraclass variability*: The unique features that are extracted from the raw images (used to create both the Enrollment) are extremely distinct from each other in the same end user population.
4. *Acceptability*: The biometric system, in general, is deemed to be suitable for use by all of the end users.
5. *Extractability*: The biometric sensor can quickly and easily extract the unique features from the raw images in a repeatable manner (this simply means that the enrollment and verification templates can be created in rapid succession between end users as they place their hand or finger onto the biometric sensor).

In the HBSI model, although the physical design of the biometric device is very important in making the end user feel comfortable by using it, the way the biometric device is permanently oriented to a fixture (such as a hand geometry scanner being mounted on a wall) can also greatly affect the way an end user perceives its level of ease of use.

In this study, the surface height on which a fingerprint recognition device was placed onto a wall was examined to see how it would affect the end user perception of it. A total of 75 end users were enrolled in the subject pool, and the results were startling:

- A counter height of 36 inches (this is measured as the distance from the surface of the floor to the bottom of the fingerprint recognition device) gave the fastest performance in terms of the biometric metrics of failure to accept, failure to reject, and the overall failure to accept rates.
- A counter height of 26 inches yielded the highest quality fingerprint images.
- Counter heights between 32 and 36 inches were deemed to be the most comfortable for end users.

As one can conclude from these results, trying to design a biometric system can yield very high-quality enrollment and verification templates, but yet keeping the design and orientation of the biometric system can be a very tricky proposition to achieve. For example, "... interfaces of security systems do not reflect good thinking in terms of creating a system that is easy to use, while maintaining an acceptable level of security."[*]

Finally, when it comes to the ergonomic design of a biometric system, there are four more variables which also need to be taken into consideration. These variables can be characterized in the sections that follow.

Privacy

As it has been stated throughout this book, privacy rights are one of the biggest issues and concerns with regard to biometric technology. This fear or public angst will probably never disappear, at least in the United States. There are many regions around the world (especially the developing nations) where privacy rights are not even an issue in the respective populations. However, in the developed nations, it still persists. Ergonomics can help to reduce this angst among the American public by designing and creating biometric systems in such a way that it does not look intimidating to the end user.

This example was alluded to earlier with the hand geometry scanner. During the lifetime of this device, for the most part, it has received lukewarm reception from the end user primarily because of the way it looks. Although this is easier said than done, the biometric industry in the United States needs to take into heavy consideration how the end user perceives the biometric device before it actually comes to market. This can probably be best achieved by conducting focus group interviews of potential end users and collect their opinions and feedback before the biometric device is actually launched.

---

[*] E.P. Kukula, S.J. Elliott, and V.G. Duffy. The effects of human interaction on biometric system performance. In V.G. Duffy (ed.), *Digital Human Modeling*, HCII 2007, LNCS 4561, Springer, Berlin/Heidelberg, Germany, pp. 904–914, 2007. http://www.icbrpurdue.org/wp-content/uploads/2014/01/Kukula-Elliott-Duffy-2007-The-effects-of-human-interaction-on-biometric-system-performance.pdf.

Reasonableness

The particular biometric technology that will be used must be in proportion to the market application from which it will serve, no more and no less. For example, it would make no point to have a retinal recognition device on a school bus in order to verify the identity of the children on board. This would be deemed to be way too intrusive. Probably, a better suited biometric technology would be the fingerprint recognition (in fact, this particular technology is already being used in public schools throughout the United States—as a means for poverty-stricken children to pay for their lunch meals through federal government-subsidized programs).

Proportionality

This variable can also be considered to be a subset of the "reasonableness" variable. The information and data that are provided by a biometric template must also be used in proportion to the market application it is serving. For instance, if iris recognition were to be used for an e-commerce site, more than likely, the end user would have much more concern about what kind and type of information was being shared with other third parties. However, if a much more compatible biometric technology was being used (for this specific market application), such as keystroke recognition, then the end user probably would not have many fears about using it.

In other words, with regard to the two variables "reasonableness" and "proportionality," the biometric technology should not "overkill" the application which it is being used for. The right biometric technology should be used in just the right manner. When this approach is utilized, any fears or anxieties about using the biometric technology should be greatly reduced.

Behavior

As it can be implied in all the chapters, biometric technology always strikes some emotion in the end user population. It can bring out mostly fear, but it can also bring out a sense of anxiety, nervousness, intrigue, wonderment, curiosity, and so on. In turn, these emotions can bring out different behaviors in people when they see the biometric device for the first time. The end users who feel fear or anxiety will be very hesitant to use the biometric device, whereas those who look at the biometric device with a sense of curiosity will want to use it but with caution.

There is no doubt that the biometric vendors want their end users not be afraid to use their devices, but rather, err more to the side of wonderment and intrigue, which in turn will lead to cooperative behavior. In other words, out of the total end user population, you would want at least 90% of it to try out the biometric device for the first time, and at least get them through the enrollment process. Again, in order to illicit this type of behavior from the end user, the biometric device must look appealing and bring out a strong perception that it is very easy to use. This can only come through when a preplanned ergonomic design is established first.[*]

FUNCTION CREEP

The fourth major variable in our study of hindering the adoption rate of biometric technology in the United States is a phenomenon known as "function creep." As it has been discussed so far in this book, biometrics are not just being used as a stand-alone application; rather the particular modalities can be used in conjunction with another, or they can also be coupled with legacy-based, non-biometric security systems. These types of applications are known more technical as "multimodal biometric systems" (this is the situation where more than one biometric device is used together), or a "multimodal security system" (this is where a specific biometric modality is used with non-biometric security technology).

Given this joint adaptability of biometric technology, there is obviously a lot more information and data that are being shared between the systems, as well as biometric templates. Normally, biometric modalities are intended to serve just one application at a time. Given this, the thinking of the American public is that the enrollment and verification templates that are created will be used solely for that application purpose alone. However, the information and data that are collected for that specific purpose can actually, whether intentionally or unintentionally, be used "or spill over" for other security applications, unbeknownst to the American public.

This spillover effect is more technically known as "function creep," and it can be defined as follows: "... [this] is the term used to describe the expansion of a process or system, where data collected for one specific purpose is subsequently used for another unintended or unauthorized purpose."[†] As it was alluded to before, this spillover tends to be more intentional based than not. After all, to some degree, it makes sense. For example, if a fingerprint recognition system was being used in a physical access entry application at the main point of entry at the place of business or organization, the same biometric templates could be used for the verification and/or identification of the same individuals

---

[*] T. Stewart. Biometrics and the User Experience, Systems Concepts, 2015. http://www.system-concepts.com/articles/usability-articles/2013/biometrics-and-the-user-experience.html.

[†] E. Mordini and S. Massari. Body, biometrics and identity, Bioethics, 22(9), pp. 488–498, 2008. http://www.hideproject.org/downloads/Mordini_Massari-Body_Biometrics_Identity.pdf.

at another physical location in which employees have to gain access to. To the upper levels of management, this is advantageous, because they do not have to invest more capital in deploying more fingerprint recognition devices.

Although this approach can be used as a cost-saving move in the place of business or organization, the repercussions that exist from this covert use of the biometric templates (as well as its associated information and data) can be quite negative, especially to the end user population who is using this particular biometric modality. For instance, to name just a few of the negativities, the miniscule trust which the American public may have biometric technology will quickly erode, and confidence in the use of any type or kind of biometric system will virtually dissipate. Also, misusing biometric templates in this fashion can be considered as a very serious ethical breach.

The function creep phenomenon can stem from three different sources.

An Absence of Policy

A formal lack of a security policy that details as to how biometric templates and their corresponding information/data can be used is probably one of the biggest reasons why function creep exists in the first place. After all without a system of accountability in place, the urge to misuse the biometric templates and use them covertly for other applications can grow very strong. However, primarily, this intended misuse of the biometric templates is often dictated by the stakeholders who are involved in the original procurement and deployment of the particular biometric modality. Even worse, the information and data that are collected from a biometric modality can be used quite opposite from its original, intended use—for example, for even launching ID theft attacks.

An Unsatisfied Demand for a Particular Business Function

The source for function creep is actually illustrated in the example just discussed. However, let us add a different twist to it. Suppose that a place of business or organization implements a fingerprint recognition device, but this particular modality is simply not living up to the KPIs and the performance metrics that the vendor claimed. Obviously, the management team will want to replace this fingerprint recognition device with a brand new one. Rather than having all of the employees re-enroll again, the existing Biometric Templates from the old system could just be used again. The "unsatisfied demand" is the result from the first Fingerprint Recognition device not performing to the expected standards.

The Slippery Slope Effect

The "slippery slope effect" refers to the fact that the unintended use of biometric templates usually occurs in a very covert fashion. This can happen in two ways. First, the function creep can transpire very slowly, or in bits at a time. For instance, this could also be the result of the incremental effects over minor changes in the original of securing a biometric system. Second, the function creep can happen just all of a sudden. This can happen when the stakeholders involved in the original biometric procurement and deployment have an ulterior motive, or even a hidden agenda in place.

In context of the slippery slope effect, the distinction needs to be made when a particular biometric modality is simply being used well beyond its technical limits, or if the biometric modality is being purposely used to generate extra information and data, which will be subsequently used for covert, malicious purposes. With regard to the former, there have been no actual, documented cases where a biometric system has literally been taxed to well beyond its limits. If this situation were to ever arise, more random access memory and other types of memory chips can be quickly and easily added into the biometric modality.

In terms of the latter, this can be also referred to as "subversive biometrics." This can also be likened to Murphy's law, which simply states that "... if any technology can be misused, it will be, and there is no reason to assume that biometrics might escape this rule."[*] This is because given the rapid advances in biometric technology, biometric templates and their associated information and data can quite easily be used for covert and malicious purposes. More than likely, it will not be the cyber attacker that will launch such types of attacks, but rather they will happen within the place of business or organization, most likely by those people who have direct access to the biometric modality. This would include the system administrators, the network administrators, and other relevant IT staff.

Thus, this is where the concept of "data minimization" must come into play. In other words, the biometric system should not generate any more information and data than what is absolutely required for the application which it serves. However, the probability of this actually occurring is low, as biometric applications will ever succeed in minimizing data capture and processing.

A prime example of function creep actually took place in the Netherlands, back in 2009. During this time, the Dutch government enacted legislation that would be used to enforce security policies on their newly implemented digital passport system (also known as the "e-passport." This involved the creation and deployment of fingerprint and facial

---

[*] E. Mordini and S. Massari. Body, biometrics and identity, Bioethics, 22(9), pp. 488–498, 2008. http://www.hideproject.org/downloads/Mordini_Massari-Body_Biometrics_Identity.pdf.

recognition databases. Although these databases were meant to be used exclusively for the e-passport, the biometric templates that were created were then spilled over to be used in the establishment of a criminal investigation database (which would be similar in nature to the biometric databases maintained by the FBI). This move by the Dutch government was totally decried by the Dutch Data Protection Authority, as well as privacy rights groups and human rights advocates based in the Netherlands.

The fear of function creep does not reside at just the place of business or organization where the biometric systems reside at. This fear could very well pervade all across the American public, stoking the fears yet once again that "Big Brother" is watching. In this regard, it would be the grave fear of the federal government taking its gargantuan biometric databases and taking the biometric information and data that reside in them and using them for other covert applications, such as keeping tabs on ordinary American citizens.

This fear is also explained well by privacy rights expert Roger Clarke: "Any high-integrity identifier [like biometrics] represents a threat to civil liberties, because it represents the basis for a ubiquitous identification scheme, and such a scheme provides enormous power over the populace. All human behavior would become transparent to the state, and the scope for non-conformism and dissent would be muted to the point envisaged by the anti-Utopian novelists."*

UNDERSTANDING OF BIOMETRIC TECHNOLOGY

The fifth major reason why biometric technology is poorly adopted in the United States is that the American public simply does not understand what the technology is all about. They do not need to be educated in each and every facet of the biometric modality in question, but they should have some idea as to how it works. As it was mentioned in the first book and in Chapter 1, biometrics is viewed as a "black box" type of technology, which means that, to some people, it is a source of intrigue, but for many others, it is a source of anxiety and misunderstanding.

Probably, one of the biggest reasons for this frustration on part of the American public is that each biometric modality is proprietary to each vendor. The technical information and data on each modality cannot be found easily, even through various Internet searches. However, if one were to look up some of the technical features of a non-biometric

---

* J.D. Woodward, Jr. K.W. Webb, E.M. Newton, M. Bradley and D. Rubenson. What concerns do biometrics raise and how do they differ from concerns about other identification methods? In *Army Biometric Applications*, RAND, pp. 21–31, 2001. http://www.rand. org/content/dam/rand/pubs/monograph_reports/MR1237/MR1237.ch3.pdf.

technology, such as that of a firewall or a router, the technical specifications can be more or less easily found.

The biometric vendors do provide this type of technical information and data only if a customer actually procures and deploys their modality. This is not to say that product- or solution-based brochures are not available, but they are often written using a language that could very well not be understood by the American public. Therefore, in this part of this chapter, we will provide a little bit of an overview, in an effort to help educate the potential end user of a biometric system.

The first and foremost component of a biometric modality is the acquisition module. Simply put, this is where the raw images of the end user are captured and processed. Each and every biometric technology has his or her own special type or kind of acquisition module. For example, a fingerprint recognition system will consist of the optical scanner to collect an image of a fingerprint; a facial or iris recognition system utilizes a specialized camera in order to capture the raw images of the face and eye; a keystroke recognition system uses the keyboard to capture the rhythmic typing pattern of the end user; and a signature recognition system uses a specialized stylus and screen to capture the behavioral mannerisms in the way a person signs his or her signature.

In the acquisition module, the raw image is converted into a digital image (it is from this particular image that the unique features are extracted from). As discussed earlier, at this stage, the ergonomic design of the sensor is extremely crucial on two fronts. First, the sensor has to be engineered in such a way that it is large enough so that a series of high-quality and robust raw images can be captured. Second, the sensor has to look "inviting" and "appealing" enough so that the end user will not be afraid, for example, to place his or her fingertip or had to the biometric device.

In the feature extraction module, it is first determined if the acquired raw images (more than likely, these raw images will be converted into a composite raw image) have achieved the actual, minimum requirements and if there are enough unique features that can actually be extracted. If so, then the composite raw image will then be transferred to the next stage, which is the unique feature extraction. The unique features vary for each type of and kind of biometric modality.

For example, with the physical biometrics, fingerprint recognition, the "minutiae" are captured (these are the various breaks and discontinuities in the swirls of the fingerprint); with iris recognition, the vector orientation of the furrows and freckles is captured; with voice recognition, various pitches in a person's voice are examined; and in facial recognition, the vector orientation and the distances between the prominent landmarks on the face are captured. With regard to the behavioral biometrics, the unique typing pattern on the keyboard and the mannerisms in which the person signs his or her signature are captured.

Once these unique features are extracted, they are then converted into the enrollment and verification templates, respectively.

In the feature matching module, the enrollment and verification templates are compared with each other. Based on the mathematical algorithms that are created and the security thresholds that are established by the biometric system administrator, if the two biometric templates are statistically close enough to one another, the identification of the end user is positively confirmed. As a result, he or she will then gain either physical or logical access to the resources he or she is seeking. However, if the two biometric templates are not deemed to be close enough in terms of a match, then the identification of the end user will not be confirmed, and they will be prompted again by the biometric system to start the verification process all over again.

The fourth and last major component of any type or kind of biometric modality is the biometrics database. In many regards, this can be considered to be the "back end" of all of the biometric modalities. This is where all of the biometric templates are stored (just the enrollment templates are stored in the database, but the verification templates are not. As the end user is in the process of having his or her identity being confirmed, the appropriate enrollment template will be called up to be compared against the newly created and enrollment template as well as of the transaction logs which of all of the activities which transpire from within the biometric system. The exact subcomponents of a typical biometric system were examined in much detail in the first book.

Therefore, as one can see from our description, there is nothing mysterious or black box about a biometric modality. It is essentially "garbage in, garbage out," just like any other type or kind of computing system. However, in order for the American public to get out of this mentality, it is very important for the biometric vendors to teach the end user populations about the major components of a biometric system and how they all interact with each other.

In order to maximize the level of acceptance, these explanations as to how a biometric system works should be given during the initial training session, in which the end user is educated on how to properly enroll himself or herself into the biometric system. The American public often likes to associate biometric technology with various "James Bond" movies and other famous crime scene programs on the major television networks, such as *CSI: Crime Scene Investigation*. This association also impedes the adoption rate of biometric technology in the United States.

In order to help alleviate these mentalities and negative associations, the deployment of biometric technologies must be a transparent and open process. The American public must have the opportunity to see not only how it is being specifically deployed, but most importantly, but also firsthand into how their biometric templates will be used and stored (from the standpoint of the database, as described previously). Finally, in an effort to make biometric technology a much more transparent process, the American public must be given the right to ask questions (but also have those questions answered) to the federal government, the biometric vendors (really, to the entire biometric industry as a whole), and their employers who will be deploying such systems.

END USER POPULATION

The sixth major reason for the slow adoption rate of biometric technology in the United States as well as its varying degrees worldwide can actually be found in the actual age groups of the end user population. Let us take the example of the United States. If the end user group consists primarily of elderly people, the chances are much lower that they will be willing to adopt a particular biometric modality for their own security and online access.

The primary reason for this is that this type of end user population probably will not embrace the latest technologies, which could add that extra layer of protection. Rather, they are more likely to stick to the more traditional ways of using technology that they are used to. For example, rather than using the latest smartphone or wireless technologies available today in the marketplace (such as tablets and netbooks), the tendency will be for this particular end user population to utilize the more conventional desktop computers.

Also, when it is the time to confirming their identity, there is also a good probability that they will be resistant to using biometric technology. Instead, they will more than likely would like to have their identity confirmed with traditional means, which includes the use of driver's licenses, usernames and passwords, challenge and response questions, and so on.

However, it has been discovered that the younger generation end user population would be much more embracing when it comes to the use of biometric technology. A primary driver for this higher acceptance rate is that the younger generation is much more affluent in terms of knowledge and usage of the latest technologies, even the latest in the security industry. They are also much more up to date about the recent technological trends; in fact, the technology surrounds their everyday lives, both personally and professionally.

In order to prove that the adoption rate of biometric technology is much higher in the younger end user population versus the older end user population, a massive research project was undertaken by the Biometrics Institute and the University of Kent, both based in the United Kingdom.[*]

---

[*] Identity and Passport Service. Perspectives on Identity, Identity Protection and Biometrics among Young People Report, 2010. http://www.eda.kent.ac.uk/material/pdf_docs/Identity.pdf.

The age group examined in the end user population was 16–25 years, and in this study, various factors were examined, including the following:

- Security threats and vulnerabilities are posed to both the personal identity and the ID theft.
- The perceptions and views are associated with biometric technology in order to determine and authenticate the personal identities of this particular end user population.

In order to execute this research, three workshops were organized as follows:

- *Workshop 1*: The ultimate goal here was to share information and data as well as identify the important social issues surrounding the use of biometric technology and analyze them as well.
- *Workshop 2*: The discussions from workshop 1 would be further applied here, but instead of just discussing about general issues, the common themes learned from workshop #1 would be carried over to much smaller subgroups of the end user population, and the issues and concerns surrounding the use of biometric technology would thus be further drilled down. One of the primary goals in this workshop was to have open and honest dialog from the end users.
- *Workshop 3*: This final workshop had four primary objectives:
  - To introduce the concepts of biometric technology to this particular end user population
  - To actually give this end user population some real-world experience in utilizing various types or kinds of biometric modalities by going through the actual enrollment and verification processes
  - To discuss more macro issues surrounding identity and identity protection in relation to social media and Internet-based communications
  - To engage this very young end user population in various activities, which would get them to research, think about, and prepare a presentation on some aspect of personal identity, using biometric technology as the main focal point

Various biometric vendors also took part in a three-part workshop, with the two main ones being Sagem Sécurité and Smart Sensors Ltd.[*] After these workshops were concluded, the researchers of this project then engaged themselves into the raw data collected in order to ascertain major findings and results, which are as follows:

---

[*] Identity and Passport Service. Perspectives on Identity, Identity Protection and Biometrics among Young People Report, 2010. http://www.eda.kent.ac.uk/material/pdf_docs/Identity.pdf.

- This particular end user population has actually, indeed, been exposed to biometric technologies, especially in their social lives. Examples include using various modalities that could be found at the major universities, child nurseries, as well as night clubs. They are also exposed to biometric technology at their places of employment (e.g., construction sites) or when they visited a health professional (such as a dentist).
- It appears that the deployment of biometric technology works much better in smaller application environments as opposed to larger scale environments (in this study, a small environment was defined as less than 1000 users, and a large environment was defined as greater than 250,000 users).
- In general, biometric technology was viewed quite positively by this end user population. For instance, it has been very popularly used in nightclubs (in fact, club owners even reported a greater uptick in good behavior from their customers once they introduced biometric technology into their establishment).
- The use of biometric technology has also received wide scale adoption and usage in the public schools in the United Kingdom, where a much younger end user population is prevalent. The primary catalyst for this has been the costly overhead associated with using cash or other types of smart card-based solutions. From the students' perception, the use of biometric technology also greatly reduced their embarrassment in case they were denied access to anything by using the traditional smart card technology.
- One of the strongest conclusions discovered was that no matter how large or small the application is, effective communications and training are still required for this young end user population despite their much higher acceptance and adoption rates.
- The end user must not be forced to use a deployed biometric system. Rather, they must be given the choice of whether to use or not, and if they opt for the latter, then other alternative authentication methods must be made available.
- The biometric industry needs to do a much better job in explaining to the end users as to how their biometric templates will be stored in the database as well as how they will be secured. This is especially true of the much younger end user population, where strong levels of nativity still exist with regard to data protection. For instance, "Data protection legislation is unknown and unloved. Young EU citizens' knowledge level about data protection laws is very low. Even lower is their appreciation of the current protection framework."[*]

---

[*] Identity and Passport Service. Perspectives on Identity, Identity Protection and Biometrics among Young People Report, 2010. http://www.eda.kent.ac.uk/material/pdf_docs/Identity.pdf.

- In terms of actual biometric modalities, it appears that finger-print recognition is the most widely accepted, whereas facial recognition is the least accepted.
- Overall, it was viewed that biometric technology helps to increase end user convenience, reduce costs, as well as improve the accuracy of the information and data that are collected.
- When extrapolating into future uses of biometric technology, this young end user population reflected that using biometric technology in health-care dispensing machines would prove to be very popular (in fact, the health-care industry in the United States has already deployed this in limited market segments).
- Another potential application that could make the strong usage of biometric technology (according to the end user population in this study) would be the payment industry, in which a cashless society would eventually transpire, as a result. However, it was also expressed that extra security checks need to be implemented, in order to ensure that the payment system could not be spoofed.
- Finally, it was deemed that voice recognition is the least intrusive of the biometric modalities that are available today.[*]

Based on these findings, the biometric industry in the United States could learn some very key lessons when it comes to increasing the adoption of biometric technology in the eyes of the American public.

- The first lesson to be learned is that, training and addressing the issues and objections raised by the end user population must be addressed and answered in a timely manner. This will only help to increase the believability of the viability of biometric technology in the American public.
- Second, the application cases in which biometric technology has been rolled out successfully in small end user populations must be illustrated to great extents to the American public to prove that biometric technology does indeed work as a strong security measure. Then from here, perhaps the acceptance of biometric technology in mainstream America will also increase.
- Third, given the very sensitive issue of privacy rights and civil liberties in the United States, alternative methods of authentication must be implemented for those end users who do not wish to use a biometric system. Not only does the biometric industry need to understand this, but the management teams at the places of business or organizations in which biometric technology will be deployed need to fully understand this as well.

---

[*] Ibid.

- Fourth, given that the Digital Era we are living will only grow at an exponential rate in the future, it is very important for the biometric industry to explain to the American public how their biometric templates will be used, how they will be stored, and most importantly how they will be secured in the biometrics databases. If this clear line of communications were to be established, then perhaps the myths and fears of "Big Brother" watching or the federal government keeping tabs on each and every American citizen would dissipate.
- Fifth, as it was reviewed previously in this chapter, it could very well be the case that perhaps the American public is not yet ready to accept the most modern forms of biometric technology that are available today, or those that are expected to be provisioned later. For example, although facial recognition technology and the use of deoxyribonucleic acid (DNA) may be accepted in the developing nations as a suitable way to confirm the identity of a particular individual, this is far from the case in the United States.
- Perhaps, in an effort to help increase the adoption rate of biometrics, only the tried and tested modalities should be used (this includes primarily fingerprint recognition and hand geometry recognition), as well as the non-contactless modalities (this would also include iris recognition and vein pattern recognition). Although using these types of modalities will just only stifle research and development efforts within the biometric industry, acceptance right now is the "name of the game," not creating more "exotic" biometric modalities. Although the technology may prove to be more effective than what is available right now, there is no guarantee that it will even be accepted by the American public.

LEGAL CONSIDERATIONS

The seventh major reason why there is a slower adoption rate of biometric technology compared to the other parts of the world is the legal considerations that are involved. It is very often the case that as technology advances at a very rapid pace, the rate at which legislation is passed to address the legal issues surrounding these new security technologies often lags at a very slow pace. This also holds true for biometric technology. Specifically, there are a number of key legal hurdles that need to be examined in this regard, and they are discussed in detail in the sections that follow.

The Legal Status of a Biometric Template

First and foremost, from a legal standpoint, the first issue that needs to be addressed is if even a biometric template is considered as either personal or public information and data. There has even been a debate as to whether or not a biometric template should even be classified as "anonymous data." Although all of this has yet to be defined and determined in the United States, biometric templates have been actually classified in the European Union as personal data, based on the "Data Protection Directive."

Keep in mind that biometric templates are not dynamic pieces of information and data. Rather, they are classified as static in nature, because once the biometric templates are stored in the database, they do not "move" anywhere, unless they are deleted from the system. Therefore, the question arises as to when (or at what certain periods in time) should a biometric template be classified as "sensitive data." According to the Directive, a biometric template should be considered as sensitive data when "personal data revealing racial or ethnic origin, political opinions, religious or philosophical beliefs, trade-union membership, and the processing of data concerning health or sex life should receive 'explicit consent' of the data subjects unless in certain listed circumstances."[*]

In other words, if a biometric template has the potential to reveal such type of information, then the consent of the end user must be obtained first before it can be used for any types or kinds of identification scenarios. In these situations then, a biometric template, under legal circumstances, can be considered to be "sensitive data." However, based on this finding, one can then pose the specific argument: How can a hacker glean such sensitive information if a biometric template is just nothing but a mathematical file? As mentioned earlier, there are two distinct ways in which this can occur. First, in theory, sensitive information can be gathered from the raw image that is collected, or it can be gathered directly from the biometric template.

More than likely, it will be the first situation in which sensitive data can be revealed about the end user. However, this is only true with the biometric technologies that require direct contact, such as fingerprint recognition and hand geometry recognition. Recent research studies have shown that latent fingerprints that are left on an optical sensor can actually be captured, and from there, the raw image can be reconstructed. However, with regard to reconstructing the raw image directly from the biometric template itself, to date, there have been no scientific studies that support this, and there have also been no actual cases of this actually occurring in real-world biometric applications.

Although the issue of how to properly classify a biometric template seems more clearly established in the European Union, in the United States it still remains a very murky issue. For example, it is often debated if the

---

[*] Y. Liu. Identifying legal concerns in the biometric context. *Journal of International Commercial Law and Technology*, 3(1), pp. 45–54. 2009. http://www.jiclt.com/index.php/jiclt/article/viewFile/41/40.

United States should take the position as that of the European Union and classify biometric templates as "sensitive data" if they meet the definition as outlined earlier, or should the biometric templates be classified under an entirely brand new category of sensitive data? Until the adoption rate of biometric technology does actually increase, it is quite possible that this debate could very well continue for a very long time in the United States.

This debate may not be solved by the Congress or the Senate of the U.S. federal government, rather it may have to be resolved in the court of the American public opinion. If the debate goes this way, then the answer is clear: No matter what the situation or application is, a biometric template must be considered as sensitive data. For example, according to a recent survey, 63% of the respondents considered biometric templates to be outright sensitive data; 30% of the respondents believed that biometric templates should be classified as sensitive data if genetic and other forms of contact information could be revealed (this would be especially the case with DNA recognition if it proves itself as a viable biometric technology); and 20% of the respondents considered biometric templates as sensitive data, which potentially reveal any sort of race or ethnic origins.

Another legal issue that has greatly slowed down the adoption rate of biometric technology has been in the area of how the biometric templates themselves are actually stored. In a technical sense, the biometric templates are just stored in a database, just like any other piece of information and data. In this sense, there is nothing special to it. The biometric databases can actually reside within the biometric device itself (this is known more specifically as "local storage") or within a server if multiple biometric devices are all networked together (this is often referred to as "central storage").

However, on a social level, the storage of biometric templates can lead to many legal issues in the American public. As mentioned earlier numerous times, biometric templates are unique in the sense that they represent a snapshot of our physiological or behavioral selves. However, it should also be noted that many of the legal and social issues surrounding the storage of biometric templates do not arise when they are stored locally. Rather, most of these issues arise when they are stored centrally in a server. Much of the reason for this is that in this type of network configuration, the biometric templates have to be accessed from multiple biometric devices. Having more biometric devices involved means that more people will be involved in the daily care of them. And of course, this means that the biometric templates are much more prone to cyber-based attacks or situations of ID theft than if they were stored locally.

In other words, when the biometric templates are stored centrally, there is a much greater chance that they could be unlawfully accessed, altered, or even disclosed to unknown third parties in covert fashions. Thus, the need for further layers of security often arises. The use of encryption has been called upon many times in this regard (and in fact, the technical details as to how this would exactly work were reviewed extensively in my first book). This technique requires the use of a private key and a public key. However, then the legal question now arises as to how these keys will be stored and who will have access to them.

There are alternative options for this. For example, they could be stored and given out to a "trusted third party," such as even a law enforcement agency. However, the legalities come into play and would be questioned seriously by the American public. For example, would law enforcement agencies actually step out of their bounds (or jurisdiction) by even being able to store such encryption keys? Would there have to be a so-called separation of duties or minimal access to what is needed policy invoked so that the encryption keys are not misused or mishandled by the particular law enforcement agency? Although these questions might seem to be very negligible on a technical level, from a social and a legal perspective, these are serious questions that need to be addressed and most importantly answered to the American public.

In the above example, the encryption keys would be given directly from the law enforcement official to the end user on an as-needed basis. Once given out, these particular keys will not reside within the law enforcement agency until they are given back by the end user. However, there is an exception to this as well. For example, a "key escrow system" could be used. In these specific scenarios, a copy of both the public and private keys is kept in the law enforcement agency, and the other copy is given to the end user. However, even this practice will raise serious legal issues, especially if the law enforcement officials misuse once again the copy of the keys. There are other legal considerations to take into account as well such as other personal information and data, which will need to be collected from the end users if an outside third party is needed for the storage of the public and private keys (in the scenarios where the biometric templates are stored centrally).

However, even to a certain degree, the local storage of biometric templates can raise some legal issues as well, although it may not be so apparent to the American public. The best example of this is the smart card. This is essentially a portable storage device, having the size and shape of a credit card. However, along with it comes a memory bank that can store all kinds and types of personal information and data. For example, your social security number, medical information, and even your biometric templates can be stored on it. In fact, the smart card is being widely used for the e-passport infrastructure so that as people travel abroad, their identity can be confirmed via the use of the biometric templates that are stored onto it.

However, this situation brings up perplexing legal considerations, which can also curtail the adoption rate of biometric technology. For example, it has been debated that although the end user has the right to his or her own smart card for purposes that meet his or her daily needs, he or she does not actually "own" those data per se. Rather, the ownership of the information and data that are stored on the smart card actually resides within the entity, which actually processed those data that are stored onto the smart card. This simply means that this entity would have the full legal rights of ownership of it, even if biometric templates are stored onto it. If this debate actually comes into fruition in terms of legal precedence, this would raise extremely a serious concern with the American public.

For instance, this would be viewed as an invasion of privacy from a different angle. The traditional view holds that privacy rights violation (in terms of biometric technology) is an intrusion into the personal life of the individual. However, with regard to the smart card, the privacy rights violation would stem from the fact that the entity that processed the biometric template onto the smart card would actually have a direct control over that particular individual's identity. It is also further legally debated that if it is indeed a biometric template that makes an individual unique from everybody else, then that particular person has legal ownership over his or her biometric templates.

Another serious legal issue that can arise from the local storage of biometric templates onto a smart card is that the American public will often not know (or not even care to know) what is actually stored onto their smart card. The question then comes about as to who is responsible for alerting the end user about what is stored onto it, especially in the way of biometric templates. The legal duties then need to be divided between the entity that issues the smart cards, the individuals involved in overseeing the data stored onto them, and the end users who use these data.

With biometric technology in particular, whenever it is utilized by an end user population, there will always be some privacy that will have to be given up in some fashion or another. In fact, this is true of really any other technology or portal in which you are required to submit personal information and data. For instance, submitting credit card information on an e-commerce site is also giving up a form of personal identity. However, we hardly ever think twice when we submit this. Therefore, why is biometric technology so prone to the arguments of privacy rights issues? Possible answer to this question has been alluded to earlier, and it will be a question that may never be completely answered.

Perhaps, the only defined answer can come from the legal system in the United States. This was clearly demonstrated in the 2002 legal case of *Messing v. The Bank of America*.* The findings from this case led the first legal precedence in the United States as to whether biometric technology can be deemed as a mandatory tool, which needs to be utilized in confirming the identity of a particular individual.

In this case, the bank was actually sued by a nonbanking customer because he or she was required to submit his or her thumbprint in a biometric

---

* *Jeff E. Messing, v. Bank of America*, N.A. No. 2646, Sept. Term, 2000.

system before he or she was allowed to cash a check. In a landmark decision, the Maryland court system "... the Bank's request of a thumbprint upon the instrument constitutes a request for 'reasonable identification' within the meaning of Md. Code, Commercial Law Article, §3-502(b)(2)(ii)."*

It has also been debated by experts that if biometric technology can be declared as a mandatory tool by business entities and organizations, there has to be an extremely large enough legal precedence for it, which means that decisions made by the supreme courts at the state level are simply not enough. These decisions have to extend to much higher levels, such as that of the U.S. Supreme Court. However, this debate has only been addressed at the macro level. The type of application environment in which biometric technology is utilized also comes under the "legal microscope." For example, it has even been further argued that in public sector applications (such as those of the federal/state/local government levels), biometric technology should not be required to be mandatory, because of other forms of authentication tools that are available and because biometric technology is a more accepted tool in this aspect.

This same argument has also been extended to biometric technology that is utilized in private sector applications, because it has been argued that businesses and entities also have a choice as to what kind or type of authentication tools they can use as well. In other words, biometric technology is not the only form of authentication that is available, and thus, "... it may not be appropriate to allow mandatory collection of biometric data from the private sector in general."†

So far, we have examined the legal perspectives surrounding biometric technology from the standpoint of the deployment of a biometric system by a business entity or an organization. However, what about from the standpoint of the American public? Under what specific criterion or circumstances do they deem biometric technology? In the United States, in accordance with the legal system, three criteria have been specifically established as to what defines the mandatory use of biometric technology for the American public. They are as follows:

1. The need exists for both "permanent" and "unique" verification and/or identification methods.
2. The explicit benefits of using a particular biometric modality far outweighs the perceived risks that are associated with it.
3. There are no other security tools that can be used to positively confirm the identity of a particular individual.

---

* Y. Liu. Identifying legal concerns in the biometric context. *Journal of International Commercial Law and Technology*, 3(1), pp. 45–54. 2009. http://www.jiclt.com/index. php/jiclt/article/viewFile/41/40.
† Ibid.

In terms of the first criterion, the fear exists among the American public that the biometric templates stored into the database could become the focal point for any "search and seizure" opportunities by the law enforcement agencies. There is also fear that covert linkage could also occur between the biometric databases and other third-party databases, and the information that resides in them could very well be used for covert and unauthorized purposes. With regard to the second criterion, there is general fear among the American public of the threats which biometric technology can bring. However, more specifically, these fears are rooted at a much more macro level, such as that of illegal surveillance and control, ID theft, and the permanent destruction of anonymity of the end user of a particular biometric modality.

It is interesting to observe also different geographic segments that mandate the legal use of biometric technology to their citizens. For instance, in the European Union, under the legislative mandate of the "EU Data Protection Directive," the governments are much more cautious about mandating the use of biometric technology. This is best exemplified by both the Swedish and Norwegian governments. With the former, fingerprint recognition has been permanently banned in the public school systems in Sweden. More specifically, this particular modality cannot be used as a means for students to pay for their school lunches (interestingly enough, this specific usage of fingerprint recognition is widely adopted in the United States). In terms of the latter, the Norwegian Data Protection Authority has also permanently banned the usage of biometric technology for very specific physical access entry applications under explicit conditions (some examples of these include airport settings, access to private business entities, and health-care facilities).

Finally, another key legal aspect that has caused a major hindrance toward the adoption and growth of biometric technology in the United States is the actual legal admissibility of biometric information and data into a court of law. For example, there are some courts that have not easily brought into trial any sort of biometric evidence, whereas other courts in other states have easily accepted this into evidence when trying to determine the guilt or innocence of a charged suspect. In other words, there is strong fear among the American public about the equity and the fairness of the consistency and balance of admitting biometric-based evidence across the entire court system in the United States.

A major part of this imbalance is actually due to the fact as to how biometric-based evidence is admitted in a U.S. court of law into the first place. For example, it is primarily up to the judge in a specific case as to whether or not expert's testimony concerning the relevance of biometric-based evidence can be utilized. In this regard, the judge performs what is known as a "gatekeeper function." Therefore, if a judge rules that an expert witness can testify before the jury and be subject to cross-examination, and also be exposed to the rebuttal process by the opposing party (with regard to the biometric-based evidence), then the jury is free to believe or disbelieve the testimony of the expert witnesses. However, if the judge rules that the expert's testimony is not relevant to the case on the biometric-based evidence, then he or she will not be allowed to take the stance, thus damaging either the prosecutor's or the defense's case.

To help determine if a technical expert should be brought into the court room and testify in a court of law with regard to biometric-based evidence, our judicial system uses two sets of standards: the Frye standard and the Daubert standard. The former is very often used in cases at the state level. For example, the judge in the case will very often ask if the expert opinion on the biometric-based evidence is established upon proven scientific techniques, which has been generally accepted. If it has been, then the expert is allowed under law to testify. The latter is primarily used in cases being argued at the federal level. In these instances, the judge in a particular case then has to take into account more variables and factors, which include the scientific approaches utilized to examine the biometric-based evidence that has been tested and evaluated by scientific peer reviews, the implications that have been derived from conducting such tests, and if too, they have been accepted by the scientific community.

It should be noted that the use of the judge as a gatekeeper role in judicial trials is only used for calling technical witnesses, and not an actual eyewitness. Why is this the case? The popular belief for this has been that juries in the United States seem to have a broader understanding of the evidence presented by an actual eyewitness than a technical expert. That is why the judge is brought in as the gatekeeper, in order to help ensure fairness and equity in a trial. However, there has been harsh criticism against this by legal experts, by making claims that this so-called gatekeeper role is based on the total subjective analysis by the judge, despite using the Frye and Daubert standards, which have been set forth in the American judicial system.

This subjective behavior thus strikes fear into the heart of the American public if fairness and justice can actually be reached in a trial and biometric-based evidence is actually presented in a legal case.

Two Worldwide Implementations of Biometric Technology

section II

Two Worldwide
Implementations of
Biometric Technology

CHAPTER 3

Biometrics and the e-Passport

As discussed throughout this book, biometric technology can serve a wide array of market applications. The most traditional markets for various biometric modalities include the following:

1. *Physical access entry*: This would primarily involve either hand geometry recognition and/or fingerprint recognition, which would be wired to an electronic access control module. This module, in turn, would then be wired into an electromagnetic lock strike, which would immediately open after the successful verification and/or identification of a particular individual.

2. *Logical access entry*: This involves granting access to a network or to resources onto a particular network segment or trunk. This also includes the local logging into a workstation, computer, or other wireless device in lieu of using the traditional username/password combination. In these types of applications, fingerprint recognition and iris recognition are the most common modalities that are utilized. For instance, instead of typing a username and a password, all the end user has to do is to merely get a scan of his or her iris or have an image of his or her fingerprint taken. After successful verification and/or identification, the end user will then be logged in automatically.

3. *Time and attendance*: This particular market segment keeps track of the hours worked by a particular employee, as well as calculates the payroll automatically. This is probably the most in-demand application for biometric technology. For example, the technologies here possess numerous and distinct advantages, which include the elimination of the old-fashioned ways of using time cards and spreadsheets; the drastic reduction of administrative paperwork and hours that have to be paid to personnel; the total elimination of the "buddy punching" phenomenon in

which an employee clocks in for another employee when he or she is not actually physically present at work. The most common biometric modalities used for these types and kinds of applications very often include hand geometry recognition, fingerprint recognition, and even iris recognition.

4. *Mobile and wireless*: This is probably one of the most recent and booming market segments for biometric technology. The most needed here is to provide the end user with another way of securing and logging into his or her particular wireless device—instead again of having to enter in a password or a personal identification number. The most common biometric modalities used here are fingerprint recognition, iris recognition, voice recognition, and even facial recognition. With a simple scan or an image taken, the end user can quickly and easily log into his or her wireless device. In fact, the major cellular operators have already implemented fingerprint recognition technology into the actual hardware of the smartphone. The best example of this is the iPhone. Starting with the 5S series, Apple has embedded an optical sensor in the casing of the iPhone. The catalyst for this was when the Apple Corporation outright acquired another biometric vendor known as "Authentec," one of the leading manufacturers at the time of fingerprint recognition sensors.

5. *Mobile and e-commerce*: This specific market application has been around for some time, ever since the dawn of the Internet Era. For instance, rather than having to visit a traditional brick-and-mortar store, an end user or a customer can just visit an online store of a merchant, and with just a few clicks of the mouse, can make his or her product selections, enter in his or her credit card information, and have them all shipped to their doorsteps in just a matter of a few days. There have been security issues here as well, such as confirming the actual identification of an end user. However, through the use of biometric technology, this almost eliminated the problem. However, now this e-commerce model has now literally deployed itself into the wireless world. For example, customers can now use their particular brand of smartphone to buy products online as they would from their desk computer or laptop. Now a variation of this has taken off in the other parts of the world, where biometric technology is now being used to help secure what is known as "virtual payments." Through the use of radiofrequency identification (RFID) technology (this concept will be discussed in much more detail in this chapter), a customer does not even have to take out his or her credit card or cash to make a payment—it can be all done by tapping his or her smartphone

on the point-of-sale terminal. Once again, Apple Corporation has pioneered the use of this technology in the United States, with their method of payment known as "ApplePay." With this, a customer can use his or her iPhone to pay for products and services. However, there have also been grave security issues, and once again, the use of biometric technology has been called upon to address and solve them.

6. *Health care*: In the United States, this is one of the largest market segments for the use of biometric technology. The primary catalysts are the recent legislations and mandates passed by the U.S. government such as the Health Insurance Portability and Accountability Act of 1996, Sarbanes–Oxley Act, and the Gramm–Leach–Bliley Act. The primary premise of these separate pieces of legislations is to, first and foremost, protect the rights and the medical information of each and every patient in the United States. For instance, all of these have to be encrypted to protect against any forms of identity theft or cyber-based attacks, and the medical personnel who are actually logging into the workstations or the wireless devices should have their identity 100% confirmed through the use of biometric technology. The most common modalities used here are fingerprint recognition, iris recognition, vein pattern recognition, and even facial recognition. The latter three are the most widely and popularly used modalities because of their non-contactless nature.

7. *The federal government*: In the United States, it is both the biggest customer of biometric technology and the largest awarder of contracts. There are many security-based applications in which biometric technology is used. For instance, this includes the verification and identification of all individuals entering and exiting the United States; protecting the northern and southern borders, especially the U.S.-Mexican border; securing all modes of transportation, which include the airports, the rail system, and the maritime ports; conducting war on terrorism; and confirming the identity of any terror suspects apprehended. In these settings, pretty much all of the biometric modalities, both physical and behavioral based, are used.

It should be noted that across all of the levels of national government, even worldwide, there is one particular application that is fast being adopted and implemented. This is known as the "e-passport," or also the "biometric passport." The most traditional means of confirming the identity of a traveler entering or exiting the United States (or for any other country for that matter) has been the traditional paper passport.

However, because of the security vulnerabilities that are inherent in it (such as its easy replication of it), governments worldwide have sought other alternative means, which are much more robust in security and cannot be easily replicated.

Thus, the use of biometric technology has come into play in this regard. It offers numerous advantages, primarily to the traveler. Probably, the biggest one is that of expedited times at both immigration and customs control. Instead of having to wait in line to have each and every individual passport stamped and processed, the traveler just has to "flash" his or her e-passport in front of a wireless reader, and within seconds his or her identity can be confirmed. However, despite these obvious advantages, the e-passport is still not widely deployed in the United States as it has been in the other geographic locations around the world. Some of the main reasons for this are the privacy rights issues associated with using it, as well as the security vulnerabilities it possesses.

In this chapter, the e-passport infrastructure will be examined in much more detail. Specifically, the following will be looked at:

- The traditional paper passport
- The transition to the e-passport
- The mechanics and the engineering design behind the e-passport
- The security vulnerabilities and weaknesses associated with the e-passport
- The social impacts of the e-passport infrastructure (such as end user and policy implications)
- Actual case studies of the deployment of the e-passport infrastructure worldwide

THE TRADITIONAL PAPER PASSPORT

The traditional passport has been used for a long period of time. The first traces of the paper passport can be found in the Bible. According to the content, in around 450 BC, Nehemiah, a messenger for the King Artaxerxes, had asked for permission to leave the Kingdom of Judah. In return, the king gave him a letter that confirmed his identity, as well as requested safe passage as he traveled across the foreign lands.

Other historical origins of the paper passport come from the medieval times as well. A form of the paper passport, known as the *bara'a*, was an actual receipt for the taxes that were paid by the citizens of various communities that existed during those times. However, it should be noted that the above two examples are just considered to be variants of the first true paper passport. In other words, these offshoots just provided the most primitive forms of confirming the identity of the citizens in question.

The first true paper passport originated during the times of King Henry V. His "cabinet" was credited with creating a paper-based identification system which enabled his subjects to prove their identity as they ventured off to visit foreign lands. The first known reference to this type of paper passport can be traced back to the "1414 Act of Parliament."

After this time, the growth and sophistication of the paper passport proliferated throughout England. By 1540, the granting of travel-related documents fell under the jurisdiction of the "Privy Council of England." Also, it was during this time frame in which the term "passport" was actually conceived of.

As time went on, the issuance of the formal paper passport fell under the auspices of the "Office of the Secretary of State" in England. Eight years later (in 1548), an entity known in England as the "Imperial Diet of Ausburg" further mandated that each and every English citizen holds a permanent passport as he or she traveled. If not, he or she faces stiff penalties, such as being permanently exiled from that country.

However, with the expansion of transportation during the nineteenth century (especially with rail travel), the paper passport system that had evolved in England over the centuries suddenly dissipated for the next 30 years. This trend continued up to World War I.

However, with the sheer amount of people now traveling across borders in the European Union, various governments reenacted the passport laws that were enacted. In fact, it was during this time frame as well that British tourists first started complaining about privacy rights violations with regard to the photographs and the physical descriptions their respective passports contained. This was referred to as a "nasty dehuminization" of the British people and the country.

The first formal gathering to introduce formal paper passport guidelines worldwide occurred in 1920, when the League of Nations held a conference known as the "Paris Conference on Passports & Customs Formalities and Through Tickets." The result from this was a set of formal paper passport guidelines and booklet designs for countries all over the world. The respective follow-up conferences were also held in 1926 and 1927.

Another follow-up meeting was held much later in the 1960s, but little resulted from that meeting. As a result, the mandates set forth in the 1920 conference still held forth. It was until 1980 that the next set of paper passport standardization protocols was established. This time, it was set forth by the International Civil Aviation Organization (ICAO). This government organization called for the radical redesign and deployment of the paper passport.

For example, the first series of "machine-readable passports" evolved. Rather than having a human make the determination of the confirmation of an individual's identity, this time, a machine would be used to do that. In order to do this, a certain area of the paper passport would have some area in which encrypted information about the passport holder would have to be contained. For example, this new textual form now consists of a set of alphanumeric characters, which can be easily deciphered by an optical character recognition device. This is illustrated in the following example:

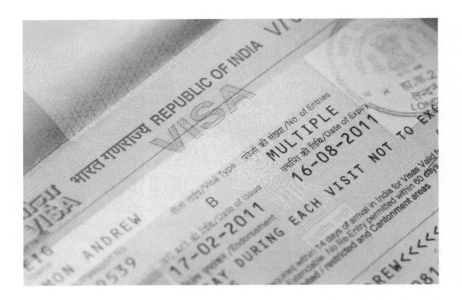

At the time, the primary advantage was that the identity of a particular traveler could be quickly confirmed rather than having to manually input the data into the computer. In these aspects, the paper passport is swiped into the optical character recognition device, and from there, the identity of the passport holder is then either confirmed or denied. The particular ICAO standard in which the mandate for this alphanumeric characterization is called for is under the "Doc 9303 Machine Readable Travel Documents."

The most recent update to this ICAO standard now calls for the use of biometric templates into the paper passport. For example, a fingerprint recognition template can be stored on an RFID computer chip, in a manner very similar to that of a smartcard.

Now, with the evolution of the biometric passport, the question often arises under what conditions can a citizen of a particular country actually obtain a passport? Obviously, the rules and the laws will vary from country to country, but in general, the established set of procedures agreed to worldwide are as follows:

- The issued passport (whether it is biometric or machine-readable based) is the sole property of the government in question.
- The passport can contain limited functionality (for instance, the issuing government may put restrictions on where its citizens can actually travel) and can be revoked at any point in time.
- The passport can be used in the judicial process of any country (e.g., an accused individual might be able to surrender his or her passport as a form of bond payment or bail).
- Some countries may require that their own citizens actually submit through an interview process before they will be issued a passport.
- Some countries (such as North Korea) only issue passports to an extremely selected number of citizens.
- A majority of countries (such as those in Europe) require that their citizens actually complete mandatory time period of military service before they will actually be granted a passport.

Within each country as well, there are different categories of issuance of the passport to citizens. These categories can be broken down as follows:

- *Multiple classes of a nationality from just one country*: There are some countries in the world, such as the United Kingdom, which possess different classes for their citizenry. This lends itself due to the fact of its rich colonial history. For example, the U.K. government issues out different types of passports for its citizens who come under different classifications. However, this has caused problems for other countries that U.K. citizens commonly visit, as the governments in these respective countries have to implement passport-processing policies for the different classes of U.K. citizens.
- *Multiple types of passports with one nationality*: There are countries, such as China, which implement this kind of system. For instance, under this passport regime, the citizens from the islands of Hong Kong and Macau are issued what are known as "Special Administrative Region" passports, whereas the citizens from the mainland are issued the traditional Chinese paper passports.

- *Passports with sovereign territory*: Geographical territories, such as that of Malta, issue special types of documents in order to gain access into the territory. In these cases, the traditional paper passport is not accepted in order to gain entry.

Also within each country, there are four different types of passports that can be issued to both citizens and government officials. These are as follows:

- *The traditional paper passport*: This has been deemed to be the most common form of paper passport, which is issued to each and every individual around the world.
- *The diplomatic passport*: These types of passports are issued to diplomats of a particular country as well as their corresponding dependants. These are used for official international travel as well as for living abroad. It should be noted here as well that the possession of a diplomatic passport does not automatically guarantee diplomatic immunity in a foreign country. This can only be granted if a diplomat has received certain accreditation levels from the country in which he or she originates from.
- *The emergency passport*: This type of passport is granted in the case a citizen loses his or her paper passport, or if it was stolen. It is issued if a replacement paper passport cannot be issued in time.
- *The collective passport*: These types of paper passports are issued for certain groups who are traveling to a particular destination. A typical example of this is school children going on a school trip to another country.

The ICAO has also set forth various protocols and standards that are required for the designs and specific formats of the paper passports worldwide. These are meant to be compatible with the ISO/IEC 7810 ID-3 standard, which calls for a paper passport size of 125 × 88 mm (4.921 × 3.465 inches).

The other requirements as set forth by the ICAO also include the following:

- *The front cover*: This normally contains the name of the issuing country, the national symbol of the issuing country, the description of the document (e.g., whether or not it is a citizen passport or a diplomatic passport), and a special symbol indicating if it is a biometric passport. This front page also consists of the "National Coat of Arms" of the issuing country. An illustration of the front cover of a traditional paper passport can be seen as follows:

- *The inside of the passport*: This normally consists of the data page, the specific information about the bearer of the passport, as well as the issuing entity. The data page is designed to consist of the numerical or alphanumerical designators assigned by the issuing authority. The inside of the passport also consists of various blank pages so that the government of entry can issue the appropriate visa type. Depending on the country in question, the visa is normally stamped in ink on these pages (which are mostly entry and exit stamps), but now adhesive stickers are used to serve as the visa. These consist of certain types and kinds of security features that do not allow for the easy replication or duplication of the visa. An example of what the inside of a paper passport looks like can be seen in the following illustration:

- *The request page*: This often consists of a message, usually near the front, requesting that the passport's bearer be allowed to pass freely, and further requesting that, in the event of need, the bearer be granted assistance. Depending on the country in question, this statement can be made either in the name of the passport issuer or in the name of the passport issuing authority (which most likely would be the government that is granting the passport to the bearer). This statement may be written in more than one language, and the countries such as Switzerland, Austria, and Finland do not have this particular statement on their paper passports. According to the standards as set forth by the ICAO, the language of the passport must be in the language of the issuing country, as well as in either French or English. For example, many countries of the European Union issue their passports in their own language as well as in either English or French.

It should also be noted that the ICAO has issued a specific set of protocols for the machine-readable passport. Primarily, these deal with the areas that need to be set aside in the passport in which the alphanumeric data can be easily scanned by the optical character recognition scanner.

THE TRANSITION TO THE E-PASSPORT

Although the traditional paper passport has been the *de facto* standard for confirming the identity of individuals as they cross into international borders, there are some serious issues associated with it. First, it is the ability to replicate the actual travel document. Although enhanced security features have been incorporated into it, there is always the possibility that it can be replicated, given the drastic sophistication level of hackers and cyber-based terrorists in today's times. Second, there are no known background checks conducted on citizens as they apply for their individual passport.

For example, if a citizen in Iraq applies for a passport in his or her own homeland, the chances are pretty high that no background check will be conducted on him or her. What if he or she has a terrorist background? Will he or she take the knowledge and experience that he or she has and conduct terrorist-based activities in another country? Or will he or she enter into another country and attempt to conduct remote terrorist-based activities in his or her homeland? These are some of the questions that need to be asked before an individual citizen of a particular country will be granted a passport.

However, of course, this same level of responsibility also lies on not just the home country that is granting the paper passport but also the country in which the citizen wishes to enter into. For example, this country will be issuing the visa for the particular citizen to enter into (as it was discussed earlier, the visa is literally a sticker that is placed inside of the paper passport—this merely signifies that the person has permission to enter into the country that issued the visa). Obviously, background checks should be conducted by the visa-granting country in order to ensure that the citizen who has applied for the visa does not possess a criminal or terrorist-based record, and that he or she does not pose a security threat as well.

In order to help combat the security weaknesses and flaws posed by the traditional paper passport, the "machine-readable passport" was first introduced back in 1981. To this date, over more than 140 countries worldwide now have implemented some sort of machine-readable passport infrastructure within their own governments. These kinds of passports contain numerous features that are different from the traditional paper passports. They are as follows:

- The passport holder's identification details.
- A digital photo or image of the face of the passport holder.
- The mandatory identity elements associated with the pass-port holder, as reflected in a two-line, machine-readable zone (MRZ), which is printed in an optical character recognition-B style and format.

Some of the benefits that can be used by utilizing a machine-readable passport are as follows:

- Given the standard, uniform layout, this greatly enhances the use of visual authentication of a passport holder.
- The machine-readable characteristics allow for much better detection of the false or fraudulent use of the passport.
- It facilitates the rapid and precise identification of foreign travelers.
- It allows for the use of "advance passenger information systems."
- It provides the improved ability to identify "problem cases" related to a particular passport and resolve quickly and efficiently.
- It allows for issuing authorities to electronically monitor and control each stage of travel document application and issuance.
- It provides a source of reliable, standardized platform from which governments around the world can build their passport infrastructures upon.
- It enhances the governments around the world to share pass-port data with the private sector with the goal to improve the detection of stolen and fraudulently obtained travel documents.
- It provides the governments around the world a cost-effective means to implement a passport infrastructure.
- For the traveler, it means that there will be much faster process-ing times at the border.
- Both the airports and the airlines adopt biometric technology for the following advantages:
  - Improved verification of document authenticity
  - Reduced time required to handle each passenger
  - There is much lower probability that undocumented or improperly documented travelers can enter into a country of destination

However, even despite the above benefits that are presented by a machine-readable passport, its biggest disadvantage is the security issues that it inherits. There are a number of key areas that need to be addressed in this regard, and they are as follows:

- The production of totally counterfeit passports
- The issuance of genuine paper passports to citizens, but this is done on a fraudulent level (such as impostors using a genuine breeder document infrastructure)
- The problems of corrupt government officials issuing paper passports when they do not have specific authorization to do so
- The issuance of truly genuine passports being given out to citizens who are illegally using different names or aliases
- The tampering of an actual, genuine passport (this would include such items as tampering with the data page or substituting a false photo)
- An impostor or even a cyber attacker posing as the legitimate holder of the paper passport when he or she really is not
- The complete loss or theft of a genuine paper passport

To address these specific security issues and threats, a newer type and kind of passport was created. This is known as the "biometric passport," or also "e-passport." When comparing these two together, the questions often asked are that how do they differ, and what other stronger advantages does the e-passport actually offer?

Essentially, the e-passport is actually a hybrid version of the machine-readable passport. However, the key differentiating factor here is that the e-passport actually contains an embedded chip (or in technical terms, a "microchip"), which has a very miniature database consisting of the information about the specific passport holder. This contains the same data as the machine-readable passport or even the traditional paper passport, but unlike these two, the e-passport also contains the biometric templates of the individual passport holder.

The type of biometric templates that are contained in this microchip of course depends on the government of the country that is issuing them, but most nations worldwide use fingerprint recognition, iris recognition, or facial recognition. Given the huge memory size of the microchip, a combination of these three biometric modalities can be stored as well, thus giving the e-passport a truly multimodal security advantage (as well as combating the security issues of the machine-readable passport).

Through the use of this specific microchip, passport fraud, forgery, and misuse of the passport are now greatly reduced. In fact, the look and feel of an e-passport is pretty much the same as the machine-readable passport, and there is one definite way to tell the two apart. The e-passport consists of a special design, which is readily displayed on the front cover of the e-passport, located at the very bottom. This is illustrated in the following diagram:

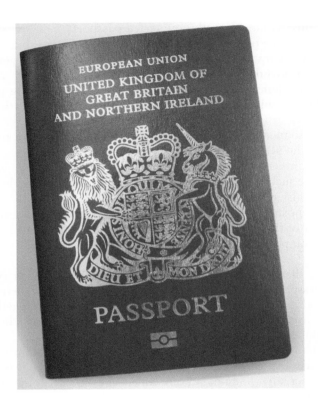

Apart from a security perspective, the e-passport also offers a significant amount of other advantages over the machine-readable passport. These are detailed as follows:

- The use of biometric technology in an e-passport infrastructure can actually help to enhance as well as improve the efficiencies and qualities of conducting a background check on a particular passport applicant (assuming that one is actually even conducted).
- Since biometric templates are unique to each and every individual, implementing them into a passport can help greatly in terms of combating any types or kinds of fraudulent misuse or potential tampering.
- The use of different biometric modalities (as previously described) can also greatly reduce the chances of identity fraud or even identity theft from occurring at the point of the issuance of the passport, as well as the immigration entry and exit points that exist in every country.

- Through the use of biometric technology, the speed and efficiency at which individuals can be processed at border crossings are greatly expedited.
- If questions do ever arise as to the authenticity of the biometric templates in the database of the microchip, these can now be confirmed by using various public key infrastructure (PKI) certificates, which can be quickly and easily downloaded from the Public Key Directory (PKD) of the ICAO.

The above are just the macro benefits of an e-passport-based infrastructure. As mentioned, the use of an e-passport at the exit/entry points and the border crossing points will have the most impact and use. The benefits here-to realized are as follows:

- The ability to 100% confirm the identities of high-risk passengers.
- Through the use of automated border control processes, those travelers as deemed to be at "low risk" will be able to enter the country of their destination without having to go through all of the hassles of the traditional immigration and customs checkpoints.
- The individuals who are crossing the borders will now be able to have their identity confirmed at rates as high as almost 100%.
- The government officials at the various border crossings worldwide will now be able to possess two mechanisms at their disposal for absolutely confirming the identity of a passport holder: a visual check of the digital photograph against the actual face of the passport bearer and the use of the biometric templates or other biographic information that is stored in the database of the microchip.

However, despite these advantages, the e-passport suffers from one serious disadvantage: the lack of a common set of protocols and standards. For instance, the e-passport has not been around for as long as the paper passport or the machine-readable passport in which time was afforded to them to develop a standard set of best practices for the countries around the world to adopt. In fact, the use of the e-passport is still relatively new, and not all of the nations have adopted such an infrastructure.

On account of this lack of uniformity with regard to the e-passport, the countries that have adopted this type of infrastructure have essentially developed their own sets of best practices and standards, which may not be compatible to other nations. Therefore, one of the biggest hurdles when adopting and implementing an e-passport infrastructure is the legal considerations that need to be taken into consideration.

Some of the legal issues surrounding the use of biometric technology were examined in detail in Chapter 2. However, those legal issues were examined based on the laws in the United States. They become much more compounded when discussing how biometric templates will be accessed, used, and stored as they travel across different countries.

Now, they do not become the focal point for the country of origination (from where the e-passport was first issued), but also for the country of destination (because it is here where the biometric templates will be accessed and processed, in order to confirm the identity of the individual passport holder).

As a result, changing the legal framework for countries around the world with regard to the deployment and implementation of an e-passport infrastructure can be quite a lengthy process, and the one that can take several years to accomplish. Some of these legal aspects any government of any country wishing to lay the foundations for an e-passport infrastructure include some of the following items:

1. How will the legal system cover the issues surrounding the collection of biometric information?

    The key points that need to be addressed here include what the collection process will look like, who will be allowed to actually collect the biometric templates of the e-passport applicants, and how these specific biometric templates will be presented to the entities who will actually store this data.

2. How will the legal system actually cover who will have access to the biometric templates and in what manner will they be specifically disclosed?

    Very detailed provisions need to be created as to who will have access to the biometric templates after they are created, as well as the specific conditions under which the biometric templates that are stored on an e-passport can be disclosed to a third party. As mentioned, this legal aspect is very much a "hot button" issue with the American public.

3. How will the legal system address the issues of the storage as well as the deletion of the biometric templates?

    Since the government of the respective country will be storing the biometric templates, very detailed legislation needs to be mandated to address these issues. In the United States, the storage of biometric templates is an issue that has received huge attention, most of it being negative. However, in other countries, such as the developing ones, the issue of the storage of biometric templates is not so much of a grave concern, as some of these geographic locations have already implemented an e-passport infrastructure.

4. How will the legal system address the need for the addition of other biometric modalities?

As just previously described, an e-passport can consist of two or more biometric templates. Although this may be good from a security standpoint, the citizens of other countries may raise serious objections of having to submit their fingerprint, eye, as well as face in the e-passport application process. It may not be so much of an issue in other countries, but it will for sure be one as the e-passport infrastructure takes off.

5. How will the legal system address the issues of how the biometric templates will be used?

In a technical sense, because the biometric templates will be used only for purposes of storage on the e-passport, that is all that they should be used for. However, because the government of the country will have oversight of these templates, the fear will then arise if they will be shared covertly and secretly with other agencies, such as that of law enforcement. Although the intentions may be good, this could lead to serious mistrust among the citizens of a country, especially in the United States. Therefore, if biometric information from the e-passport infrastructure is to be shared with other government agencies, whether domestic or foreign, special laws then need to be established and set forth to protect the interests of the e-passport holder. Also, the use of the biometric templates for any other purposes other than the e-passport needs to be disclosed to the citizens of the respective country.

6. How will the legal system address the issue of privacy rights associated with the e-passport?

As it has been described throughout this book, the issue of privacy rights is one of the biggest impediments to the adoption and growth of biometric technology in the United States. However, in some areas around the world, especially those in the developing nations, the issue of privacy rights is not even given a second thought. Regardless of the geographic region, the issue of privacy rights, especially when it comes to the e-passport, needs to be addressed by the legal infrastructure. In the end, every citizen is entitled to the same level of keeping and

ensuring that his or her biometric templates (and their associated information) are kept private and not shared with any
other outside third party.

Apart from both the legal and security issues, another major disadvantage of the e-passport is its cost of deployment and implementation. Given
that the traditional paper passport has had such a deep history and largely
embedded infrastructure, creating the machine-readable passport was
simply an add on. In other words, the traditional paper passport already
possessed the key features that were needed for the machine-readable passport. All that simply had to be added on was the alphanumeric portion.

However, deploying and implementing an e-passport infrastructure
cannot be considered simply as an upgrade to the machine-readable passport. After all, the memory chip, as well as the biometric templates, has
to be included. Thus, for any country wishing to undertake an e-passport
infrastructure, it can be an expensive proposition. This is further compounded by the millions of citizens who are needing to replace their traditional paper passport or machine-readable passport with the e-passport.

This greatly increased cost for the e-passport infrastructure stems
primarily from the following areas:

- The software development and related hardware costs
- The new equipment that is needed
- The integration of the microchip into the e-passport
- The deployment of new security measures not only in the
  e-passport itself but also in the e-passport infrastructure
- The training that is needed to educate the necessary personnel
  into the administration and management of the e-passport and
  its infrastructure
- Other backup mechanisms that might be needed in the face of a
  natural or manmade disaster posed to the e-passport infrastructure

Under normal circumstances, the government of the country will fund
the e-passport infrastructure. However, if it is a developing nation that
is involved, the respective government thus may not have the assets to
deploy it. Under these circumstances, other sources of financing are
available, such as the following:

- Money donated from the private sector
- A combination of money from both the public and private
  sectors
- Monetary assistance from a developed country (e.g., the United
  States giving money to a developing nation in Africa wishing to
  deploy an e-passport infrastructure)

THE MECHANICS AND THE ENGINEERING DESIGN BEHIND THE E-PASSPORT

As mentioned earlier in the last section, deploying and implementing an e-passport system can be very expensive for any country. The primary reason for this is that the country in question is not just deploying an upgrade to the machine-readable passport—rather, an entire information technology (IT) infrastructure has to be created to accommodate the use of the e-passport. This type of infrastructure has to exist in the country that is deploying the e-passport system; most nations also should have an e-passport system in order to process the foreign travelers who are entering and exiting with their e-passports (but this is in theory only—as reality dictates, there are still countries that need to adopt the e-passport, in particular the United States).

For instance, an IT infrastructure at the facilities where the e-passport is actually issued, as well as the international airports so that the foreign travelers can be processed in a quick and efficient manner. The entire IT infrastructure for the e-passport for any country involves the following components:

1. The software for the IT structure
2. The hardware for the IT structure
3. The e-passport readers

The Software for the IT Structure

This consists of the IT assets that are needed to produce the actual e-passport, the scanning equipment, the required network protocols for the transfer of the biometric templates (as well as their associated information), the databases needed for the storage of the biometric templates as well as for the verification and identification transactions to take place, as well as the needed exchange for the biometric templates between other government agencies, both domestic and worldwide. However, in this aspect, the software component is the most crucial in the IT infrastructure for any e-passport system. The following are a few examples in which software development and applications are needed the most:

- *Software for the capture of the biometric information*: With the example of a fingerprint recognition system, along with the optical sensor, special software needs to exist within the capture data in order to process the raw images that are collected, as well as to convert them into the actual biometric template (which again is just a mathematical representation of the raw images; in this case, it would just be a binary mathematical file).

- *Software to ensure quality assurance*: With the advancements made into various biometric technologies today, software now exists in them as well, which can double the integrity of the raw images that are collected from the sensor, as well as the biometric templates that are created from them.
- *Database software*: Specialized software needs to be developed and created so that the biometric templates can be stored readily in a database as well as accessed for later activity transaction analyses.
- *Data warehouse software*: Since the e-passport is and will be continuously used by millions of end users worldwide, the databases that contain the biometric information from them will, in turn, need to be equally large as well. Therefore, the concepts of data warehousing will present themselves well here. For instance, special mathematical algorithms can be created to comb through and analyze all of the transaction data to discern any hidden trends among the foreign travelers entering and exiting a particular country.

The Hardware for the IT Structure

Although the software is a critical piece for the e-passport system, the hardware that is needed is equally important. Examples of what are needed to support and maintain an entire e-passport infrastructure is further discussed in this section.

The contactless integrated circuit chip is a very important component of the e-Passport. For example as discussed earlier in this chapter, the microchip is embedded in the e-passport. In this particular microchip, the biometric templates as well as any other information or data about the traveler can be stored. However, there are many types and kinds of microchips which an e-passport can readily use; there is no standard among the countries as to which specific microchip to employ. For example, some can be very generic in design (thus making the cost of implementing them into the e-passport much cheaper), whereas some other microchip designs are much more sophisticated in nature (thus driving up the cost of implementation much more). The microchip is considered to be the contributor to the performance of the e-passport; the governments around the world need to select a microchip design, which is optimized to the level of performance that is required.

Other factors that affect the performance of the microchip embedded in the e-passport include the specific classification of the microchip and its associated data processing rate. For purposes of the e-passport, the ICAO has mandated the use of either two types of microchips: type A and type B. The former is the more generic type, whereas the latter is the much more sophisticated version and is much more suited to contain multiple layers of biometric templates. The ICAO has also mandated the data processing rates of the microchip that is embedded in the e-passport. For instance, the processing rates have to be either 106 or 424 kbps. It should be noted that the data rate that is selected also has a strong bearing upon the microchip to e-passport reader communications.

The software that resides in the microchip of the e-passport can also have a strong bearing upon its performance. It resides in the actual operating system of the microchip, as well as in the logical data structure (LDS) applications. The LDS specifies the exact format in which the biometric templates will be stored on the microchip. Also, the physical size of the microchip can be a key performance factor. In order to determine the optimal size of the microchip, several factors need to be taken into consideration as well. These include how much biometric information will be stored, as well as the data compression rate of the microchip in question. For instance, the more biometric templates are stored on the microchip, the longer the processing time will be for the foreign travelers at both the entry and the exit points.

The e-Passport Readers

This is deemed to be the next critical component for the IT infrastructure of any e-passport system. When a foreign traveler enters into the country of destination, the e-passport is merely "flashed" in front of an e-passport reader. The biometric information that is stored on the microchip are then collected by the reader and processed in order to confirm the identity of the foreign traveler. There are three key components that comprise the reader subcomponents in an e-passport system. These include the following:

- The actual e-passport reader itself
- The software development kit (SDK) that comes with it

- The host system (this would be the servers that are connected to the e-passport reader)
- The host application (this would be the specific type of border application that is created in order to help confirm the identity of the foreign traveler)

The choice of SDK that is offered with the e-passport reader subcomponent can also have a huge bearing on the overall performance of the e-passport system. For instance, if an "issuance quality analysis" application is developed and created, this can greatly hamper overall performance. For instance, the factors that will affect the processing time from which the foreign traveler "flashes" his or her e-passport to the reader and by the time his or her identity is confirmed include such variables as the real-time referencing of the biometric databases, the execution of cryptographic functions (which is often used in a PKI—this will be discussed shortly), as well as the modular application design of the software that manages the interactions between the microchip and the e-passport.

As it will be addressed later in this chapter, the e-passport system does suffer from an entire host of security issues as well. One of the biggest concerns is regarding how the biometric templates (as well as their associated information) will be kept secure although they are in the transmission stage between the actual e-passport itself and the e-passport reader. The principles of cryptography have been called into play as a result. The basic premise here is to use the principles of encryption to further scramble and unscramble the biometric templates. This is also known as "biocryptography," and in fact, an entire chapter was devoted to reviewing this in our last book.*

To help create a secure e-passport processing environment, the use of the PKI has also been called into use (and the concepts of a PKI were addressed in our last book as well). Essentially, with a PKI, a pair of both public and private keys are created in order to not only ensure the security of the biometric templates but also maintain the integrity of them (in other words, providing assurances that the biometric templates in transit have not been altered or manipulated in any way or fashion).

In fact, the ICAO has set forth the standards and protocols for the creation of a PKI, which is designed specifically for an e-passport infrastructure. The e-passport PKI scheme includes the following two components:

1. *The Secure In-Country Key Generation*: In this fashion, each and every country involved with the creation of its own e-passport infrastructure will actually build its own secure facility from which

---

* R. Das. *Biometric Technology: Authentication, Biocryptography, and Cloud-Based Architecture*, CRC Press, Boca Raton, FL, pp. 329–354, 2014.

the private and public keys will be generated. Although these key generation facilities will be run by the government of the respective government, the ICAO-based Document 9303 will be strictly enforced to help that global interoperability is strictly maintained.

2. *The ICAO Directory Services*: This is essentially a PKD that is made available from the ICAO to all members participating in an e-passport infrastructure. With this type of service, all of the information from the public keys from all of the countries worldwide is stored in a respective PKI directory. This will be made accessible to all countries (e.g., India can access the public keys provided by Germany in order to facilitate the border crossings of German citizens wishing to enter the borders of India).

The PKD helps to provide border officials with much greater levels of security than what is afforded by the machine-readable passport. The public keys will be validated certificates, which can be easily downloaded by border crossing officials in order to help further validate the authenticity of the biometric templates that are stored on the microchip of the e-passport.

Also, the ICAO-validated public keys can also be used to help combat identity theft, especially when it comes to the financial transactions that are made by the foreign traveler in the country of destination. The PKD as established by the ICAO also consists of the Document Signer Certificates as well as the Certificate Revocation Lists. There are also three subcomponents that are included in an e-passport-based infrastructure, which are as follows:

- The Country Verifying Certificate Authorities
- The Document Verifiers
- The Inspection Systems

As one can see thus far, the microchip and its respective memory bank that it possesses are at the heart of the e-passport. Although it may seem to be a simple and straightforward task as to where to place it in the e-passport, it can be a complex issue to decide among the participating nations. This is due to the fact that the e-passport utilizes a wireless protocol known as the "radio-frequency identification" or "RFID" protocol. It should be noted that this specific protocol makes use of three subsystems, which are as follows:

1. *The RFID tags*: They are embedded in the e-passport.
2. *The e-passport readers*: They collect the biometric information from the microchip in the e-passport in order to confirm the identity of the e-passport holder.
3. *The RFID antenna*: This transmits the biometric information that are stored on the microchip to the e-reader and can be found embedded in the RFID tag.

The e-passport readers traditionally operate at a wide range of frequencies, power, as well as reading ranges. There are two types of RFID tags, which are as follows:

1. *Active tags*: These are run and operated by battery power.
2. *Passive tags*: These do not use battery power; rather, they operate from the power of the radio signals that are generated and harnessed from the e-passport reader at the point of entry.

For the e-passport, the passive tags are most commonly used, given their low cost and ultra read ranges from the e-passport to the e-passport reader. These tags that are used in the e-passport have dimensions of 125 mm × 88 mm and operate specifically at the 13.56 MHz radiofrequency to the e-passport reader.

The RFID protocol makes use of electromagnetic fields to transmit, or transfer data from one source to another. It makes use of tags that are attached to different kinds and types of objects, which permit for this transfer of information to take place. Therefore, for instance, an RFID tag would be placed in the e-passport, and there is also an RFID tag at the point of the e-passport reader at the entry point of the country of destination. From here, once the traveler flashes his or her e-passport to the reader, the biometric information that is stored on the microchip are then transferred via the wireless RFID protocol. The tag at the e-passport reader captures this information, and in just a matter of seconds, the traveler's identity can then be confirmed.

As it will be addressed later in this chapter, one of the major security vulnerabilities of the RFID protocol is that the information that is transmitted can appear as "plaintext." For example, an attacker with the right network attack device can literally capture the data that are transmitted and quite easily decipher it. In an effort to make this more secure, rather than placing in an RFID tag directly into the e-passport, participating nations are now making use of a very miniature antennae that are placed into the e-passport in lieu of the RFID tag.

In order to help ensure the more secure transmission of the biometric information from the e-passport to the reader, the microchip can be placed strategically at four points within the e-passport. These two points are as follows:

1. The biographical page of the e-passport holder (which is located just inside the front cover).
2. Between the end paper and the cover, which is located at the back of the e-passport.
3. In between the middle or the center page of the document (this is where the binding of the e-passport is easily visible).

4. In its own special page in the e-passport. In these cases, this particular page is actually sewn into place, and thus, it cannot be used as either a visa or a travel stamp page.

Another key factor in determining how the microchip will be placed is how it will actually be used for confirming the identity of the passenger at the country of destination. For example, the biometric information from the microchip embedded in the e-passport can be transmitted if the e-passport is either in the open position (this is where the cover is open and the microchip is exposed to directly to the e-passport reader) or in the closed position (this is where e-passport is closed and the microchip is not exposed to the e-passport reader). The microchip can be literally placed into a very thin plastic sheet in the e-passport, or it can also be easily inserted into the front or back cover of the e-passport.

Since the e-passport is meant to be a rugged device that should be able to be used in all types and kinds of environments, the microchip must be of a similar quality as well. In other words, the durability of the microchip in use becomes a crucial factor in this regard as well. It is recommended by the ICAO that the e-passport and the microchip it contains should last for a minimum of 10 years, and should also be able to withstand any type or kind of application it may serve (for instance, the e-passport may not just be a travel document per se; it can also serve as a national identification card in some countries). Thus, the manufacturing process that is involved in creating the e-passport should thus be double checked to ensure the highest levels of quality assurance. In this manner, both functionality and usability testing need to be conducted in different stages throughout the entire process.

Just as much as the placement of the microchip in the e-passport is crucial, so is how the biometric information that is stored on it. This is primarily because the e-passport will exchange many hands in many countries of entry and exit. Thus, interoperability is the key here, as these data must be able to be read quickly and easily by all foreign governments. In order to facilitate this, the ICAO has mandated exact specifications and standards as to how the biometric templates must be stored.

These standards are as follows:

- *The ISO/IEC 19794-5 specification*: This applies to the storage of facial recognition templates.
- *The ISO/IEC 19794-6 specification*: This applies to the storage of iris recognition templates.
- *The ISO/IEC 19794-4 specification*: This applies to the storage of fingerprint recognition templates.

- *The ISO/IEC 19794-2 specification*: This applies to the storage of fingerprint minutiae information.
- *The ISO/IEC 1974-3 specification*: This applies to the storage of the fingerprint pattern information.

It is interesting to note here that the ICAO has also mandated that a miniature image of either the face, the fingerprint, or the iris must be stored on the microchip, along with the respective biometric templates. This requirement as set forth by the ICAO thus can lead to quite a bit of confusion among participating countries, and even lead to a greatly increased false rejection rates among the foreign travelers. For example, as just discussed, the current mandate calls for that the e-passport must be durable for 10 years. If, for example, a facial recognition image is stored, along with the respective biometric template, a strong mismatch can occur.

It is well known through scientific studies that the structure of the face can change greatly, due to massive weight loss or massive weight gain. Therefore, if the facial image of a particular individual is taken when he or she has experienced massive weight gain, and if the corresponding biometric template reflects this in the e-passport and then all of a sudden the next year this individual has experienced massive weight loss, and he or she still uses the same e-passport, the chances are much greater that he or she will thus be falsely rejected by the e-passport system.

In other words, the physiological and biological structures of the individual can change greatly over time, and the e-passport will not be able to capture this unless a new e-passport is issued each and every time. Perhaps, a potential work around this is to issue a mandate which specifies that citizens must submit new raw images and the corresponding biometric templates at certain intervals.

The biometric information that is stored on a microchip in an e-passport can be processed in numerous different ways (via the use of protocols), and they are as follows:

1. *Passive authentication*: The biometric information that is stored on the microchip of the e-passport is actually not processed; however, it must be shown at the time of identification that the contents contained within the e-passport (as well as the microchip) have not been changed or altered in any way. It should be noted that this protocol is actually mandated by the ICAO. Rather, the RFID tag that is placed into the e-passport is not involved in any processing, and simply put, it just plays a passive role; thus, it has been given this name purposely.
2. *Active authentication*: This involves the explicit and known processing of the biometric information that is stored on the

microchip of the e-passport. This authentication method differs from the passive authentication method in that not only does it have to be proven that the content of the e-passport has not changed, but also the microchip has not been substituted in any way in shape or form. In other words, the microchip that was embedded when the e-passport was first issued is still the very same microchip at the point of entry when the time comes to confirm the identity of the foreign traveler. This is not a mandated protocol by the ICAO; rather, it is an optional one that can be implemented by the participating countries into their e-passport system. With this particular protocol, a challenge–response system is utilized in order to confirm the validity of the microchip. In these cases, the RFID tag in the e-passport will contain a public key, as well as a hashing algorithm. In return, a private key is also stored in a separate section of the RFID tag. In order to validate the authenticity of the microchip, the e-passport must "prove" to the e-passport reader at the point of entry that it does indeed possess this specific private key.

3. *Basic access control*: This is an optional protocol (which is not mandated by the ICAO). However, the difference between this and the other protocol just described (active authentication) is that it too takes a passive role, in that it only makes an attempt to help ensure that the e-passport readers at the point of entry can only access the biometric information of that particular passport, which is "flashed" in front of it. In other words, the use of this protocol is designed to help the inadvertent theft of biometric information from e-passport holders in front of the individual whose e-passport is currently being scanned, as well as the e-passport holders behind this individual. In order to engage the e-passport reader in this protocol, the e-passport must contain a pair of private keys (which are stored in the MRZ section of the e-passport), which can be deciphered by the e-passport reader as it scans the e-passport.

4. *The extended access control*: This is a newer type of authentication protocol that has been applied to the second generation of e-passports (as opposed to the previous three protocols, which have been applied only to the first generation of e-passports). The primary objective of this protocol is to implement a more comprehensive suite of subauthentication protocols in order to add more assurances that the biometric information contained in the microchip of the e-passport are indeed authentic. Also, this protocol allows for multimodal biometric templates to be stored on the microchip of the e-passport (e.g., instead of using just facial recognition templates, both iris and fingerprint

recognition templates can also be stored). The subauthentication protocols include the following:

a. *Chip authentication*: If the extended access control protocol is to be utilized, then this specific protocol is mandatory. The primary objective of chip authentication is to replace the active authentication protocol, in order to better detect the e-passports that may have been cloned or maliciously duplicated. In order to accomplish this task, a new set of public and private keys is automatically generated, utilizing the Diffie–Hellman encryption algorithm.

b. *Terminal authentication*: This specific subauthentication protocol is only used if access to the more secure biometric information that are stored on the microchip is required. It utilizes a challenge–response system that allows the RFID contained in the e-passport to validate the e-passport reader, which is capturing the biometric information from the microchip. In return, the e-passport reader then "proves" to the RFID tag contained in the e-passport that it has been duly authorized, in general, to read all sorts of RFID tags.

5. *The password-authenticated connection establishment*: This specific authentication protocol has been applied to the third generation of e-passports. This protocol was specifically designed to replace the basic access control protocol. In a manner similar to the terminal authentication protocol, this protocol enables the RFID tag contained in the e-passport to confirm that the e-passport reader that is capturing the biometric information from it has been actually validated for use. Once again, the Diffie–Hellman encryption algorithm is used to facilitate this process.

6. *The types of passwords*: This authentication protocol actually allows for the use of passwords to be used in the communication process between the RFID tag in the e-passport and the e-passport reader. Two specific types of passwords can be created, which are as follows:

a. *The card access number*: This can be either a dynamic or a static password. If the created password is static, it is merely represented in a scrambled format in the e-passport. If it is created to be dynamic in nature, the RFID tag contained in the e-passport will actually create a random password, and it will display it on the e-passport.

b. *The MRZ password*: This is actually a public key that is derived and created using the principles of symmetric cryptography in the MRZ portion of the e-passport.

7. *Terminal authentication version 2*: As the name implies, this is the second version of the terminal authentication protocol. In this latest version, the RFID tag that is contained in the e-passport is given the "opportunity" to confirm the validity and authenticity of the e-passport from which the biometric information will be scanned. The RFID tag also gives "permission" to the e-passport reader to access the more secure biometric information, which are the multimodal biometric templates (primarily the fingerprint recognition and iris recognition templates). This protocol also utilizes a challenge–response system.

8. *Chip authentication version 2*: As the name implies, this too is the second version of the chip authentication protocol. However, with this latest enhancement, this protocol can only be executed after the terminal authentication protocol version 2 has been executed.

As a prelude to the next section, there have been scientific studies that have researched the use of the RFID protocol in the e-passport and the security vulnerabilities that are associated with it. One such study was conducted by Blundo and colleagues.[*] In this research work, the authors have pointed out specific requirements that are needed to effectively implement an RFID-based protocol, which would allow for an effective communication between the e-passport and the e-passport reader. These scientific properties can be described as follows:

1. *Nontransferability*: In this property, the biometric information that is contained in the microchip of the e-passport must be protected in such a way that after it has been transmitted to the e-passport reader and the identity verified by the passport official, it cannot be used by the latter for malicious purposes. Let us illustrate this with an example. Suppose that a foreign visitor is about to embark on the entry points of the destination country. However, before he or she is allowed to enter into the country, his or her identity must be first confirmed by the passport officer who is monitoring the e-passport reader. Obviously, this particular person will have access to the biometric information after it has been transmitted. The key here is that although this particular individual will have access to this, he or she will not be able to use this biometric information for launching a subsequent identity theft campaign. In this fashion, the principles

---

[*] C. Blundo, G. Persiano, A.R. Sadeghi and I. Visconti. Resettable and non-transferable chip authentication for e-passports. In *RFIDSec08*, 2008. http://libeccio.di.unisa.it/Papers/EPass/NonTranChipAuthentication.pdf.

of biocryptography would be most applicable here (as discussed earlier in this book). Essentially, the biometric templates (and any types or kinds of information) would be encrypted and decryptyed up to the point where the foreign traveler's identity will be positively confirmed.

2. *Resettability*: With regard to this property, the notion is that the biometric information that is stored on the microchip cannot be tampered with or altered in any way. In more technical terms, whatever resides in the memory of the microchip cannot be "reset" in any way, shape, or manner. With regard to the e-passport, it is especially prone to the fact that more than one instance of a biometric template can be stored on it. For instance, if the biometric templates of one foreign traveler are to be captured, they can be very covertly injected into the microchip of the e-passport of another foreign traveler, thus causing even more confusion as to what the actual identity of the foreign traveler really is. As a result, this may even lead a legitimate foreign traveler from being entered into a country, if he or she falls victim to this type of attack. In fact, it has been cited in this research study that numerous e-passports have actually been altered in this fashion.

3. *Practical setup assumptions*: In order to allow for the smoothest possible level of communications between the microchip of the e-passport and the e-passport reader at the point of entry via the RFID protocol, the overall infrastructure must have the lowest overhead as possible. In other words, if a PKI is employed as the primary crux of the e-passport infrastructure, the least minimal amount of both public keys and private keys needs to be used. In order to facilitate this effort, the public and private keys that are used must be afforded with the highest levels or layers of encryption as much as possible.

4. *Operational efficiencies*: In the entire e-passport infrastructure, one of the most important aspects in terms of efficiencies that need to be considered is power consumption. If a particular e-passport requires a huge power overhead, then of course, the system will not become efficient for large-scale uses. Thus, the level of power consumption that is utilized must be kept to the most minimal possible. This is especially true of the e-passport readers that are located at the point of entry into the country of destination, as well as the battery power that is required by the microchip embedded in the e-passport. Lower power consumption in these aspects will then translate into a much more efficient handling of the RFID protocol.

THE SECURITY VULNERABILITIES AND WEAKNESSES ASSOCIATED WITH THE E-PASSPORT

Just like the biometric technologies themselves, the e-passport infrastructure is also prone as well as susceptible to many types and kinds of security breaches. One of the reasons for this major weakness is that despite the standards, best practices, and protocols set forth by the ICAO, many participating nations still implement their own specific version of the e-passport that is not compatible with these specific guidelines. In other words, the e-passport infrastructure set forth and established by the Chinese government may not be compatible with the e-passport infrastructure of that of Sweden.

On account of these differing e-passport infrastructures, the biometric information that is stored on the microchip may not be able to be picked up by the e-passport reader in the destination country. It is because of these differences that security holes and gaps exist. Some of the major security threats and risks that are posed to any e-passport infrastructure are explained as follows:

1. *Cloning attacks*: This was touched on a little bit earlier at the beginning of this chapter. This type of attacks occurs when a newly issued e-passport actually contains the biometric information of a stolen or hijacked e-passport. A successful attack means that a foreign traveler with a newly issued e-passport cannot have his or her identity confirmed by the e-passport reader in the country of destination. This basically means that this particular foreign traveler will be barred from entry, or if his or her e-passport was cloned with the biometric information of a known criminal or terror suspect, he or she could very well be apprehended. To combat this security vulnerability in the e-passport, the active authentication protocol (as reviewed in this chapter) was utilized in the first-generation passports. The basic premise for the use of this specific protocol was that the RFID tag in the newly issued e-passport contained a highly encrypted private key (assuming that a PKI-based e-passport infrastructure is being utilized). However, as the first generation of e-passports continued to evolve, scientific research showed that this protocol was prone to "side-channel" attacks. To further combat the issues of these side-channel attacks, the chip authentication protocol was thus created. As it was also reviewed in this chapter, the wireless communications between the RFID tag embedded in the e-passport and the e-passport reader at the point of entry is automatically reset after the microchip in the

e-passport has been authenticated. In return, after this process has been completed, another protocol, known as the "reader authentication protocol," which makes assurances that only valid and authentic e-passport readers can access the secondary security system (or the multimodal biometrics, which include the fingerprint recognition and iris recognition templates).

2. *Eavesdropping attacks*: This type of attack occurs when a malicious third party (such as a corrupt government official reading the biometric information) actually gets access to the biometric templates that are stored on the microchip of the e-passport, which are in transit from the RFID antenna in the e-passport to the e-passport reader. The communication between these two entities is also known as a "conversation." To help mitigate this type of security breach, "Faraday cages" or "Faraday shields" are often used. This is essentially an enclosure in the e-passport, which is formed by a conducive material, or even a mesh. This particular enclosure helps to block both external static and nonstatic electric fields by channeling the flow of electric current around the conducive material of the e-passport, and not directly into the line of communication with the e-passport reader. However, in the second and third generations of the e-passport, the use of Faraday cages was dropped, and its replacement became the "terminal authentication protocol." The use of this protocol helped to guarantee that only validated and authenticated e-passport readers could communicate with the RFID tags embedded in the e-passport. An attack similar to this is also known as a "Clandestine attack." This occurs when an RFID tag can essentially broadcast the biometric information the microchip possesses over hundreds of meters away from the point of origination. As a result, it is almost impossible to shield the radio emissions that are generated by it.

3. *Adversary attacks*: In this type of security vulnerability, the biometric information that is stored on the microchip of the e-passport is literally "skimmed" or hijacked directly via the RFID tag. This can all occur very quickly, in just a matter of seconds, without the knowledge of the e-passport holder.

4. *Weak entropy of the basic access control keys*: Rather than being a direct security threat, this is much more of a security vulnerability in the weakness of this protocol. As it was mentioned earlier in this chapter, the basic access control protocol can also be used to help curtail any types or kinds of skimming and eavesdropping attacks posed to the e-passport. However, in more technical terms, the major crux underlying the security of this protocol is based directly on the entropy of the access keys it uses from the data

that are available in the MRZ section of the e-passport. Although the encryption level is at 56 bits, these particular access keys can be guessed by a very well-versed cyber attacker. For example, all he or she would have to do is to merely reduce the encryption level of these access keys in order to guess to gather the information contained in these access keys. In fact, it has been discovered that several German and Dutch passports had their respective encryption levels dropped to 25–35 bits, and as a result, the cyber attacker could then very covertly gain access to the RFID tag for the lifetime of the e-passport in which it was embedded in.

5. *Lack of access rules*: This is much more of a security weakness than an actual threat. This was mostly prevalent in the first-generation e-passport. On account of the confusion surrounding who could have access to the e-passport, any government official could very easily get hold of the secondary level of biometric information that was stored on the microchip. However, this easy access was not just limited to government officials, but research has also shown that even labor workers could gain access to it, provided they had a stolen e-passport in their possession and had the rudimentary knowledge needed to untap this very private information.

6. *Once valid readers*: As it was also pointed out earlier in this chapter, the microchip contained in the e-passport is by nature considered to be "passive." In more technical terms, this simply means that the microchip does not possess an internal time clock; it can only read time once it has been activated by an e-passport reader on which the identity of the foreign traveler is to be confirmed. As a result, an unvalidated e-passport reader (i.e., one that has expired certificates in them) can actually read the biometric information stored on the microchip, which can be easily intercepted and read by a nonauthenticated e-passport reader. This can only happen in the cases in which the e-passport has not been used for a very long time (and where the RFID tag has not been activated), such as in the cases of the very infrequent foreign traveler.

7. *Denial-of-service attacks*: This security vulnerability was actually examined in much detail in our last book. The basic premise of this kind of attack is that a server can literally come down to its knees and become crippled if it is basically flooded with gargantuan amounts of network traffic and malformed data packets. This example can also be extrapolated to the level of the e-passport. Although it does not take enormous levels of bandwidth to stop the proper functioning of the RFID tag and the microchip, a maliciously configured e-passport reader can

flood an RFID tag with malicious PKI certificates, thus rendering it inoperable.

8. *Leakage of biometric data*: Although encryption protocols are utilized to help secure the biometric templates that are stored on the microchip of the e-passport, a phenomenon known as "biometric data leakage" could still remotely occur, especially if latent fingerprints are discovered either during the enrollment or verification processes.

9. *Cryptographic weaknesses*: Some of these include the following:
   a. *A weak encryption key*: This can lead the cipher (this is the mathematical algorithm that is used to encrypt and decrypt both the public and private keys) to behave in an undesirable way and fashion, which could result in the disclosure of encrypted biometric information.
   b. *Man-in-the-middle attacks*: This occurs when a hacker tries to intervene in the line of communications between the e-passport and the e-passport reader, in an attempt to hijack the biometric information, or in worse cases, gain the ability to guess them.
   c. *No key revocation*: Based on the principles of cryptography, keys, whether public or private, should be refreshed at random or differing intervals. In other words, the original public or private key should be revoked, and new keys should be established as their replacement. However, this is not the case with the e-passport reader. The public keys as well as the private keys used to create the secure line of communications (to the e-passport) are partially stored here. These keys are not refreshed at random intervals, and the same keys have been known to be stored and used for up to 10 years.

The security threats and vulnerabilities just described above are those that are posed directly to the RFID tag, the microchip, and the biometric information (as well as the biometric templates), which are contained within the e-passport. Although these vulnerabilities are platforms from which identity theft campaigns can be leveraged, there is also another security vulnerability that poses direct harm to the e-passport holder himself or herself. This is known as a "traceability attack," and specific scientific research was conducted on this by a team of researchers at the School of Computer Science in the University of Birmingham, located in the United Kingdom.[*]

It should be noted that a traceability attack does not lead to the actual compromise of the biometric information that resides in the e-passport.

---

[*] T. Chothia and V. Smirnov. A traceability attack against e-passports. In R. Sion (ed.), *Financial Cryptography and Data Security*, LNCS 6052, Springer, Berlin/Heidelberg, Germany, pp. 20–34, 2010.

Rather, this form of attack can lead to ascertaining the actual identity of a foreign traveler. For instance, other scientific studies have shown that merely placing a very covertly placed locator, say at a door, can trigger an alert to the attacker that a specific individual is present, and from there, an identity theft campaign could be launched. Although these types of attacks require some sort of direct contact with the individual, with the traceability attack, these same concepts can also be applied to non-contactless devices, in particular the e-passport.

The basic premise behind the traceability attack is that the RFID chip that resides within the e-passport is actually in an "always on" mode. This fact always remains unknown to the unsuspecting foreign traveler, and he or she will never know indeed that his or her biometric information is being eavesdropped on. When an e-passport is first presented to a particular e-passport reader, a cryptographic-based secure session is first established between these two mechanisms using any sort of protocol (or even a combination of them) as reviewed earlier in this chapter.

For example, if the basic access control is being used, the e-passport generates what is known as a "nonce." In the world of cryptography, a nonce is merely a random number that is assigned to the source of communication in any secure session. The nonce (or the arbitrary number that was assigned and allocated) is primarily used to help ensure that the secure line of communications that was first established between the e-passport and the e-passport reader cannot be used again in order to launch what is known as a "replay attack." However, before the biometric information can be transmitted from the microchip embedded in the e-passport to the e-passport reader, the latter must first encrypt the nonce using the e-passport's public key.

In addition to this, the line of communication between the e-passport and the e-passport reader also establishes what is known as a series of "machine authentication codes" (MACs) for each level of secure communications, which is established between the two distinct entities. The origination of the MAC streams originates from the e-passport's own unique MAC-based key. The use of the MAC key helps to ensure that the secure line of communications between the e-passport and the e-passport reader is indeed authentic, and that all of the biometric information that is transmitted between these two entities remains unaltered or unchanged.

However, if any of the biometric information that is transmitted from the e-passport to the e-passport reader is rejected in this established, secure line of communications, a rejected or corrupted error message will be displayed. Thus, it is possible to tell if a specific e-passport was rejected because of a corrupt nonce or a malformed MAC encryption key. This specific scenario thus sets up the framework for a potential traceability attack.

For purposes of illustration of the nonce and the MAC-based encryption key, the secure line of communications between the e-passport and the e-passport reader is first established when the e-passport reader sends what is known as a "challenge" to the RFID tag embedded in the e-passport. In return, this same RFID tag then sends its own 64 bit message back to the e-passport reader. Then, it creates its own nonce and a new random message, which is also 64 bits long. This is all encrypted and sent back and forth from the e-passport to the e-passport reader, culminating in one round of message exchanges. In this, a MAC-based encryption key is also computed, in order to ensure the integrity of the messages. This is detailed in the next paragraph.

When the RFID tag first receives the message from the e-passport reader and verifies the validity of the MAC encryption key, it then checks that the returned nonce (which first comes from the e-passport reader) is indeed correct. In return, the RFID tag that is embedded in the e-passport then transmits its own 64 bit message and sends this back to the e-passport reader. However, in this case, the order of the nonce is now reversed, and the e-passport reader now double checks for the integrity of the MAC encryption key and its corresponding nonce.

In this research, the scientific investigators actually simulate an eavesdropping attack on a legitimate, secure line of communications between an e-passport and its associated e-passport reader, and record any error messages, which may occur as a result of this. In order to identify a particular e-passport (and subsequently its owner), the specific error message is replayed. The hypothesis in this specific study is that if the original error message that was recorded was the result of a malformed MAC encryption key, then the original e-passport was not utilized. However, if the error message was the result of a failed nonce check, then it can be safely assumed that the MAC encryption key was not malformed in any way shape or manner, and that the original e-passport was used. Therefore, the owner of this particular e-passport can be "traced" back, and from here, potential identity theft campaigns can then be launched.

In order to prove this hypothesis, an ACR122U e-passport reader was purchased (at the time this scientific study was conducted, the manufacturer of this hardware was known as "Advanced Cards Systems Limited"). This was deemed to be one of the cheapest e-passport readers at the time, and the primary reason why this was purchased was that the scientific investigators wanted to also prove that sophisticated equipment and hardware are not required in order to launch a stealthy and covert traceability attack. To conduct these tests, the following e-passports were selected:

- Three U.K.-based e-passports
- Two German-based e-passports
- One Russian-based e-passport

- Two French-based e-passports
- One Irish-based e-passport
- One Greek-based e-passport

It should be noted that although the ICAO does indeed specify the specific language and syntax which should be used in constructing these error messages (primarily for the purposes of standardization and uniformity), each country has created its own version of these error messages. For example, many countries that have developed their own e-passport infrastructure utilize the "Answer to Reset" error message, provided that they have embedded the ISO 7816 microchip in their e-passports. Along with this particular message, information on the microchip's manufacturer and how the microchip should be read is also displayed. By contrast, if a particular country uses the ISO 14443 microchip, the error message reads either "Answer to Select" or "File Control Information."

In the e-passports that were tested in this scientific study, each country had utilized its own version of the "Answer to Reset" error message. For instance, the German-based e-passport (at the time this study was conducted) has been recently updated to include both an alphanumeric based e-passport number and the fingerprint biometric templates of the e-passport holder. It was further discovered that the "Answer to Reset" error messages derived from this latest generation of the e-passport was far different than its predecessor.

This finding underscored another security vulnerability of the e-passport in that not only does the "Answer to Reset" error message allow to clearly identify the issuing nation of the e-passport, but also the version number of the specific e-passport can be discovered. This is turn makes it easy for the hacker to guess the basic access control encryption key as well.

Of all the e-passports that were tested, it was also discovered that the French-based e-passports displayed different error messages, thus making them the most vulnerable to a traceability attack. In this case, the two differing error messages that were displayed are as follows:

1. *Error 6300*: No Information Given
2. *Error 6A80*: Incorrect Parameters

Interestingly enough, the e-passports of the other nations in this scientific study revealed the same error message (Error 6300) in all instances of testing, thus making them much less vulnerable to the traceability attack. This type of attack to the French-based e-passport can be launched in numerous ways, which include the following tactics:

- If the e-passport is read by the e-passport reader when the foreign traveler is in a stationary mode (i.e., they are standing still, although their identity is being confirmed), all the hacker has to do is to just send one random replay message to the e-passport, and if there are specific time intervals that are noticed as the e-passport is being processed by the e-passport reader, then the hacker can more or less be sure that the same e-passport is being used.
- If the e-passport is read by the e-passport reader when the foreign traveler is in a nonstationary mode (i.e., they are in movement, although their identity is being confirmed), all the hacker has to do is to launch a series of random replay messages to the e-passport, and if there are any variations in the specific time intervals that are noticed as the e-passport is being processed by the e-passport reader, then the hacker can more or less be sure that the same e-passport is being used.
- If the hacker covertly observes numerous e-passports that are being processed by different e-passport readers, all he or she has to do then is to merely record the error messages that are presented and test this same error message on other e-passports, which are being processed at different time intervals. In order to do this, the hacker must secretly transmit a "GET CHALLENGE" response to any e-passport which is in plain sight. If an "Error 6300" message is displayed, it means then that the MAC security check has failed (as explained previously); however, if an "Error 6A80" message is displayed, then the MAC check has succeeded, so this means that the same e-passport is being used; thus, it becomes a prime target for traceability attack.

In order to mitigate the security risks and vulnerabilities that are posed by a traceability attack, the scientific investigators have proposed a number of key findings, which are as follows:

- All e-passports, regardless of the issuing nation, must issue the same type and kind of error messages, and this should be strictly enforced by the ICAO.
- If the basic access control protocol is utilized, then the specific e-passport in question must encrypt the error message with the nonce before it is transmitted.
- Before implementing any type or kind of authentication protocols in the secure line of communications between the e-passport and the e-passport reader, the MAC key must be first checked for any security vulnerabilities which it may possess before it is decrypted.
- If contact-based e-passports were mandated (such as using a smartcard vs. an RFID tag), then the traceability attack would

never occur in the first place. The use of such technology also provides the same benefits of those with an RFID tag, such as high transfer rates of the biometric information from the micro-chip embedded in the e-passport to the e-passport reader.

THE SOCIAL IMPACTS OF THE E-PASSPORT INFRASTRUCTURE

As it has been discussed in detail not only in this book thus far but also in our last book, biometric technology is one of those security modalities, which is the most prone to privacy rights and civil liberties violations, compared to the other security technologies, if they are viewed on a spectrum. The primary reason for this, as also reviewed in detail, is that it is a piece of our individual physiological/biological as well as behavioral mechanisms, which are being captured in order to fully confirm our identity.

The biggest fears in letting the governments around the world use such features that foreign travelers have no idea how this information will be used (unless the point of entry of the respective government tells each and every foreign traveler how his or her biometric templates stored on the e-passport will be specifically utilized), and also biometric templates are permanent identifiers.

If any biometric template from the e-passport were to be hijacked, there is nothing that can be done to mitigate any subsequent that may occur. The only thing that can be done is to have the foreign traveler go through the entire enrollment process again and have new biometric templates created.

As mentioned, the magnitude of the level of the issues of privacy rights and civil liberties violations depends largely on the geographic segment that is being examined. In general, the citizens of many of the developing nations do not have too much of an issue when it comes to submitting and using their biometric templates, whereas in the developed nations, such as the United States, the American public would raise many issues. One of the primary reasons for this is that the American citizens have certain, inalienable rights, which are afforded to them by U.S. Constitution.

When we examine the particular issues of privacy rights and civil liberties violations, we are primarily examining them from the basis of individual nations. However, with the e-passport, the problem becomes that now all of a sudden, many nations are involved at once when the time comes to process the biometric information of people entering and exiting any country. Thus, when you have this sheer conglomeration of people, the issues of privacy rights and civil liberties violations certainly come into the foreplay now, at a much more magnified level and spectrum.

In other words, there will be brand new processes and systems, which will have to be integrated in order to not only process brand new e-passports to individuals in a certain country but also process the e-passports of foreign travelers entering into that same country.

There will be not only a certain amount of time required to implement these new processes and systems at a technical level, but also a substantial amount of time needed to be devoted for government officials who will be issuing and processing the e-passports to be fully trained and completely understand this brand new infrastructure.

It is much better for the government of a country to take the time required to deploy an e-passport infrastructure in order to ensure that all project milestones have been successfully implemented, and that there will be no major obstacles forthcoming as both citizens are issued their brand new e-passports, and as foreign travelers are processed into the point of their destination.

The e-passport, in certain ways, have now become the embodiment of a national identity for many citizens around the world. Therefore, an e-passport infrastructure will have a great impact on the "wider socio-economic realm" of all nations concerned and involved in an e-passport infrastructure. However, when differing nations, as well as many millions of people, are involved, there will be many differing, personal views on what exactly constitutes privacy rights and civil liberties violations when it comes to the use of biometric technology. It is nearly impossible to address all of these concerns on an individual basis, but they do need to be addressed at a general, macro level by the government officials of the countries in question.

One area that will need major effort undertaken by a foreign government is in explaining to their citizens what the benefits of using an e-passport actually are. For instance, citizens may seriously question why they should spend forth the extra time and money required in obtaining an e-passport when the traditional paper passport would work as well in order to confirm their identity. Also, at the outset, there could be a lot of hesitancy for the citizens of a particular country to adopt to a new process—in other words, the fundamental resistance to change will come into play here.

However, above all, the citizens need to have, and are deserved to have, specific explanations as to how their e-passports will be used, how the biometric templates will be stored, what safeguards will be used to protect them, and how the associated information will be utilized for any other purposes except for confirming their identity at a foreign point of entry.

If this benefit/risk analysis is not undertaken and used to explain the overall net gains to the citizens of a foreign country with regard to the e-passport, certain risks could evolve, which include the following:

- A very slow adoption rate of the e-passport (although the citizens will be required to obtain e-passports, the specific timing as to when they will be issued will be greatly affected) or even total rejection of it.
- A severe degradation of the efficiencies as well as the economies of scale of an e-passport infrastructure.
- The quality of the enrollment process will also suffer as a result of uncooperative e-passport holders.
- A total lack of faith as well as a huge sense of skepticism on part of the citizens with regard to the entire e-passport infrastructure and its interrelated processes.
- On a much macro level, a sense of much reduced credibility in the eyes of other nations around the world.

In order to ensure that the e-passport will have the highest levels of adoption as possible, and to help guarantee the cooperativeness of the citizens of a particular country, foreign governments need to address the concerns and issues discussed in the sections that follow.

Privacy

This issue again goes back to the problem of the citizens of a country having the fears of their own government utilizing the e-passport infrastructure in order to keep tabs on them and keep track of their every move. To allay all of these, governments around the world must explain to their citizens as to how the e-passport agencies and their respective agents will protect the privacy of the biometric templates (as well as their associated information) and what specific security protocols will be used to secure them as well as to maintain its integrity. Obviously, with the latter scenario, the government of a specific nation should not disclose in detail about what security protocols are being used, but give out just enough information to satisfy its citizens. Giving out too much detail, of course, will then lead to subsequent and much graver security breaches. Also as mentioned previously, the government of a nation that has just deployed an e-passport infrastructure also needs to disclose and 100% ensure its citizens that the biometric information that will be collected will only be used for the purposes of confirming their identity as they travel abroad. If such information is intended to be used for any other reason or be given away to a nonrelated third party, then explicit permission must be given by the e-passport holder. In other words, the biometric templates are not owned by the government; rather, they are explicitly owned by the bearer of the e-passport.

Also as mentioned throughout this book, one of the biggest topics to be also addressed with regard to privacy rights and civil liberties violations is how the biometric templates will be stored in the respective databases. This specific topic needs to be addressed by the government of a country not only in the short term but also in the long term. A well-maintained biometrics database will involve the right security protocols in place to protect the biometric templates, but there will also be strict governance in place as to who and how the biometric information will be accessed, regular audits conducted with regard to the access control policy of the biometric database as well as ensure the integrity and unalteration of the biometric templates, and also ensure that the line of communications between the RFID tag embedded in the e-passport and the e-passport reader is secure with the latest encryption protocols. In the end, if the government has taken the necessary steps to implement all of these, there will be nothing to hide from the eyes of its own citizens.

Another issue that needs to be addressed with regard to privacy rights and civil liberties by the government deploying an e-passport infrastructure is the security vulnerability of the biometric information that is stored on the e-passport. The list of protocols to ensure the mitigation of this vulnerability was discussed in detail in this chapter. However, not all countries implement the same protocols as mandated by the ICAO. In fact, some nations probably do not even implement tight security procedures at all. Therefore, without question, one of the biggest fears on part of the citizen is the covert hijacking of the biometric templates from the e-passport when an unsecure line of communications is used. However, this is not a fear that is just isolated to just one particular country; rather this is a fear of all citizens of all nations involved.

One of the best tools that a government can use to address these security concerns is to craft and implement the right type of legislations with regard to these security issues and make every effort its enforcement in any type or kind of e-passport infrastructure. However, drafting these certain types of legislations will be a very complex process and will require the involvement of many related government entities (such as any data protection authorities, computer and IT specialists, and privacy rights and civil liberties groups).

Also, to help ensure the security as well as the integrity of the biometric information that resides in the microchip, the ICAO has mandated and set forth protocols to allow e-passport holders to gain access to specific e-passport readers in order to confirm the validity of their respective biometric templates.

Many countries have already addressed these issues as established in this section, as well as passed the appropriate pieces of legislation to the nations, which include Australia, China (Hong Kong), South Korea, Malaysia, the Philippines, Singapore, and Thailand.

Usability and Accessibility

Chapter 2 looked at one of the major issues, which is impeding the growth rate of biometric technology in the United States: the ergonomic design of the biometric modalities available in the marketplace today. In other words, the biometric technology that is being used in any type or kind of market applications must be perceived by the end user which is easy to use. If it is not, the chances of it being accepted and utilized by the end user are extremely low. This case in point was illustrated with the hand geometry scanner. Although it is very useful for large-scale market applications (e.g., using it for time and attendance applications in large square footage warehouse), it is not compatible to be used for small-scale applications, such as single sign-on solutions. In this specific regard, the hand geometry scanner would be perceived as very "intrusive" to be used. Therefore, other more smaller biometric devices have been created and developed for this specific type of application. These devices appear very simple to use; therefore, the acceptance rate of them is quite high.

However, apart from having a strong sense of ease of use, the biometric modality in question must also look aesthetically pleasing and blend into the environment easily and efficiently. In other words, if a fingerprint recognition device is to be installed onto the wall of an office or a place of business or organization, it should not the direct focal point of daily activity; rather, it should only be "noticed" during the times and circumstances it is needed (such as for providing access to a secure room within the office area). The same issue of biometric-based ergonomics also holds true for an e-passport infrastructure. However, in this regard, a distinction has to be made. There is no need for ergonomic considerations in the actual design of the microchip of the e-passport that contains the biometric templates. All that will be done is that this microchip will be presented to the e-passport reader in order to fully confirm the identity of the e-passport holder. The only consideration that needs to be taken into account in this regard is that the construction of the e-passport must be viable enough so that the biometric information in it can be captured readily by the e-passport without any major issues.

However, in order to capture the biometric templates that will be stored on the microchip of the e-passport, the citizens of a country have to be present at a government-based e-passport office in order to have their fingerprint, face, or iris scanned. In order to do this, these biometric modalities must be deployed. Therefore, in this regard, the ergonomic design of the biometric modality being utilized must take a top priority.

For instance, the particular biometric modality must be simple enough for the government official to use in order to capture the biometric templates of the potential e-passport holder; however, it must also look aesthetic and pleasing enough to the citizen so that he or she will not be frightened to present his or her fingerprint, face, or iris for scanning purposes.

Thus, in this regard, the following considerations need to be taken into account when deploying biometric modalities in an e-passport office:

- *Physical access*: Can the potential e-passport holder (the citizen) easily present his or her face, iris, or finger to the biometric modality in order for him or her to be scanned? It is important to keep in mind here that the physical needs of all citizens have to be taken into account, which can include many factors and variables.
- *Access for citizens with physical impairments*: This consideration is especially true for those who are disabled and are required to use a wheelchair. The biometric modality must be placed in such a manner at the e-passport office so that there will be no extra effort or any pain inflicted on the citizen as he or she has his or her fingerprint, face, or iris scanned.
- *The location of the e-passport reader at the point of entry*: Although the e-passport reader does not consist of any biometric technologies directly per se, the same ergonomic factors need to be taken into consideration here as well. For example, probably one of the biggest considerations that need to be taken into account is that the e-passport reader must be deployed in such a way that the biometric information that resides in the e-passport can be collected quickly and processed, so that the identity of the e-passport holder can be confirmed in just a matter of seconds.
- *The physical environment for the biometric modalities*: The fingerprint reader, or the iris and facial scanner, which is deployed at the e-passport office must be in an environment that is free from any contaminants of the external environment. Also, the environment must be stable enough so that quality biometric templates can be collected (for instance, in the case of facial recognition, the lighting must be constant and not change).
- *Network capacity*: In an e-passport office, there will obviously be more than one biometric modality that will be used, as well as different types and kinds. More than likely, all of these biometric modalities will be interlinked together via the use of network protocols, such as transmission control protocol/ Internet protocol. Therefore, enough network capacity needs to be planned at all e-passport offices so that it can handle and process a large volume of citizens with a quick turnaround time.

- *Fallback mechanisms*: Backup procedures need to be put into place in the case of total biometric modality failure at the e-passport office, or in the case where a citizen simply cannot have a biometric template(s) due to any physical ailments he or she may possess.

Health and Safety

As also discussed throughout this book, one of the biggest concerns that are impeding the growth rate of biometric technology at least in the United States is the perception of health and safety issues. At least with the physical-based biometric modalities, many of them still require full contact, especially in the cases of hand geometry scanning and fingerprint recognition. Depending on the type and kind of applications these certain biometric modalities serve, there could be many individuals who are placing their hands on the optical sensor in order for the raw images to be collected. On account of this sheer number of end users using these systems in order to have their identity confirmed, there is often a grave fear of the medical unknowns of them. As a result, the anxieties and concerns if germs or contaminants exist upon the optical sensor arise, and thus, the panic of contracting an ailment. To date, there are no known serious illnesses or diseases, which have been contracted through the direct contact with a particular biometric technology. Nevertheless, the fear still exists. In this regard, it is thus very imperative for the operator of the biometric modality to follow the cleansing procedures of the device as it has been outlined by the biometric vendor who manufactured it. As a result, in large part to these public fears, the biometric industry has adopted a trend of developing biometric modalities that do not require contact or interface with the optical sensor on part of the end user. Thus, the use of vein pattern recognition (this is the modality in which the end user merely shows his or her palm on top of a sensor, which in turn flashes an infrared beam of light in order to illuminate and capture the unique patterns of blood vessels) and iris recognition is starting to catch hold in numerous applications. One example of this is the health-care industry, in which hygiene is of paramount importance.

As countries around the world continue to proliferate and grow their e-passport infrastructures, the issue of hygiene will take place again, but probably at a much higher and deeper level. Again, this will not exist at the point of entry in the destination country for the foreign traveler; rather, it will exist at the point of origination, the e-passport office. Here, there will be citizens from all walks of life and different countries that will have their physiological/biological features captured and analyzed. Thus, the fear of contracting any illnesses or ailments through the direct contact with the optical sensor (this will be especially of that with regard to fingerprint recognition) will greatly escalate. The following are other factors and variables that could further exacerbate this particular fear when it comes to deploying an e-passport infrastructure:

- Although iris recognition is a non-contactless biometric modality, there is still strong angst that subsequent medical issues could very well arise (such as that of blindness and glaucoma).
- Cross-contamination issues, for instance, if latent fingerprints are left behind on an optical sensor by a foreign traveler, could the next person in line waiting to go through the process of enrollment be affected if the other person has some sort of physical ailment?
- Although there is no direct correlation attached with it, there is also fear that some sort of psychological disorder could be contracted through the direct contact and interface with a biometric technology (to another extreme, fears also exist if certain more serious degenerative diseases, or even any physical disfigurements, can be contracted).

There are really only two possible solutions in which a government can implement if it is going to deploy an e-passport infrastructure, and they are as follows:

1. Assure to the citizens who visit the e-passport office that all biometric equipment and devices being used to collect their raw images are indeed being kept clean and inspected for any outside contaminants on a daily basis.
2. Implement non-contactless forms of biometric modalities, such as iris recognition and vein pattern recognition.

Social and Cultural Differences and Considerations

It should be noted that biometric technology is a security tool that is implemented on a world-wide level. There is not one country that is not using it, whether it is for the smallest applications (such as single sign-on solutions) or for the largest applications (such as e-voting, which will be examined in Chapter 4). Given the privacy rights and civil liberties issue it faces, biometric technology also faces a huge social and cultural divide. For example, in the United States, many religious groups view it as the "mark of the beast"; in other places in the Middle East, the use of facial recognition is forbidden to be used by women there because of the head clothing which they are required to wear; and even in a modern and developed country such as Japan, the use of fingerprint recognition is almost banned because of its hygienic issues (in this case, vein pattern recognition is used instead, especially in the financial system).

Thus, these types and kinds of social and cultural differences must be taken into heavy consideration as governments around the world deploy their e-passport infrastructures, as well as permit the entry of foreign visitors. These differences need to be taken into account at two separate places:

1. At the e-passport office, where the citizens and/or foreign travelers will have their biometric templates processed into their respective e-passports
2. At the point of entry into the destination country, where the identity of the e-passport holder will be confirmed

There are also other reasons why these social and cultural differences exist with biometric technology and how they relate to the e-passport infrastructure, and they are as follows:

- *Religious factors*: In many places in the Middle East region, women cannot be literally "unveiled" in the presence of other men. Rather, they can only present themselves when other women are around. This can cause huge problems at the e-passport office, and in these cases, a woman government official must aid the female citizen in having her raw images collected and biometric templates processed.
- *Personality issues*: Citizens from different countries may be afflicted with certain types and kind of disorders; thus, they may be shunned away by the public and, as a result, may be quite fearful of being enrolled into a biometric system.
- *Personal victimization*: In some countries, such as the developing ones, cases of identity theft may not be taken so seriously by the legal system of these governments, as opposed to the governments of the developed nations such as the United States, where identity theft is taken very seriously by the legal system. In this regard, victims of identity theft who have not been taken seriously will of course be fearful and skeptical of being enrolled by a biometric system and having an e-passport issued to them, where the fears of identity theft are abundant and plenty.

When it comes to the e-passport infrastructure, the only solution that is available to governments around the world is to follow a strict policy of tolerance. And in cases in which this may not work, other backup systems will have to be implemented in order to accommodate the foreign travelers who have a very strong objection as to using biometric technology in confirming their identity. This case in point is well illustrated by the government of South Korea, where, if a foreign traveler has serious objections of submitting his or her fingerprints, backup alternatives are available.

To help increase the social perception and the worldwide acceptance of e-passport infrastructures, governments around the world can engage in the following programs of dialog in order to educate their respective citizens into the awareness of the benefits that biometric technology brings to the table:

- Explaining at a high level what biometric technology is all about and how it works within the confines of the e-passport infrastructure
- Explaining how biometric technology can be used to confirm the identity of a particular individual, as he or she travels overseas
- Explaining how the e-passport can be used to facilitate the safety and security of traveling overseas
- Most importantly, explaining how the biometric information will be stored in the databases, how they will be made secure, and who will have access to it

Of course, the above is not at all an inclusive list of what governments around the world can implement in terms of education and awareness. Other programs can be implemented, based on the needs of the citizens of that particular country. In other words, any biometric-based education effort with regard to the e-passport needs to address the factors that impede the acceptance and adoption of e-passports on part of each and every citizen. These include the following:

- The understanding of the perceived benefits and ease of use of an e-passport infrastructure
- The level of technology experience and understanding the citizens possess
- The level of trust the citizens have in their own government
- The level of visibility and transparency that an e-passport deployment is made to the citizens of a particular country
- The level of perceived convenience and reliability of the e-passport system
- How the costs of implementing an e-passport infrastructure will be absorbed by the government of a nation (e.g., will this mean increased taxes or other surcharges to the citizens of a country?)

- The perceived level of invasiveness that the use of e-passports brings to the citizens of a country
- The nature of the security threats and risks associated with the implementation and use of an e-passport infrastructure

Numerous countries have already launched certain public awareness campaigns in the efforts to boost the national acceptance of their e-passport infrastructures. Some of these countries include the following:

- *Australia*: A massive public relations was launched prior to the deployment of its e-passport infrastructure, which included the following:
  - How the e-passport can be used to provide a more secure and positive means to confirm the identity of a foreign traveler
  - How the e-passport can be used to combat the threats and risks posed by identity theft
  - How biometric technology embedded in the e-passport can be subsequently used to access automated border controls
- *Malaysia*: Public education campaigns were launched through various channels, which include social media, the traditional print press, and various Malaysian government websites. As a result of these types and kinds of efforts, the number of applications for an e-passport by Malaysian citizens has increased by at least 20% every year. Special emphasis was placed as to how an e-passport infrastructure can be used to help detect and combat forged travel documents.
- *Thailand*: The government here used various media to introduce its e-passport infrastructure to its citizens. This included the use of traditional newspaper print and radio broadcasts. Its citizens were even required to participate in a mock border crossing, in order to completely understand firsthand how an e-passport infrastructure actually works.

ACTUAL CASE STUDIES OF THE DEPLOYMENT OF THE E-PASSPORT INFRASTRUCTURE WORLDWIDE

So far, this chapter has covered a lot of theoretical aspects concerning the e-passport. This chapter has examined the historical background behind the paper passport, the transition to the e-passport (which covered its history as well), provision of a review of the technical components covering the e-passport, the security vulnerabilities and threats posed to any type or kind of e-passport, as well as the social implications and factors that would impact the current as well as the future usage of any e-passport infrastructure.

In this chapter, it is now important to review some actual, successful implementations of various e-passport infrastructures that have been deployed successfully worldwide. This will serve as the framework for Chapter 5, which will review in detail how biometric technology can be successfully adopted and deployed, especially in the United States.

BIOLINK SOLUTIONS AND THE E-PASSPORT IN SENEGAL

Senegal is a country that is located in the extreme western portion of the African continent. The name of the country is derived from the Senegal River, which borders the nation from both the eastern and northern borders it possesses. The Senegal covers a total geographic territory of 76,000 square miles and has an estimated population of well over 13 million citizens. The Senegal's largest city is its capital, which is Dakar.

BioLink Solutions, a major biometric vendor based in the United States, has recently won a contract with the government of Senegal in order to register each and every one of its citizens into a biometric-based database. From here, this biometric information would then be processed into an e-passport infrastructure, which of course is ICAO compliant.

However, from the outset of the project, only a small sample of the population would be initially enrolled into the biometrics database, which accounts for three million, or about 27% of the total population. At the time of the contract awarding, there was only one main passport processing office, located in the capital city.

One of the main goals of this new e-passport infrastructure was to increase the total number of passport processing offices to eight nationwide, with other passport offices located worldwide. The other main goal was to provide the citizens of the country with a means to combat the threat of identity theft via the use of a machine-readable passport.

In addition to this, another objective was to streamline the immigration activities and processes at the international airports located in Senegal, as well as keep tabs of the foreign visitors entering and exiting the country.

As this e-passport project was being deployed by BioLink Solutions, the Dakar International Airport was equipped and further enhanced with four Immigration Autogates (e-gates), which has allowed for the safe, swiftless, and effortless flow of foreign visitors entering and exiting the country. BioLink Solutions has been primarily responsible for implementation of the biometric technology in the Senegal's e-passport infrastructure.

This included providing the live scan fingerprint readers deployed throughout the nation's e-passport offices, as well as the related software and databases that were required for the management and matching of the fingerprint recognition templates.

Also, in order to facilitate the processing of the country's citizens at the newly established e-passport offices, BioLink Solutions also provided a dedicated biometric management server, along with eight heavy-duty biometric matchers (which consisted of two quad-core processors) in order to process the millions of fingerprint raw images into their respective biometric templates.

The matching (or comparison) between the enrollment and verification templates has been accomplished with BioLink Solutions's proprietary mathematical algorithms, which is also compliant with both international and industry standards that are as follows:

- ISO/IEC
- ANSI/NIST
- ANSI INCITS
- WSQ

To assist in the development of the Senegalese e-passport system, BioLink Solutions also partnered with another biometrics vendor known as IRIS Corporation Berhard, which will provide e-passport-based support services for the next 20 years.

NEUROTECHNOLOGY AND THE POLISH E-PASSPORT SYSTEM

Poland is a county in the European Union that contains one of the largest populations. In fact, over one million traditional paper passports have been issued there on an annual basis. However, as of 2009, newly enacted European Union Law all of the paper passports issued in Poland and other "Schengen" nations were now required to convert their existing, paper-based passport infrastructures into an e-passport based infrastructure. This called for the use of both fingerprint recognition and facial recognition.

The Schengen is essentially a group of 25 E.U. nations, which have enacted a borderless zone that allows for the free travel and movement of citizens within this specific geographic area.

The main passport issuing authority in Poland, known as the Polish Security Printing Works (with over 130 offices located throughout Poland), selected a biometric vendor known as "neurotechnology," based in Lithuania. In order to establigh the fingerprint recognition component of the Polish e-passport, this office decided to utilize the "VeriFinger" SDK. This particular software has received worldwide acclaim for its very fast and highly accurate 1:1 based verification algorithms, and can also work very easily in a wide variety of both programming and software environments. As Polish citizens now visit their local passport offices to apply for their new e-passports, their fingerprints are scanned in automatically with a Dermalog-based ZF1 fingerprint scanner.

After the raw image of the fingerprint has been collected, the VeriFinger SDK is then used to evaluate the quality of the particular image taken. If the image is deemed to be of high quality and caliber, the raw image then makes its way through the process of being converted into a biometric template to be stored on the microchip of the e-passport.

Before the Polish citizens receive their e-passports, the applicants must submit their fingerprints again using the same scanning hardware. The VeriFinger SDK is then used again to compare this new set of fingerprint images with the set of images taken previously. If there is a positive match and both sets of the fingerprint images are deemed to be of good quality, the applicants are then finally issued their e-passports. In this same manner, the set of facial images is also captured, utilizing an entirely different software component.

The requirements to us, both fingerprint recognition and facial recognition, were mandated by the European Union Council Regulation Number 2252/2004. The information that is contained in the Polish e-passport consist of the following:

- The passport holder's surname
- The passport holder's given name
- The passport holder's date of birth
- The passport holder's birthplace
- The passport holder's fingerprint recognition and facial recognition biometric templates

The VeriFinger SDK also allowed for the capacity to allow the e-passport applicant to submit his or her both rolled and flat fingerprint images, which in turn allowed for a wide variance of translation, rotation, and deformities in the fingerprint image.

Finally, a number of key benefits were also derived by using the VeriFinger SDK into the Polish e-passport infrastructure. These are as follows:

- *Reliability*: A high degree of accuracy as well as a greatly increased speed in biometric template matching has been achieved by the Polish e-passport infrastructure.

- *Flexibility*: The Polish e-passport infrastructure can now quickly and easily accommodate Polish with all types and kinds of physical ailments, which would normally otherwise impede their ability to be issued an e-passport.
- *Support*: Through the use of the VeriFinger SDK, all e-passport offices in Poland now have access to a wide range of support services to further enhance their services. These include samples, documentation, and tutorials.
- *Financial value*: By using the VeriFinger SDK in large volumes, the Polish Security Printing Works was able to cost-effectively issue over a million e-passports on an annual basis.

CHAPTER 4

Biometrics and e-Voting

Chapter 3 reviewed in detail the background, technical concepts, as well as the various issues surrounding the deployment, implementation, and use of the e-passport infrastructure. As it was explained, e-passport has now become a replacement for the traditional paper passport, as well as the latest versions of any type of machine readable documents.

E-passport is also becoming to be known as the "biometric passport," and essentially consists of a microchip (which contains the biometric templates of facial recognition, fingerprint recognition, and iris recognition), as well as an radiofrequency identification tag and miniature antennae, in which the biometric information can be transmitted to the e-passport reader in the destination country.

After the transmission of the above-mentioned information, the identity of the foreign traveler can be confirmed, in just a matter of seconds. However, if the identity of the person cannot be positively confirmed, then other manual checks will have to be utilized.

The e-passport not only allows access to various points of entry around the world, which is a much more safe and robust means of securing their own individual borders, but it has also been designed in such a way as to provide a much convenient traveling experience.

For instance, rather than having to wait for hours in order to get processed through the immigration and customs lines at international airports, as previously mentioned, this certain processing time is now reduced to just a matter of seconds. In the past, only frequent business travelers could afford this luxury; however, now, every citizen around the world can enjoy this newfound freedom, provided that their country of origin mandates the implementation of an e-passport infrastructure.

Specifically, Chapter 3 covered the following points regarding an e-passport infrastructure:

- Overview of the history regarding the traditional paper passport
- Evolution of the e-passport
- Technical aspects behind the e-passport

- Nature of security risks and threats associated with an e-passport infrastructure (regardless of the nation in question)
- Social implications surrounding the use of an e-passport to the infrastructure of the countries who use it
- Actual implementations of an e-passport infrastructure in selected countries

Chapter 5 looks at the use of biometric technology from a different perspective, but still from the angle of a large-scale deployment, which not only involves the governments of various countries but also every citizen. This is the concept of e-voting. For the most part, voting, in which the citizens cast their votes in order to help elect the government officials of their choice, has existed since centuries.

In these instances, the candidate receiving the majority of the votes after the election will be the elected official(s) or leader(s) (except in the United States, where the presidential candidate who has the most number of electoral votes actually wins the election—only 270 votes are required, and the presidential candidate who gets this number first actually wins the election).

However, in casting the vote among the nominated candidates, the citizens of a country normally have to cast their vote via a designated ballot. After the ballot has been cast by a particular citizen, it is then delivered into the collection medium, and at the end of the voting period, these ballots are then examined individually to determine the total number of votes that each candidate has received. This method has existed literally for centuries—whether it is circling "yay" or "nay" by the name of each candidate, or punching those choices with a pushpin attached to the voting booth.

However, with the passage of time, these traditional methods of casting votes and ascertaining who won a particular election possess a certain number of disadvantages, which include the following:

- The time taken to process every ballot.
- Errors made by misreading a certain punch or circle.
- The overall flaws in the manual processes of tabulating the total number of votes for each candidate, especially in very closely held elections. This was best exemplified by the 2000 U.S. presidential election. The difference in the number of popular votes between George W. Bush and Al Gore was a mere 543,895 votes. This razor thin margin led to the famous recounts of every ballot in four primary counties of Florida—Broward, Miami-Dade, Palm Beach, and Volusia. All of these recounts yielded different results, ultimately the U.S. Supreme Court decided the

stalemate, which gave George W. Bush the competitive edge in winning the election.

- The covert nature by which tabulation of the ballots occur, which could also be very easily influenced by social or political pressures
- Cases of voter fraud (which primarily involves the use of driver's licenses or identification cards of deceased individuals)
- Voter errors caused by hanging, dimpled, or "pregnant" chads (this term refers to the fragments that are created as a result of punching holes next to the name of each candidate on the ballot card)

Over the years, because of these critical flaws in the manual system of tabulating ballots, many reforms have been called for modernizing the current election systems when it comes to counting the total number of votes associated with each candidate. These flaws were best exemplified by the problems exhibited in the above-mentioned counties of Florida. In these circumstances, both the design and the usability of the voter ballots caused many problems.

For instance, the so-called "butterfly ballot" triggered the most headaches when tabulating the total number of votes. This type of ballot is essentially a paper-based punch card, and because of the manual and subjective processes which are involved in tabulating the final votes, both overvoting and undervoting transpired.

These reforms have been triggered primarily by the 2000 U.S. presidential election. On account of the closeness involved in the total number of popular votes between Al Gore and George W. Bush, both the numerous committees at the level of the federal government and both the state and local levels called for major election reforms.

These changes were supposed to have been implemented by the 2004 U.S. presidential election, but once again, given the bureaucratic nature of the voting system, some of these recommendations have still to be implemented. Thus, the new system of voting would now call for the use of electronic means of casting a ballot, also known as "e-voting." The concept of e-voting has actually been around since the late 1960s, but its use did not start to proliferate until the 2004 U.S. presidential elections actually took place.

The use of e-voting technology can take place in many forms, which include the following:

- Optical scanning voting systems
- Specialized voting kiosks
- Direct recording electronic systems (commonly known as "DREs")

- The transmission of electronic ballots via the use of telephone modems, virtual private networks, and even the Internet

In the United States, e-voting can take place in the following two distinct formats:

1. Voting stations that are governed by representatives of government or other independent electoral authorities; these voting stations are deployed at approved polling stations.
2. The use of remote e-voting, where the voter casts their ballot via an electronic means (such as those described above); there are neither any voting officials to confirm the voting transactions that take place nor is there any receipt of the actual e-ballot.

The primary advantages of using the e-voting technology are that the votes can be processed quickly, and the total number of popular votes can be counted with much more accuracy than with the traditional, manual methods (although this latter advantage is still highly refuted among voting and election scholars). Despite these major advantages of e-voting technologies, still some major security vulnerabilities are associated with it.

Probably the biggest security disadvantage of e-voting is in confirming the identity of the voter who cast his or her ballot. This is not so much of an issue if a voter appears directly at a polling station (after all, there are government officials who can check the identification document of a particular voter, but again, there are also security issues), but this becomes much more of a security vulnerability if the voter casts his or her e-ballot remotely, especially from his or her home or office. In these cases, the actual cases of voter fraud can exponentially increase as opposed to using the traditional, manual means of casting a ballot.

Similar to the e-passport infrastructure, the use of biometric technology has been called upon in order to provide irrefutable proof of the identity of a particular voter. Thus, the utilization of biometric technology in e-voting is the premise of this chapter. Specifically, this chapter is further divided into the following sections:

- History of voting
- Traditional methods of voting
- Problems with the traditional methods of voting
- Transition to e-voting
- Security vulnerabilities of e-voting
- Use of biometrics with e-voting
- Case study of e-voting with biometrics

HISTORY OF VOTING

As briefly mentioned in the beginning of this chapter, the actual act, or the mechanism, involved with voting has been around for centuries. In some fashion or another, voting among citizens can be considered as a ritual that is observed by most nations worldwide.

However, the extent to which a citizen can actually vote depends upon the type and kind of government that is installed in the country in question. For instance, in a Communist regime, there is virtually no voting allowed for the citizens. Since post-Cold War, only three primary Communist regimes of China, North Korea, and Cuba have remained.

However, there are also other countries where some sort of monarchy-type government is witnessed, such as that in Europe and in the Pacific Rim. Thailand is another prime example. This nation has what is known as a constitutional monarchy, which oversees the parliamentary demo-cratic structure. In fact, the current monarch, King Bhumibol Adulyadej, has been deemed to be the world's longest reigning royalty, having assumed power back in 1946.

From this point onward, the citizens of Thailand are free to vote for the candidates of their choice in the national elections, which involve the various campaigns for both the executive and the legislative branches of the Thai government, as well as the prime minister. Then, there are those nations that are purely democratic in nature, with the United States being a prime example. The term "democracy" can be specifically defined as "… a government by the people, a form of government in which the supreme power is vested in the people and exercised directly by them, or by their elected agents under a free electoral system."[*]

In other words, in a purely democratic society, the votes of every individual, at least in theory, are counted, and whoever wins with the majority of these votes becomes the elected leader. However, it should be noted that this only holds true for those elections that are held at the local and state levels.

At the national level, especially in the presidential elections, the candidate who has the largest popular vote in a particular state will win the total number of electoral votes it has to offer. Then, the candidate who first gets the required number of electoral votes (in this case, 270) becomes the president of the United States.

The primary goal of this chapter is not to delve deep into the history of the evolution of voting of other nations, but rather the intention is to focus exclusively on the U.S. voting system. Therefore, the remaining sections of this chapter will focus upon the voting as well as the e-voting

---

[*] D. Archibugi. *The Global Commonwealth of Citizens: Toward Cosmopolitan Democracy*, Princeton University Press, Princeton, NJ, 2008.

issues that are found here, with the exception of Chapter 5, which will focus upon case studies of the successful deployment and implementations of e-voting systems worldwide.

The actual history of voting in the United States is very rich and a unique one, and in fact, it has had a strong impact upon how the concept of voting and the technology has evolved today. For example, when the U.S. Constitution was first ratified and the government was declared to be a democracy, not every citizen could enjoy the right to vote. This right was first reserved exclusively to Caucasian males, if they owned a certain minimum amount of property. In fact, when the Constitution was first written, it was not spelled out clearly who was actually eligible to vote.

Later, over an extremely slow rate of time, the right to vote as spelled out in the Constitution was further granted to women and non-Caucasian males. However, once again, the key factor was that an individual, in order to exercise their right to vote, had to own a minimal amount of defined property.

Despite the fact that Article VI of the Constitution explicitly states that "no religious Test shall ever be required as a Qualification to any Office or public Trust under the United States," each individual state was still allowed to establish its own rules and regulations as to who could vote in elections, based primarily in part of skin color and the economic background of the citizen in question.

In order to "discriminate" against certain demographic segments of voters, the states administered things such as literacy tests, religious tests, and even levied higher taxes in an effort to prevent naturalized citizens, non-Caucasians, and Native Americans from exercising their right to vote.

On account of these large-scale discriminatory practices, the federal government enacted a number of key pieces of constitutional amendments, which are as follows:

- *Fifteenth Amendment*: This right to vote cannot be determined by "race, color, or previous condition of servitude."
- *Nineteenth Amendment*: The right to vote cannot be discriminated on account of the gender of the citizen.
- *Twenty-Fourth Amendment*: The right to vote cannot be determined via the use of poll taxes, or be based upon the socioeconomic class of the U.S. citizens.
- *Twenty-Sixth Amendment*: U.S. citizens who are at least 18 years of age shall possess the full right to vote in all kinds of elections.

Therefore, as one can see from the passing of so many pieces of individual legislations, the equality of the right to vote in all classes of U.S. citizens has been a hotly contested issue, and in fact, even to this day, remains an issue in certain geographic segments of the country with the advent of the e-voting infrastructure. Part of the reason for this was the passage of another piece of legislation commonly known as the "Voting Rights Act of 1965."

This law basically stated that the state governments had to literally redistrict or redefine their population sizes based on the census results, occurring every 10 years. As a result, there have been many claims that a certain biasness can exist favoring the local government officials whose districts have displayed a larger population size when compared to the previous census.

The following timeline discusses the key events that have transpired in the United States, greatly influencing a citizen's right to vote, and the e-voting process in general:

- 1776: The United States declares its independence; the basic right to vote is now born. However, there are still very extreme limitations, as only male Caucasians above the age of 21 could initially cast their ballot (as mentioned earlier, the other prime requirement was that these individuals had to own a certain amount of land property).
- 1856: Only male Caucasians above the age of 21 could still continue to vote, but the requirement of owning land is abolished.
- 1870: The Fifteenth Amendment has been passed, thus in theory, extending the right to vote for all U.S. citizens (except for women and Native Americans). However, as discussed earlier in this section, many states have passed their own requirements, which mandate the use of literacy tests and poll taxes to discriminate against voters.
- 1920: The Nineteenth Amendment has been passed, thus extending the right to vote to women in the United States.
- 1924: Legislation is passed by the U.S. Congress that now extends the right to vote to Native Americans, but many states still deny this right.
- 1943: The Chinese Exclusion Acts are repealed, thus extending the right to vote to the U.S. citizens who are of Chinese descent.
- 1961: The Twenty-Third Amendment is now officially passed, which extends the right to vote to U.S. citizens residing in the District of Columbia. However, they can only vote in the presidential elections and not in the congressional elections.
- 1964: The Twenty-Fourth Amendment has also been passed, which totally abolished the use of poll taxes (at this time, five states were still using it).
- 1965: The Voting Rights Act is passed, and this piece of legislation outlaws any racial or ethnic barriers in the ability for U.S. citizens to cast their ballot in any type or kind of elections.

- 1970: The voting age has been lowered from 21 years to 18 years for all U.S. citizens.
- 1982: The Voting Rights Act is now extended to include the right to vote for those U.S. citizens who are blind, disabled, or deemed to be illiterate or incompetent to understand the voting process.
- 2006: The U.S. Congress extends the mandates of the Voting Rights Act for the next 25 years, thus allowing every citizen the right to vote (in theory) in any election they choose to participate in.
- 2009: The Military and Overseas Empowerment Act is established, which allows for U.S. troops and expatriates to cast their ballot via any type or kind of electronic means.

It should be noted despite the passage of the Voting Rights Act that there is still some discrimination experienced by U.S. citizens in the voting process at levels of government (whether it is federal, state, or local). For instance, those citizens residing in the District of Columbia still have no representation in either the Congress or the Senate; convicted felons cannot exercise their right to vote after their release.

Quite surprisingly, the exclusive right to vote is still not explicitly stated in the U.S. Constitution. This stands in stark contrast to those fledgling democracies in Afghanistan and Iraq, where the right to vote is explicitly stated in their respective constitutions.

TRADITIONAL METHODS OF VOTING

Now that a brief history of the right to vote in the United States has been examined, it is equally, if not more, important to now review the types of voting mechanisms (specifically the kinds of voting machines) that have been utilized in order for U.S. citizens to be able to cast their ballot, as well as for them to be counted and tabulated in order to distribute the total number of votes to each nominee. The history of these specific voting mechanisms has also had a strong impact on the engineering and design of the e-voting machines that are used today.

The first methods of voting were invented obviously when the very first ballot was cast in 1776. During those times, many of the polling stations actually evolved at the stairway of the courthouses in every state. In these situations, the respective courthouse judge administered an oath to every voter before they could cast their ballot.

The would-be voter would then merely place his or her hand on the Bible, and make a sworn statement that they have the right to vote, and has that they have not cast their ballot previously.

It is interesting to note that during those times, there has been no recorded use of any type of voter registration methodology. Rather, the concept of implicit trust was widely used, but this too was abused by voters. In other words, any particular individual could come and cast their vote repeatedly, thus obviously greatly skewing the election results for the candidate of their choice. The only way to determine if a voter double casted (or even "multiple" casted) his or her vote is if somebody actually recognized such person's presence on the premises of the polling station multiple times.

In fact, during those times, the concept of "secret ballot" was totally unheard of. The only way voters could cast their ballot was by simply yelling out their choice for the candidate whom they wanted to see elected. In turn, the votes were recorded by the various election clerks who would be sitting on the porch of the courthouse, right behind the judge. The use of a poll book was mandated, where the name of the voter was written down, as well as their corresponding votes.

Of course, during those very early times, there was a very large margin for errors in counting and tabulating every vote, and the reason for this lay in the overhead in terms of manpower and administration which was required to maintain multiple poll books by every election place. The use of "voice voting" continued well into the 1900s, and in fact, campaigning by the various candidates at the polling places was allowed until literally the very last minute the court house closed for the day.

Under these circumstances of very primitive voting, there were obviously no issues or concerns of voter or ballot fraud, of course, only if the voter appeared multiple times at the courthouse. For example, the election clerk very easily maintained an independent tally of the voice votes and the final tally, but it is from these early voting mechanisms that the privacy rights surrounding casting a ballot first started to arise. The voters were very prone to bribery and intimidation (in this particular scenario, a voter could have very easily been bribed to vote in a certain way in order to affect the outcome of an election).

These very early processes of voting over time became much more clearly defined as countless and numerous elections subsequently occurred in the United States. Technology has certainly evolved during this time, especially during the past decade, with the availability of online voting and possessing the ability to cast a ballot remotely from any part of the world. However, one factor is still prevalent in voting stations throughout the United States: the human element.

Certified as well as qualified government officials are still necessary in order to ensure that the voting process remains very smooth and that its integrity is maintained; they are needed in order to not only count the total number of votes but also tabulate which election nominee has a percentage of the total popular vote. As it has been illustrated with the example of voting in the early 1700s and 1800s, security has always remained and will continue to remain a serious issue.

For example, there is always the risk that voting officials could be bribed in order to affect the outcome of a particular election. Also, on the other side of the equation, there are the security risks posed by the voter themselves. Probably one of the largest security threats in this aspect is if a certain voter really claims who they are to be. For instance, is he or she genuinely whom they claim to be, or are they actually representing somebody else, using stolen credentials? (Of course, this would be a case of identity theft, which is one of the most serious security risks prevalent at voting stations.)

These fears of identity theft have become greatly proliferated now with both the Internet and remote-based voting. Thus, biometric technology has been utilized to confirm, with 100% certainty, the identity of the voter in question.

However, similar to the discussion in Chapter 3 regarding the e-passport infrastructure, one cannot rely upon technology completely. It takes a combination of both a human presence and the technology in order to guarantee as well as ensure the highest levels of security possible. Therefore, in the case of e-voting, although biometric technology can be used to confirm the identity of a voter, election officials will need to be present to not only serve as a backup in case of technology failure but also serve as a "double check," confirming the identity of the voter. For example, after voters have had their identity confirmed via fingerprint recognition, a voting official can also confirm the voter's identity by double-checking their documents, such as their driver's license and state ID card.

On account of the rich U.S. history with the democratic voting process, four very unique and distinct stages have been developed for the citizens. These stages can be described as follows:

1. *Polling place voting*: In the United States and in a majority of other countries around the world, the ballots for the various nominees in the elections are cast and tabulated in these types of venues. In these specific scenarios, there are two types of mechanisms presented to the voter in order to cast their ballot:
   a. Paper ballots (or other assistive ballot-marking devices).
   b. Software interfaces where the votes are stored and tabulated via computer memory. In these situations, voters have literally cast their votes by using a touch screen, which in turn interacts with the software interface.

   It should be noted that a combination of paper ballots and optical scanners are used most commonly throughout voting stations in the United States.

2. *Accessible voting*: Through the passing of the "Help America Vote Act of 2002" (HAVA), every polling place in the United States is now required to provide voting equipment with assistive features for those voters who may have a particular disability. The following three different approaches are currently being utilized in order to meet the mandates of this legislation:
   a. The use of DREs.
   b. The use of a combination of an optical paper scan and a DRE.
   c. The use of specialized ballot marking systems. These are essentially paper ballots and are physically counted and tabulated in counting the final votes for each election candidate.
3. *Early voting*: With this special provision, voters have the choice if they prefer to vote weeks and even days ahead of time of the official Election Day. If this option is utilized, not every polling station is open. Rather, only the central polling station is open, but all of the same types of voting equipment that would be used on the official Election Day are also utilized.
4. *Absentee voting*: This mechanism of voting is now available across all of the 50 states in the United States. In these specific circumstances, the voter simply mails in their voting ballot to the main election headquarters of the state where they reside. In order to count and tabulate all of these absentee ballots, most state jurisdictions utilize optical scanning technology. This can come in the form of either "central count systems" or "precinct count systems." Some state jurisdictions even transfer the paper ballot votes to DRE-based technology, and still a fewer amount actually tally up the number of absentee ballots by hand, or other types of manual processes.
5. *Provisional ballots*: The Help America Vote Act of 2002 also established certain provisions that allow a voter to cast what is known as a "conditional ballot." This legal precedent has been established for those cases where a voter believes that he or she has the right to vote, but for some reason or another, his or her name does not appear in the polling books located at the polling stations. The use of a provisional is actually warranted in three specific situations:
   a. The voter refuses to produce any sort of documentation that will help confirm his or her identity (this is also used in the cases of e-voting, e.g., if a particular voter refuses to submit his or her biometric templates from being processed).
   b. The voter's legal name cannot be found in the poll book at the voting precinct.

c. The voter's registration record consists of either inconsistent or outdated biographic information (such as a wrong address or even a misspelled name).

However, it should also be noted that provisional ballots are not counted until after usually 7–10 days after the Election Day; as a result, these types of votes typically do not affect the outcomes of the initial results of any particular election. Moreover, provisional ballots can be counted and tabulated either manually or using optical scanning technology.

These types of voting mechanisms just described have led to a major contribution in the kinds of voting technologies that are available in the United States today. As it was reviewed earlier in this chapter, the first types of voting "technologies" that were predominant was the "voice ballot." This means that there were no paper ballots, and the only way that a particular vote could be kept track of was by manually recording it in the poll book after the voter had announced their particular choice for a candidate.

Moreover, as alluded to earlier in this section, this open outcry system of casting votes led to many errors in tabulating the final votes; both the voters and the election officials at the courthouse were very much prone to the issue of bribery—this means that they would be paid a large sum of money by an outsider in order to skew the results of the election toward the briber's favor. Given these disadvantages, it came to no surprise that soon the American population and the government at that time would look toward other means of casting and tabulating votes, which would not only be much more accurate but also secure.

As a result, the next logical choice was to look into machine-based voting. Of course, at this time, the electrical and electronic engineering components were far from heard of at the time, so the next logical choice was to look into creating voting machines that made use of the principles of mechanical engineering. The first concepts of such mechanical voting machines actually originated in England from the early days of paper voting, and then made its way to the United States by the late 1800s.

The first known group of people who envisioned this type of mechanical voting machine was known as the "Chartists," dating all the way back to 1838. In fact, they had even created their own version of a Constitution, which became known as "The People's Charter." The provisions laid in this charter called for equal rights to vote by all, not by open outcry, but by the concept of a secret ballot. This simply meant that a voter in England could go to a polling station and cast his or her vote on a piece of paper anonymously. To some degree or another, it was viewed that this would ensure the privacy rights of the individual voters.

In their particular Constitution, the Chartists established two distinct sections as regards to provisions related to voting. They were known quite simply as "Schedule A" and "Schedule B." The former laid down the principles as to how a polling place should be established and run, and the latter described, for the first time, how a mechanical voting machine was used at the various polling stations.

This gave birth to the very first mechanical voting machine in England. In this scenario, each individual voter was given a brass ball. This ball would then be dropped into the appropriate hole at the top of the mechanical machine by each candidate's name. To a certain degree, the problem of a voter casting multiple votes was actually eliminated, because each voter was only given one brass ball. After the ball was dropped into the mechanical machine, it would advance a clockwork counter for the candidate of choice for the voter. As the brass ball made its way through the mechanical machine, it then fell out of the front from a designated slot, and from there, it would be given to the next voter, so that he or she could then cast his or her ballot.

The first true mechanical voting machine, which made its way into the United States, was envisioned by Henry Spratt. In 1875, he received a patent from the U.S. government that called for the development of a mechanical voting machine, which would consist of an array of push buttons, where each respective button would represent each individual candidate in an election. However, based upon this particular design, each voter could only cast a fixed number of votes and could only cast them in just one election.

However, as the concept of the political party started to evolve in the 1800s (as opposed to just having separate candidates), the demand for complex mechanical voting machines also grew. In this regard, by 1881, Anthony Beranek patented the first true mechanical voting machine that could be used in general elections all across the United States. Thus, this also gave birth to the notion of having a common set of standards for the voting process in general for all elections. This new design called for the use of a wider array of push buttons to be developed and utilized. One row of buttons would be used to represent all candidates in a particular election, and a column of buttons would further represent each political party involved in the election. The use of mechanical interlocking systems prevented the risk of a voter from casting multiple votes, in addition to resetting the machine to a null value after the voter had done casting his or her ballot.

Over time, the sophistication of these mechanical voting machines grew, and in fact was in use until the twentieth century. In fact, the last known use of mechanical voting machines dated back to 1996, when almost 21% of the American voting population used them. The following is an example of a twentieth century mechanical voting system:

Paper-based voting systems were the next type of voting technology to evolve after mechanical voting machines. From within this category, the first paper-based voting technology was that of the "hand-counted paper ballot." In these scenarios, the voter was literally given a paper ballot, which consisted of the names of each candidate, and the respective political party that they represented. Using nothing more than a simple pen or pencil, the voter would mark off their choices in a private booth, and after they were done making their selections, the marked ballot would then be handed to an election official, who in turn would then push the ballot down the slot of a locked box.

After the hand-counted paper ballot showed its security vulnerabilities and greater increased cases of counting errors and voter fraud, the next paper-based voting technology that evolved was that of the "punch card voting system." In this particular voting methodology, the voters designate their choice of candidate by punching a hole next to the name via the use of a specialized punch device in the punch card given to them. After the voter is done punching his or her candidate's name in the punch card, it is then handed over to the election official to be placed in a locked box for tabulation later, or it can be manually fed into an electronic vote tabulating machine. This was the first time in the U.S. voting history where counting the total number of votes that each candidate has received was done in real time. The punch card voting system was last used in 2014 by two counties in the state of Idaho.

The first form of the use of electronics in voting systems came with the evolution of the "optical scan ballot system." A digital image scanner is utilized in this technology. This in turn scans the marked paper ballots and tabulates the number of final votes that each candidate has obtained. A specialized type of paper is used in these instances, and depending upon the make and vendor of this paper ballot, a voter will mark their respective vote on the following:

- Oval (if either an ES&S or Premier/Diebold optical paper ballots are used)
- Arrow (if a Sequoia optical paper ballot is used)
- Box (if a Hart/Intercivic optical paper ballot is used)

Similar to the punch card voting system, the optical paper ballots can be scanned on a real-time basis, or they can be inserted into a locked box for subsequent, *en masse* scanning.

Although the optical scan voting system is still being used in certain geographic segments of the United States, the next major upgrade is the creation and development of the DRE. With this type of voting methodology, a voter can cast their ballot using one of three systems:

1. Push button
2. Touch screen
3. Telephone dial in

Once the voters cast their ballot, the votes are then stored into a computer memory bank (which can be a tape cartridge, cassette, or even a smart card). The first generation of DRE voting systems utilized a push-button interface, and the DRE voting systems of today use a combination of the touch screen and/or telephone dial in. The DRE technology is also equipped with what is known as "voter verified paper audit trails" (VVPAT paper records). This simply allows the voter to confirm their ballot selections on an independent paper record before their selections are stored into the memory banks of the computer. This paper record is kept for a long period, in the cases of a voting audit or county/state wide recount.

PROBLEMS WITH THE TRADITIONAL METHODS OF VOTING

The traditional methods and the associated technologies in which U.S. citizens can participate in (as detailed in the previous section) are now fraught with doubts in both security and technical issues. Apart from these aspects, voting in the United States also suffers from a serious set of flaws from a social perspective. In fact, the turnout of voters in recent elections has been among the lowest levels recorded in a long period.

There are many reasons that can be cited for this low turnout, including:

- Overall dissatisfaction with the candidates in time of election.
- The current economic conditions in the United States. This is the predominant factor affecting votes—for instance, if the current economic conditions are good, there is generally a higher optimism among the voters, thereby translating to a higher turnout, whereas if the current economic conditions are weaker than normal, optimism among voters will be much lower, thus affecting overall voter turnout in a given election. In fact, the economy is the primary variable that affects if an incumbent presidential candidate will be reelected or not.
- *Electoral competitiveness*: Research has shown that the voter turnout in any given election can actually be greatly affected by each individual state. For instance, in the 2012 presidential elections, surveys conducted revealed that while there was a 76% voter turnout in the state of Minnesota, there was a much lower voter turnout in the state of Hawaii—only 45%. These research studies have also indicated that the competitiveness of an election becomes much more complex at the state and local levels. For instance, there could be many coinciding elections taking place at very close periods from one another, such as a state senatorial and governor races. Election research has also indicated that the voter turnout in the 12 most competitive states can reach as high as 66%, but voter turnout can be as low as 57% in the lesser competitive states.*
- *The type and kind of election*: The magnitude of the election that takes place can also have a great social impact upon the level of voter turnout. For example, in a presidential election, people tend to pay much more attention to the voting issues, and thus there is a tendency for a voter to have the view that his or her vote will actually make a difference in deciding who is elected as the next U.S. president eventually. However, once again, the social feelings on part of the voter as regards the issues at the state and local levels do not hold nearly as high of a precedence. This can be attributed to the fact that the issues at this level do not get as much of the media coverage as opposed to the issues that are debated at the federal level. For example, in a

---

* The Center for Voting and Democracy. What Affects Voter Turnout Rates, Fairvote, Takoma Park, MD, 2014. http://www.fairvote.org/research-and-analysis/voter-turnout/what-affects-voter-turnout-rates/.

2013 study based upon 340 mayoral elections across 144 major U.S. cities, voter turnout was at a very low—25.8%.* Moreover, if a winner cannot be declared in an election, then a run-off election must be held to determine the winner a second time around. At this point, voter fatigue can set in, thus affecting voter turnout. In other words, if in an election, the results are too close to call, the voters will have to turn out for a second or even a third time to cast their ballots to determine the winner.

The specific demographics of the voting class can also determine the level of voter turnout in a given election. Some of the variables are as follows:

- *Age*: Although this trend appears to be changing somewhat, younger voters tend to turn out less than the older voters during election time. For example, between 1972 and 2012, the voting age group of 18–29 years old turned out at polling stations at a 20% lower rate than voters who were 30 years and older.†
- *Race and ethnicity*: Ethnic origins also affect voter turnout. For example, the general trend is that both Caucasian and African American voters tend to have a much higher turnout (at almost 66%) versus Latino voters (this group has a voter turnout of 48%) and Asian American voters (this group has a voter turnout of 47%). However, it is interesting to note that in the 2012 presidential elections, the number of African American voters far surpassed that of the Caucasian voters.
- *Gender of the voter*: Gender can also play a huge role as regards to voter turnout in a given election, affecting the overall results. In this regard, the total number of women voters appearing at polling stations and casting their vote has far surpassed that of men voters. However, age plays an important role as well. It turns out that the voter turnout percentage for older women is far less than that of the older men (65% vs. 73%, respectively).
- *The socioeconomic situations of a particular voting class*: It is a fact that wealthy and affluent American citizens possess a much higher voter turnout rate than that of the much lesser affluent American class. Studies have shown that in the 2008 presidential election, the voter turnout among people making $15,000 or less was only 41%, as opposed to those people whose income was $150,000 or higher; their voter

---

* The Center for Voting and Democracy. What Affects Voter Turnout Rates, Fairvote, Takoma Park, MD, 2014. http://www.fairvote.org/research-and-analysis/voter-turnout/what-affects-voter-turnout-rates/.
† Ibid.

turnout was as high as almost 80%.* This stark contrast in voter turnout can have a huge impact on policy creation, as politicians are more likely to be much more responsive and attuned to the needs of their wealthier constituents. As a result, the less affluent voters have the feeling of hopelessness that their vote will not really matter in the end, thus affecting voter turnout in future elections.

- *Hereditary factors*: Recent studies have also shown that the genes an individual has and other hereditary factors can also have a strong impact upon voter turnout. The premise here is that if parental voter turnout is low, the statistical probability that their children will vote in future elections will also be very low. This finding may also help explain the fact why voting tends to be a habitual process. In other words, past voting behavior in general elections makes a very good predictor as to how a particular individual will vote in future elections.

- *Voter fatigue*: In the political world, a phenomenon known as "voter fatigue" can set into a society if the citizens are first and foremost required to vote (in other words, it is compulsory that the citizens of a particular country have to cast their ballot), and if too many elections are held in a very short span of time. However, this needs to be distinguished from the term known as "voter disenfranchisement." This situation occurs when a particular group of voters is not allowed to vote, or if a citizen cannot vote due to physical disabilities.

- *International comparisons*: Comparatively, voter turnout in the United States is much lower than other geographic segments. For example, it has been proven that the countries of Asia, South America, and Canada exhibit a much higher voter turnout percentage. On average, the countries of the European Union have an average voter turnout rate of 77%, and South America has a turnout rate of 54%. A number of factors have been cited as to why these nations have a much higher voting rate than the United States, and these are as follows:
  - *Cultural factors*
    - The overall trust in the respective governments
    - The amount or level of partisanship in the citizens of a particular country
    - The level of interest in politics
    - The level of belief in the effectiveness of the voting system in the respective countries

---

* The Center for Voting and Democracy. What Affects Voter Turnout Rates, Fairvote, Takoma Park, MD, 2014. http://www.fairvote.org/research-and-analysis/voter-turnout/what-affects-voter-turnout-rates/.

- *Institutional factors:* This simply refers to the mechanics and procedures the government of a particular country puts forth for nominating a candidate, defining the election process, which will take place for nominating a particular candidate to office, and how those votes will be counted and ultimately tabulated. The variables that can affect this entire process include the following:
  - Process of voter registration
  - *Concept of compulsory voting:* A few nations require their citizens to vote; if not, it could be viewed as a potential violation of a law. Some of these countries include Australia, Bolivia, Mexico, Brazil, Venezuela, the Netherlands, Greece, and Belgium. In some cases, compulsory voting can be a positive experience, as in the case of Australia. The Australian government has enacted this type of legislation since the 1920s, and the voter turnout has been as high as almost as 93%. However, in countries such as Bolivia, implementation of compulsory voting has not worked well.
- *Level of saliency:* This refers to the fact of how the citizens in a particular country will perceive the effectiveness of their votes in an upcoming election.
- *Degree of proportionality:* The closeness of the election results of a nation reflects the views as well as the needs of the citizens in general. Of course, the higher the level of the proportionality, the greater will be the statistical probabilities of a higher voter turnout. However, the converse is also true. If this proportionality is very low (such as the low approval ratings for the U.S. Congress), then the statistical probability of a very low voter turnout will occur. In fact, in recent times, this has been one of the reasons cited for the declining voter turnout percentages in the United States.
- *Ease of voting:* In order to increase the level of voter turnout, many governments have now implemented the use of e-voting and Internet-based voting systems, as opposed to the traditional methods of voting, as outlined earlier in this chapter. It is also very interesting to note that in this aspect, many other countries have actually adopted, deployed, and implemented an e-voting infrastructure of some sort very similar to that of the e-passport infrastructure. Efforts have been made in the United States to adopt an e-voting infrastructure, but so far it has been severely lacking. A lot of this has to do with both privacy concerns and security issues, which the following section will address.

TRANSITION TO E-VOTING

As it has been mentioned throughout this chapter, the traditional methods of voting are no longer able to keep up with the rapid pace of technology, nor are they able to keep up with the world's growing population of people wanting to vote in their country's elections.

The process of registering every voter with these traditional methods is simply not enough to keep up with this growing demand. In other words, the citizens around the world, and especially in the United States, want to have a much quicker and more rapid way of being able to vote and cast their ballot.

Not only is the standpoint of having the ability to vote quickly is fast gaining attention but also the candidates who contest in an election want to know the results as quickly as possible, in order to determine if they are winners

Both government and election officials want to also have a method in which an audit trail can be created easily if votes have to be recounted again in the case of a very close election or an election runoff.

As it was demonstrated with the 2000 U.S. presidential campaign (which was also reviewed earlier in this chapter), recounting the total number of paper ballots can be a very laborious and time-consuming process. Moreover, this form of manual recounting can lead to a wide margin of errors, thus defeating the purpose of a recount in the first place.

Thus, the concept of "electronic voting," or "e-voting," is now receiving wide attention. With this newer technology and form of voting, some of the primary advantages include rapid voting, instantaneous updates of the total votes garnered in an election in real time, and a much quicker way of recounting votes if the conditions or situations warrant it. However, if one thinks of an e-voting process, many images are conjured up, causing great confusion as to what it exactly is.

A definition of e-voting is as follows: "Voting systems where the recording, casting, or the counting of votes in political elections and referendums which involves the recording, casting, or the counting of votes in political elections and referendums which involves both information and communication technologies."[*]

E-voting technology does possess a number of specific key advantages over traditional voting methods, and they are as follows, at high-level overview:

---

[*] International Institute for Democracy and Electoral Assistance. Introducing Electronic Voting: Essential Considerations, Policy Paper, IDEA, Stockholm, Sweden, 2011. http://www.eods.eu/library/IDEA.Introducing-Electronic-Voting-Essential-Considerations.pdf.

- It can often be viewed as a means to advance democratic principles (especially in the Middle East countries such as Afghanistan and Iraq)—for example, the use of e-voting can greatly enhance the credibility and efficiencies in a given election.
- The use of e-voting, in theory at least, can greatly eliminate the statistical probability of voter fraud from occurring.
- It can make the voting much more accessible and convenient to all classes of citizens of a particular country.
- In the long run, the use of e-voting technology can actually help to reduce the costs of elections and referendums.
- E-voting technology evolves at a very rapid pace—therefore, it can adapt very quickly to the election needs of any given country.
- A much faster vote count and tabulation results are made available.
- The use of e-voting technology provides much accurate results as opposed to the traditional voting processes.
- Since e-voting can take place in the home of an individual voter, there is a much greater level of convenience. It is hypothesized that this in turn should help greatly stimulate voter activity and turnout at the election polls.
- In more advanced societies such as the United States, the use of e-voting now permits voters to cast their ballots on their wireless devices.
- With the advent of the e-voting infrastructure, voters suffering from any physical ailments have greater accessibility to the polling stations.
- U.S. citizens who come from a multicultural background can now cast their voting ballots much easily using an e-voting interface.
- The use of an e-voting infrastructure (if it has been planned out and deployed properly) can actually result in great cost savings for the government of any nation. For instance, poll workers do not have to be paid. There is a substantial reduction in cost for the production and distribution of paper ballots—in these instances, the government of a country may still wish to deploy traditional methods of voting along with an e-passport infrastructure—in addition, there is very little logistics overhead involved if Internet voting is used in an e-passport infrastructure.

However, the use of e-voting technology also poses its set of inherent disadvantages:

- Since the implementation and deployment of e-voting infrastructure are still a relatively new concept in most countries, there can be many legislative and technical challenges as well as hurdles that still need to be overcome.

- In certain regions of the developed world (such as the United States), e-voting is still viewed with great skepticism, and in fact, even citizens of many countries strongly oppose its use.
- When compared to the traditional methods of voting and casting ballots, an e-voting infrastructure can be quite complex to deploy and maintain, thereby incurring an enormous capital expense.
- The concept of an e-voting infrastructure is very often poorly misunderstood by the public at large; only those government officials who are involved in the deployment of a particular e-voting technology understand it the best.
- The use of e-voting technology is often viewed as a "black box" phenomenon (similar to the biometric technology). This means that there is no transparency attached to the e-voting process for voters to question, which is often found in the traditional voting methods and techniques.
- If the e-voting infrastructure is not carefully planned, its haphazard deployment can actually undermine a general election.
- Similar to the biometric technology, the use of an e-voting infrastructure can raise very serious issues of privacy rights as well as civil liberties violations in certain geographic regions (e.g., the United States).
- Since most modern e-voting technologies use Internet-based protocols, where a voter can cast their particular vote, there is a high probability of, identity theft if the principles of encryption are not utilized.
- Presently, similar to e-passport infrastructure, there is no common set of best practices established for countries to follow when deploying and implementing their e-voting infrastructure.
- Any e-voting system deployed (at least in the United States) must be certified by an accredited government body, but at present, there are no common set of standards or best practices set forth in establishing the definition of a proper certification.
- There is a potential for the principle of the "secrecy of the vote," in that only a few people can actually have access to the inside workings of an e-voting technology.
- From a security standpoint, the following are inherent risks from within an e-voting infrastructure:
    - The risk of technology manipulation either via social engineering tactics or by cyber attackers from the outside.
    - The increased chance of fraudulent activities taking place.
    - There is a greater need to secure the e-voting infrastructure during and between elections, including during transport, storage, and maintenance periods.

- There is a higher tendency to depend solely upon the e-voting vendors (those that supplied the technology) for support and maintenance of the systems as opposed to the traditional voting processes (where the government has much greater control).
- There is a greater need for voter education on how to cast their ballot when the e-voting infrastructure has been deployed and implemented for the very first time.

As previously mentioned, e-voting infrastructure is much more complex than that of the traditional voting methods. In fact, the first true version of an e-voting technology has been the DRE devices (which were also reviewed earlier in this chapter). Today, e-voting technologies possess a set of common features, which are as follows:

- *Electronic voter lists*: One of the primary advantages of an e-voting system is the total elimination of a paper-based polling book, as it has been illustrated earlier in this chapter. This polling book has been used throughout several decades in the United States across a majority of the polling stations, and it has been used primarily as a means to keep track of the voters who have come to cast their ballot. However, with the advent of e-voting, the paper method has totally been replaced with an electronic list that can be stored upon a wireless device. With this methodology, the names of the voters who come to cast their ballot can be easily queried for and found, and this data can be easily uploaded to a computer for later processing and analysis in order to determine the total percentage of voter turnout in any given election. However, using this electronic means is also prone to security risks and threats, such as the covert hijacking of information by a cyber attacker.
- *Poll worker interfaces*: Under the traditional methods of voting, the lines can very often become blurred as regards the job responsibilities of the election officials. For example, although one person may be delegated to keep track of the voters registering, he or she may be called upon later to actually participate in the tabulation process, when they have not received any type or kind of training in doing it. However, with the e-voting infrastructure, different special functionalities can be created that will designate the actual work duties and responsibilities of every election official and worker. This is done via specially created interfaces and modules. For instance, there are separate modules for opening a polling station, closing a polling station, as well as transmitting the raw voting information and data to the central server, so that the final votes can be tallied and counted.

- *Interfaces for voting*: With the traditional methods of voting (except for the case when a DRE device is used), the paper ballot has always been utilized. As it has been illustrated with the example of the 2000 presidential election, the use of paper ballots can literally create a gigantic nightmare when it comes to having to recount every vote. This can be a very time-consuming and laborious process and also cost the state government a lot of money. However, with an e-voting infrastructure, the use of paper ballots is virtually eliminated. For example, with an e-voting infrastructure, computer-based touch screens, electronic buttons, touch sensitive tablets, specially designed web pages, or even customized software applications are used in order for the voter to cast their ballot. As a result, this leads to a much cleaner election and voting process.
- *Special interfaces for disabled voters*: The latest e-voting technologies allow disabled voters to cast their ballots with greater ease and efficiency than what the traditional voting systems currently offer. For instance, Braille and audio input devices are included, so that visually challenged voters can also cast their ballot. This is a far cry from having to cast a paper ballot, and having an election official guide a visually impaired person through the completion of their ballot.
- *Interfaces for displaying the output/results of an election*: With the traditional means of voting, the counting and tabulation of the final votes has always been a very cumbersome process. But what is even more of an administrative "headache" is actually placing confidence that the total number of votes counted is indeed authentic, and convincing that to the voters (in this case, it would be the American public). Once again, the 2000 presidential elections is a prime example of this. For example, after the secretary of state of Florida actually certified the total number of votes for both George W. Bush and Al Gore, there was still huge skepticism as well as doubt that these were the official votes. In fact, the American public felt that the total number of votes had been purposely manipulated to favor George W. Bush. But in stark contrast, with an e-voting infrastructure, the possibilities of skewing the total number of votes to one candidate is virtually eliminated. With e-voting technologies, there are electronic audit trails incorporated into the system in order to ensure the integrity and the nonfraudulent activities of the entire voting process. In this regard, digital displays as well as various output devices are used in order to provide irrefutable evidence of the final counts and tabulations not only to government officials but also to the American public in order to quell any doubts or skepticism.

- *Results transmission systems*: With an e-voting infrastructure, since everything is done electronically, the total number of votes can be counted and tabulated either locally or centrally. Locally, the total number of votes can be ascertained using the e-voting technology at the polling stations, but if tabulation occurs centrally, as the votes are submitted, they can actually be transmitted to a remote server (via the use of a results transmission system) and processed there. While this situation may not be warranted for a local election, it would be used primarily in the federal elections, where there are obviously many more votes to be counted and tabulated. In addition, if Internet voting is the primary means by which a voter can cast their ballot, then this latter type of technology would be primarily utilized.
- *More modern means of displaying election results*: Given the advances of technology in general, even after the results of a general election have been ascertained, they can be posted almost immediately (such as across the major cable news networks). However, with use of an e-voting infrastructure, the results of an election can be posted very quickly across all forms of medium, which can include the following:
  - Websites
  - Social media sites
  - Wireless devices
  - Audio and video media sites
- *Confirmation code systems*: When using the traditional voting methods, the only way it can be determined if a voter has actually cast their ballot is if their name has been checked off in the poll books before they are allowed to actually vote. The premise here is that each vote should be kept anonymous. Nevertheless, with the e-voting infrastructure, a special control code can be associated with the voter's ballot. However, this option is only used for very special circumstances, for example, to conduct research on voting trends, the psychological motives as to why voters cast their ballots the way they do, and specialized demographic studies.

The beginning of this chapter examined in detail the various classifications of the traditional voting that are available today. There are five major categories in this area, and e-voting infrastructure has a number of different classifications as well. The types of e-voting technologies to be used primarily depend upon the geopolitical climate of the country in question and the type of election. For example, if it is just a local election, then just one classification of an e-voting infrastructure may be utilized. But if it is a national election, then a combination of different e-voting technology classifications may have to be used, in order to accommodate all of the citizens of a particular country.

The major classifications, or typologies, of e-voting technologies are as follows:

- *DRE Voting Machine*: As discussed, this has been deemed to be the first true e-voting technology; its specific functionality and use have been discussed earlier in this chapter. This type of e-voting technology can come also with an audit paper trail, if the need or situation warrants its usage.
- *Optical mark recognition (OMR) system*: This type of e-voting technology essentially makes use of present-day scanning systems. Under this particular classification, an OMR machine can recognize the votes a particular voter has cast on specialized machine-readable paper ballots. This type of e-voting technology can be used either as a "central count system" or as a "precinct counting system." With the former, the specialized e-voting ballots get scanned and tabulated at specialized vote counting centers; in the latter scenario, the actual scanning and tabulating can take place at every polling station. In these instances, the voter can feed their e-voting ballot directly into the scanning machine.
- *Electronic ballot printer system*: This type of e-voting technology classification is very similar to that of the DRE technology, just discussed. But rather than just using a specialized type of paper, an electronic can also be used to record the voter's choice of nominees. This too can be fed into a special type of ballot scanner, which can then automatically count and tabulate all of the votes in a given election.
- *Internet voting system*: This type of e-voting technology is starting to become the most popularly demanded technology today. The primary reasons for this are speed and convenience. For instance, a voter can cast their ballot at anytime or at any place they want to, without leaving their home. The voters can vote directly through their computer. In this regard, every vote cast is counted and tabulated at a centralized counting server. Internet-based e-voting systems can also be made available at the polling stations.

These major e-voting typologies can be utilized in two types of environments: controlled or uncontrolled. With the former, the e-voting mechanisms and the processes associated with casting a ballot are made available only at the polling stations, or at the election headquarters. With the latter, the e-voting mechanisms are often based upon using the Internet, and in this regard, the voter is free to cast their ballot from wherever they want to, as long as they have a computer (either hard wired or wireless) and a good Internet connection.

Another factor that differentiates between e-voting in a controlled and a noncontrolled environment is in the involvement of the government or election officials themselves. For instance, once again with the former, election and/or government officials are on hand at the polling stations in order to administer the e-voting machines and to troubleshoot any problems that might exist. However, with the latter, there is no administration or oversight in the e-voting process by government or election officials. Although the voters have the freedom to cast their ballot from wherever they want or desire to, there is also no guarantee that their vote will be processed, counted, or even tabulated in case of any technological failure. In these cases, if the voter suspects any issues in this regard, he or she will then have to visit an election polling station and recast his or her vote.

Although the use of e-voting technology in an uncontrolled environment does possess its benefits, it also has a number of disadvantages. For example, issues regarding voting ballot secrecy as well as the technological integrity of the voting device (such as a laptop or a wireless device) often come into serious questioning.

To equate this with the traditional methods of voting, e-voting in a controlled environment can be viewed as casting a paper ballot at a polling station; e-voting in an uncontrolled environment is often viewed as casting an absentee ballot and sending via postal mail.

However, probably one of the biggest differentiators between e-voting in a controlled environment versus a noncontrolled environment is that of the audit trail that is created, and the confirmation if an electronic vote has been casted and tabulated successfully. For example, if a voter casts his or her vote at an e-voting-based polling station, he or she is very often given (under normal circumstances) a receipt of the confirmation that his or her vote has been successfully processed.

This type of confirmation receipt can especially be useful and handy if the results of an election need to be independently verified. Although this process may work very well for the local or even state elections, this would not be so efficient at the national level, as there would be millions upon millions of receipts that would have to be counted manually. Therefore, in these cases, only a random sampling of the e-voting polling stations throughout a particular country is utilized.

However, in an uncontrolled environment, there is no physical evidence presented whatsoever to the voter that his or her ballot has been processed successfully. Thus, this could lead to a false sense of confidence that an actual e-vote has been counted and tabulated, and the lack of the physical evidence makes recounting votes a very difficult process in the event of an extremely close election. As a result, the only remedy to this solution is that the total number of ballots casted by an e-voting system can only be indirectly verified.

This process entails the use of a strict certification process, along with a very rigid security policy, which must be enforced at every step of the way in order to ensure the integrity of the e-voting recount. This will also result in the lack of a transparent process, thus casting more doubts into the minds of voters about the validity of an election based purely on an e-voting infrastructure.

However, on the opposite side, while adding an audit trail or vote confirmation functionality to an e-voting infrastructure does have its benefits, there is also one serious disadvantage to it. That is of added expenses, administrative overhead, and extra complexities to the e-voting infrastructure. It should also be noted here that even incorporating an audit paper trail or the confirmation of a ballot casted by an e-voting machine has its set of disadvantages.

For instance, at the polling station, once a voter is given his or her particular receipt, the statistical probabilities are high that it will be simply discarded. On the other hand, if a paper audit trail is not implemented into an e-voting infrastructure, this is one of the first aspects that will be judged (or even criticized at) in the event of an election recount.

Given the electronic nature of an e-voting infrastructure, many of the interfaces that are available to both the election/government officials and the voter are developed from the use of software programming languages, simply known as "software code." The programming language utilized in an e-voting infrastructure can be either closed source or open source in nature. With the former, the source code that is used to create the e-voting interfaces is proprietary in nature, whereas with the latter, the source is available for any software developer to use quickly and easily.

Presently, most of the software components associated with an e-voting infrastructure are based upon closed source platform. As a result, the vendors that manufacture the e-voting technology (such as Diebold Systems) are often very reluctant to make the software code they have utilized known to government and election officials. But given the fact that the use of e-voting technology is now coming under close scrutinization by the public as well as by the federal government, many e-voting vendors are now being more open minded in revealing a small portion of the source code they have used.

However, in sharp contrast, if e-voting technology is created using an open source programming language, then the software code can be made easily available to the public as well as to government and election officials. The time at which this can become an issue is that if a recount is needed in a hotly contested election. In these cases, all of the technologies that make up the e-voting infrastructure can come into some very serious questioning by the government at all levels.

Although creating an e-voting infrastructure using an open source programming language may mean much lower procurement and implementation costs for the government deploying it, security experts have pointed out a number of serious threats and risks associated with this. For instance, the security weaknesses of an e-voting infrastructure can be readily known to the public, and worst yet, to cyber attackers who could potentially exploit the system and even affect the outcome of an election, or worst yet, launch instances of identity theft.

However, proponents of open source programming languages in an e-voting infrastructure claim that this will lead to a much quicker resolution of any technical setbacks or glitches that may potentially occur. They have also pointed out that by using an open source programming language, the entire e-voting infrastructure will be much more transparent (from a technical standpoint) in the eyes of the American public.

These proponents have also claimed that the use of closed source programming languages will lead to a phenomenon known as "security by obscurity," which means that only few individuals (the government and election officials) will have true knowledge of the security weaknesses and vulnerabilities of an e-voting infrastructure.

It should be noted that with the present e-voting infrastructure, one of the biggest security issues is voter authentication. With the traditional means of voting, all a voter has to do is merely produce an identification document (such as a passport, a driver's license, or even a state identification card) and present it to the election official. The name and the address on the identification document are then compared to the information present in the polling books.

If everything matches correctly, the voter is then allowed to proceed to the voting machine, and cast his or her ballot. However, the issue of voter authentication becomes much more of a security issue in the case of an uncontrolled e-voting environment, where the voter can cast his or her ballot from literally anywhere around the world.

For example, if John Doe submits his e-vote via an Internet-based mechanism, how much certainty is there that it is really John Doe himself who casted that particular ballot? Although e-voting technologies do possess some sort of authentication method (such as that of the usage of a username or password, or using a challenge/answer response system), these have their own inherent security vulnerabilities and issues. For instance, a cyber attacker can easily hack into the computer or wireless device of John Doe, assume his identity, and cast a ballot under false pretenses.

Apart from this technical perspective, there can also be the social issue of an e-voting infrastructure having too much of a close coupling between the voter identification module and the actual e-voting module (the mechanism in which the voter actually casts his or her e-vote). In other words, there have been claims by the American public, especially those of privacy rights and civil liberties, that the e-votes cast are truly not kept private and secret, as they would be with the traditional voting methods.

Thus, there have been calls for the establishment of various efforts in order to keep these two e-voting modules separate from each other, and to avoid any possibilities from them being linked to each other in any form. In order to achieve this specific goal, biometric technology has been deployed in e-voting infrastructure.

The biometric modalities that would be used (and in fact, to some degree or another, already have been) are fingerprint recognition, iris recognition, hand geometry recognition, and even facial recognition.

SECURITY VULNERABILITIES OF E-VOTING

As it has been described throughout this chapter, the concept of e-voting consists of many electronic components working together in unison for a voter to cast their ballot seamlessly in any given election. However, given the technological advances witnessed in e-voting infrastructure on an almost daily basis, the inherent security threats and risks are even further magnified than those of the traditional voting methods, which were outlined earlier.

The security vulnerabilities associated with the traditional voting methods have been primarily rooted in the following scenarios:

- *Voter fraud*: This occurs when a voter is either intentionally or unintentionally wrongly identified and authenticated to vote; this can happen when an election or government official does not even double-check the identity documents of the particular voter and just logically assumes that he or she claims to be who they are. The result of this is that a voter can assume the identity of another voter under false pretenses.
- *Improper security measures on the boxes containing the votes*: Under the traditional methods of voting, the paper ballot is often used widely. After the voter has cast his or her ballot, it is then dropped into a secure box until after the election is over. At this stage, the box is then unlocked (or, however, opened depending upon the security measures that have been out into place), the paper ballots are then collected out of it, and either via machine

or by manual methods, counted and tabulated in order to ascertain the final vote count. All of this happens under the assumption that the ballot box is securely locked at all times. But what if it is not securely locked? What if the election or government official actually forgets to lock the ballot box after it has been opened initially? And, who are the individuals that have access to this particular box? Are there certain rules established in place as to who can access and when? What if the ballot is not locked, and somebody accesses it, and actually discards some of the votes? These questions illustrate some of the major security vulnerabilities that are present in the traditional methods of voting.

- *Election corruption*: Under the traditional methods of voting, this is probably one of the greatest security vulnerabilities present. For example, bribery taking place among the election or government officials can greatly affect the outcome of a particular election, or social engineering taking place in order to make the election or government officials to act peculiar can also adversely skew the results of an election. Alternatively, bribery can also take place by basically paying the voters a certain amount of money if they vote for a particular candidate that was not their original choice.

- *Voter identity authentication*: As mentioned previously, with the traditional methods of voting, the only way the identity of an individual can be confirmed is through the appropriate usage of identification documentation. But what if this particular piece of identification documentation has been actually altered or reproduced in some malicious manner, so that the voter can actually assume the identity of another individual? For example, there have been reported cases where a voter has reproduced the identification documentation of a deceased individual and had the ability to actually cast his or her ballot under those false pretenses. For example, as alluded to earlier, what happens if these individuals simply enter an e-voting kiosk through the voting lines without even confirming their identity? Alternatively, what if they do check the identification documents of the voter, but it is done in a haphazard fashion? (e.g., the data on the identification document may not be matched up against those available in the polling books. In this regard, the traditional methods of voting can also be viewed as a much more subjective approach to casting a ballot—this is an area in which the use of e-voting infrastructure tries to resolve).

The above-mentioned security threats and risks of the traditional voting methods are also equally prevalent in the e-voting infrastructure.

However, the security threats and risks in e-voting are much more prevalent and compounded due to the fact that (as also mentioned previously) the electronic component is now introduced into the voting process. Given its advantages, a voter can now cast his or her ballot from far and remote places away from the actual polling stations.

As it has been termed, in these uncontrolled environments, a voter can cast his or her ballot not only through the normal postal mail but also through any wireless device that has a Web browser and is connected to the Internet. Therefore, the same security threats and risks that are prevalent in today's Internet environment are also equally prevalent in the present e-voting infrastructure. In other words, if a virus can affect a computer in a non-voting environment, it can also affect a computer that is used in an e-voting infrastructure to cast a ballot.

In general, the security threats and risks associated with an e-voting infrastructure can be outlined as follows:

- *Adware, malware, and spyware*: In this grouping, the most pronounced security threat is that of Trojan horses (these are individual pieces of software that can be injected into a computer, a wireless device, or even the e-voting kiosk at a polling station, and even trick a voter to cast his or her ballot in a particular way). In addition, special types of virus software are created and deployed to specifically infect an e-voting infrastructure. The only countermeasure to this is to use antivirus software, and make sure that all information technology (IT) assets in an e-voting infrastructure are updated on a regular basis. However, even this may not be enough if specific software code obfuscation techniques are utilized.
- *"Buggy" software*: This refers to the software that has been developed to create the electronic interfaces used by both the government/polling officials and the voters themselves. These software applications can be developed using either closed source software or open source software, but the key thing is that these applications must be tested first before they are implemented into an e-voting infrastructure. If not, security gaps and holes could still be remnant from the time when the applications were being developed. A prime example of this is known as the "backdoor." These are used in any software development process to give the developers quick and easy access to the actual software code. If these are not double-checked and removed before deployment, any cyber attacker can gain access to an e-voting infrastructure through the manipulation of these backdoors. The only known countermeasure to this is to once again test the e-voting software before it is deployed to the e-voting infrastructure.

- *Distributed denial of service (DDoS) attacks*: This occurs when a server is literally bombarded with malformed data packets, and as a result, the processing and computational power of the server comes to a grinding halt. This type of attack can also be used to hit the servers utilized in an e-voting infrastructure, and can greatly slow down the speed of an election process or vote tabulation. DDoS attacks can be quite complex, and presently, there are no known effective techniques to combat these against an e-voting infrastructure.
- *Insider attacks*: This can happen when an election or government official who has knowledge of the inner working secrets of an e-voting infrastructure manipulates those for personal gains, or for changing the outcome of an election. The countermeasures include the use of the separation of duties concepts and principles, independent or third-party audit checks of the e-voting infrastructure, and maintaining a physical control over IT assets that are used in an e-voting infrastructure.
- *Spoofing*: These are a special type of Trojan horse viruses, and they can be created to specifically steal, or even maliciously hijack the votes that are processed by the e-voting infrastructure.
- *Man-in-the-middle attacks*: This type of security threat can be defined as "An **attack** where the attacker secretly relays and possibly alters the communication between two parties who believe they are directly communicating with each other."* When this is used to attack an e-voting infrastructure, a specialized type of electronic device is implanted into the e-voting kiosk. The primary intent here is to interfere with the transmission process of voting. In these situations, a logic analyzer can be used, which lets the cyber attacker see the exchange of information and data that is being sent back and forth between the e-voting kiosk and the server(s) that are processing the e-votes. The idea is to mimic this information, so that false e-votes can be cast and tabulated, thus changing the outcome of an election. This type of security threat preys upon the use of open standard communication formats present in the e-voting infrastructure. The only known countermeasure to this is to implement visual inspections of all of the e-voting kiosks at a polling station, and make sure that "nothing out of the ordinary" exists among them.

Many scientific studies have examined the security weaknesses and vulnerabilities of an e-voting infrastructure. For example, these studies have

---

* W. Trappe and L.C. Washington. Security protocols. In *Introduction to Cryptography with Coding Theory*. p.257, Pearson, New York. 2005. https://www.en.wikipedia.org/wiki/Man-in-the-middle_attack (last modified January 18, 2016).

examined the issues not only from the standpoint of the e-voting kiosk itself at the polling stations but also from the standpoint of when the voter casts his or her ballot remotely in an uncontrolled environment, most particularly when he or she is using the Internet to submit his or her vote. As it was examined, whatever security threats and risks are associated with the Internet, the very same security vulnerabilities will be prevalent on an e-voting infrastructure.

One of the more recent scientific studies that has examined these types of security vulnerabilities was the research conducted by Estehghari and his colleagues, in their work entitled "Exploiting the Client Vulnerabilities in Internet E-voting Systems: Hacking Helios 2.0 as an Example."* The basic premise of this study examines the e-voting infrastructure from the standpoint of when a voter casts his or her ballot using the remote device connected to the Internet.

In such Internet-based voting systems, often two subsystems are utilized in order for the ballot to be cast: the client side and the server side. The former is a specialized piece of software, or even a dedicated website (which is most often the case these days), which the voter can access to cast their vote on his or her laptop or wireless device. The latter is a computer from within the e-voting infrastructure to which votes are electronically transmitted, processed, and tabulated.

In this scientific research, the client-based e-voting software known as "Helios" is examined. This piece of software is commonly utilized in e-voting infrastructure; it supposedly uses state-of-the-art security and cryptographic principles and concepts in order to assure the voters that their particular ballot will be cast in a seamless, secure, and in a very private manner. Despite these, there is one inherent security weakness in Helios: The voter could very easily be spoofed into using a fake ballot to cast his or her vote.

This occurs when a cyber attacker actually inserts a PDF file into an e-voting website. This document can consist of the political views of the nominee, in order for the voter to be enticed into voting for him or her. However, this specially crafted document also consists of a special link that will direct the voter to another website, so that they can see more information and data about the nominee and learn more about their election views and stances.

This link actually takes advantage of a serious security weakness found in the Adobe Acrobat Reader (this software is commonly used to access and interpret PDF-based files). As a result, when a voter clicks on the link, as just described, it actually exploits this security vulnerability

---

* S. Estehghari and Y. Desmedt. Exploiting the client vulnerabilities in internet e-voting systems: Hacking Helios 2.0 as an example. In *Proceedings of the International Conference on Electronic Voting Technology/Workshop on Trustworthy Elections*, Article No. 1–9, USENIX Association, Berkeley, CA, 2010.

in the software to install malicious Web browser extensions in the voter's computer or laptop or wireless device. These extensions, in turn, will lead the voter into casting their vote to the spoofed ballot (as just described) that favors the nominee of the cyber attacker, thus adversely affecting the outcome of an election.

However, it should be noted that this type of security breach can only occur with those e-voting infrastructure that utilizes the Helios software package. This specialized platform is available on both the client side and the server side, and this attack takes advantage of the security weaknesses that are found on the client side.

More specifically, in this study, the Helios 2.0 software platform is examined. It is a Web-based voting application, which also makes heavy usage of the JavaScripting language. Furthermore, the Java virtual machine is also required to be installed in the voter's computer or wireless device. The voter's identity and his or her ballot are encrypted from the Web browser itself (in reality, any Web browser can be utilized, such as the Internet Explorer, Google Chrome, and Mozilla Firefox).

However, in this specific scientific study, the researchers have used the Google Chrome, and have created a malicious extension known as "BROWSERSPY" in order to take advantage of the security vulnerabilities of the Adobe Acrobat Reader. These types of malicious extensions can be covertly installed anywhere in the Web browser, but in this scientific study, it was purposely installed in the Google toolbar extension).

It should be noted that the Adobe Acrobat Reader also makes heavy usage of the JavaScripting language. For example, using a very specialized JavaScript "application program interface" (API), designed for this software, a voter not only can view and print a PDF-based file, but he or she can also digitally sign PDF-generated documents. However, it was also discovered that this API is very much prone to what are known as "buffer overflow attacks."

This specific type of attack occurs when excess amounts of data are actually written into the buffer areas of the computer's memory banks. As a result, the boundaries of these buffers can extend greatly beyond their prescribed limits, thereby overwriting the existing data that is held in other areas of the memory banks. This, in turn, becomes a very serious security breach regarding the safety of the computer's memory banks.

In turn, this gives cyber attackers a very strong potential to inject their own malicious code (which are in technical terms known as "payloads" or "shellcodes") into these corrupted memory banks, thus giving them direct and ultimate control of the computer or server in the end. This example of a memory buffer overflow attack is also used in this study.

In addition, the concept of "browser extensions" is utilized in this scientific research. Essentially, these are simply additional functionalities that are added into a Web browser in order to give the voter additional features, which he or she may require in order to make the voting process a more seamless experience. The browser rootkit is available across all of the major Web browser brands, most notably Internet Explorer and Mozilla Firefox. Once again, these extensions are also prone to cyber attacks.

For example, after an attacker has gained access to a particular computer, malicious add-ons can also be injected into the Web browser, in which private and confidential data stored in the computer can be easily accessed. Worst yet, the voter can also be easily spoofed into installing these malicious add-ons in their computer. More specifically, these infected add-ons are also known as "browser rootkits."

In this scientific study, the attack on the security vulnerabilities that are found in the client side of the Helios e-voting platform is launched as follows: The cyber attacker injects the malicious code into the PDF file of a particular candidate that exists on the e-voting website. Then, using social engineering tactics, the voter is tricked into clicking on the link to download further information about the candidate.

After this link is clicked, a specific type of memory buffer overflow will be created, and the resulting shellcode is then injected into the memory banks of the voter's computer. This in turn will also create a browser rootkit, which will then be incorporated into the Web browser that the voter is using in order to cast their ballot. At this point, the voter is tricked into restarting his or her Web browser and is prompted to visit the e-voting website in order to cast his or her ballot.

The malicious add-ons that have been created because of the browser rootkit will ultimately gain full control over the client side of the Helios software platform. Consequently, the behavior of the e-voting application that Helios uses will be altered, and in the end, the voter will be directed to a spoofed ballot upon which he or she will ultimately cast their vote.

The researchers of this scientific study have offered the following solutions in order to prevent this type of attack occurring in an e-voting infrastructure that makes use of the Helios platform:

- *Disabling the JavaScripting functionality in the Adobe Acrobat Reader*: It should be noted that one of the best ways to prevent such attacks from happening is to simply disable the JavaScripting functionality in the software. Very often, the voter will be prompted with this type of message just before the PDF file in an e-voting website is opened (or for that matter any PDF file):

    "This document contains JavaScripts. Do you want to enable JavaScripts from now on? The document may not behave correctly if they're disabled."

    It is only human nature to trust the essence of this message and enable the use of the JavaScript functionalities. However, it is important that the voter heed this type of message much more seriously, as this type of attack which has been reviewed can be simply avoided by clicking on the "No" option available in the dialog box of the message.

- *Implementing the use of independent, third-party verifiers*: The utilization of such groups will allow for the unbiased auditing of the Helios software platform, from both the server side and the client side. Through this process, any kind of security vulnerabilities or risks will more than likely be found, addressed, and resolved.
- *Avoiding the Helios software platform altogether*: In hindsight, this may appear to be the easiest solution to implement, as there are other types of e-voting software platforms that possess the same functionality as that of Helios. However, in reality, this may be much easier said than done, because the Helios software platform is so deeply engrained into the existing e-voting infrastructure already. In response, the researchers of this study have offered an alternative solution: the use of "code voting." This process simply works when the voter is given specific codes that are associated with each of the nominees in an election. Therefore, rather than inputting or selecting the name of the nominee the voter wishes to choose, all he or she simply has to do is enter in the code into their computer or wireless device of the nominee of their choice. Although this methodology is still in theory and not has been practiced in reality, there is strong potential that it could work. For example, a client-side attack (as illustrated by this study) could not only be mitigated but also the privacy and the anonymity of the voter will still be kept intact.

Given the security vulnerabilities and threats associated with the e-voting systems and infrastructure, cryptographic principles have been utilized to help further fortify both the level of security and the level of authenticity of the e-votes that have been casted and in the process of being tabulated. Rather than using the principles of cryptography at all levels of the e-voting infrastructure in a haphazard fashion, it is thus important to pinpoint strategically where in the e-voting infrastructure they need to be utilized widely.

In this regard, one of the most important areas to apply the principles of cryptography is at the application layer. It is here where most interactions take place between the election and government officials as well as the voter with the e-voting infrastructure. As a result, the cryptographic principles that are employed at this level are known as "application level cryptographic voting protocols."

These layers of protocols are deemed to be all inclusive in that "… [they] prescribe the steps and actions to be followed in casting a ballot remotely, both by the voter's device and by the corresponding vote collection server. The protocols also determines the cryptographic actions that must be done to open a digital ballot box to tabulate the ballots, and also to verify the election results."[*]

Given the importance of the application level cryptographic voting protocols, the security requirements it must meet or exceed for an e-voting infrastructure are stringent and precise. The exact requirements are defined as follows:

- *It must ensure privacy*: This simply means that it must be impossible to associate an e-vote with a specific voter, except in the cases where the voter is given a confirmation that their e-vote has been successfully processed (as discussed earlier in this chapter).
- *It must preserve the authentication process*: These encryption protocols must not only protect the particular authentication process, which is in place in order to confirm the identity of the voter (e.g., using biometric technology), but it must also ensure that the integrity of the process cannot be tampered with or altered in any way or fashion.
- *It must ensure the level of accuracy of the e-voting infrastructure*: These encryption protocols must also ensure that once the e-voting process starts, it cannot be manipulated or compromised in any way. Furthermore, the protocols must have the capability to inspect and discard any type of invalid e-votes.
- *It must ensure to maintain the secrecy of the e-voting process*: The application level cryptographic voting protocols have to be implemented in such a way that the e-vote counting and tabulation processes must be kept secret until the election is over.
- *Non-coercion by third parties*: The cryptographic principles employed must be able to prevent the "selling of e-votes," and also help the government and county election officials from having independent third parties coercing voters to vote for a certain candidate who is not their original choice.
- *It must ensure to establish the verifiability of the e-voting process*: The entire e-voting infrastructure must possess the capability to refute any claims of fraud via the use of electronic audit trails and mechanism.

However, certain distinctions have to be made regarding the last category. For example, two levels of verifiability need to be taken into account. The first level is the assurances, which are provided to the e-voter that

---

[*] A. Riera. Communications-Electronics Security Group. Comments on the Report "e-Voting Security Study." Scytl Online World Security, Barcelona, Spain, 2002. http://www.scytl.com/wp-content/uploads/2013/05/Comments_on_the_report_e-Voting_Security_Study_UK.pdf.

the votes that they have casted have actually been processed and tabulated without any manipulation or interference. The second level of verifiability is that the voter can actually check the presence of his or her own e-vote when the election results have been released (in these specific instances, the e-voter would have his or her own login credentials and access a specialized portal in order to confirm this).

One of the latest application level cryptographic voting protocols to have been developed, which addresses all of these security requirements, is known as "Pynx," which was created by a business entity known as "Scytl," who are known for conducting pioneering research and development in the e-voting industry. Their product is a result of eight years of research. The basic premise behind Pynx is that it assumes a so-called mutual suspicion across all parties and entities who are involved in the e-voting infrastructure.

This simply means that a bare, minimal level of trust is initially utilized by Pynx, and it has to be "earned" by all of these parties. In the end, after a certain level of "trust" has been built up, the goal of this specific cryptographic software package is then to "… to protect every party [involved in the e-voting infrastructure, even from collusions between other legitimate parties."*

The components that make up the layers of the application level cryptographic voting protocols in the Pynx software package include the following:

- *Key principle*: This level discerns the so-called mutually suspicious parties in an e-voting infrastructure, meaning that it is assumed there will be internal attackers present in the system; therefore, only minimal levels of trust are initially established between all of the parties.
- *Service protection*: There are clear boundaries and distinctions made between the actual e-vote collection and tabulation processes.
- *Security techniques*: The legacy security system measures which are already in existence with the traditional methods of voting are in existence from within and e-voting infrastructure, but the application level cryptographic voting protocols are added into them, thus offering much greater levels of confidentiality, integrity, and privacy.
- *Restricted computational processing demands*: Whenever a server or computer is being taxed in terms of its processing power, it is always pushed to a higher level, being prone to

---

* A. Riera. Communications-Electronics Security Group. Comments on the Report "e-Voting Security Study." Scytl Online World Security, Barcelona, Spain, 2002. http://www.scytl.com/wp-content/uploads/2013/05/Comments_on_the_report_e-Voting_Security_Study_UK.pdf.

security threats and risks. Therefore, when using the Pynx software package, on the client side (such as the e-voter's laptop or other wireless device he or she may use when casting their ballot), minimal processing power is utilized.

- *Use of audit trails*: In an e-voting infrastructure, these are normally "turned on," unless otherwise dictated by government officials.
- *Principle security requirements are met or exceeded*: The key principles of privacy, authentication, accuracy, secrecy of e-vote processing, noncoercion, and verifiability are all taken into account and addressed.

Apart from these specific technological components, the Pynx software package also consists of the following cryptographic components:

- Cryptographic hashing functions
- Encryption keys
- Digital signatures

With respect to the first item, these very sophisticated mathematical algorithms are used to check for the integrity as well as the authenticity of the electronic components that comprise the e-voting infrastructure. It can also be considered as a "digital fingerprint."

In these specific scenarios, binary mathematical files are utilized to also check for the integrity of the e-voting electronic-based module. However, it should be noted that the use of these so-called digital fingerprints, although good enough in theory to confirm the integrity of the e-voting electronic modules, often dictates the opposite in reality.

Therefore, it is very important to include another cryptographic-based component when it comes to checking for the integrity of an e-voting infrastructure. Such a tool, which is very useful in these circumstances, is known as the "secure hash standard" (SH-3).

This is also a high-level, complex mathematical algorithm and can be used in an e-voting infrastructure in order to help double check for electronic components that are running on compromised or flawed software. This type of mathematical algorithm is very often used in conjunction with the digital fingerprint, in order to provide a multimodal layer of security to an e-voting infrastructure.

The principles of encryption were discussed in detail in our previous book, *Biometric Technology: Authentication, Biocryptography, and Cloud Based Architecture*.[*] Essentially, two types of encryption environments can be utilized in an e-voting infrastructure. This includes both the symmetric and the asymmetric methodologies. With the former,

---

[*] R. Das. *Biometric Technology: Authentication, Biocryptography, and Cloud-Based Architecture*, CRC Press, Boca Raton, FL, pp. 329–354, 2014.

only one set of encryption keys is used, traditionally known as "private keys." With the latter, two sets of encryption keys are used: "private keys" and the "public keys."

In essence, these keys are used to scramble any type of information that is in transit across a network medium irrespective of the methodology used. Therefore, with regard to an e-voting infrastructure, either the private key or the public key (depending upon the methodology used) can be used to scramble an e-vote that has been casted by the voter in an uncontrolled environment (such as when a laptop or a wireless device is used).

Both the private keys and the public keys are based upon separate available mathematical algorithms. One such algorithm is known as the "advanced encryption standard" (AES) or "Rijndael."

This high-level mathematical algorithm is primarily used for the encryption of electronic data that is in transit across a network medium. In the case of an e-voting infrastructure, this would be the e-vote that has been cast from the voter's computer or wireless device and is on its way to the e-voting infrastructure's servers to be processed and tabulated.

However, despite using a robust cryptographic tool such as the AES, there is no guarantee that every bit of data will result in differing ciphertexts (this is merely the scrambled state of the data).

Therefore, for example, if the AES were used to scramble the state of two distinct e-votes cast by two different and distinct voters, the resulting ciphertext (which would be these two e-votes) may not appear as being two distinct entities to the servers of the e-voting infrastructure. This would pose a very serious flaw, as each e-vote needs to be processed as unique and distinct entities.

Digital signatures are used to authenticate and verify the bits of information after they have been both encrypted (in other words, rendered into its scrambled state) and decrypted (meaning the scrambled state of the pieces of information are now rendered back into its original state, and now can be deciphered and understood by the receiving party).

Therefore, in the case of an e-voting infrastructure, digital signatures can be used to verify and confirm the authenticity of a particular e-vote after it has been both encrypted (once it leaves the voter's computer or wireless device) and decrypted (once the servers of the e-voting infrastructure receive the e-vote and has to be descrambled, so that it can be processed and tabulated).

In these specific instances, where every e-vote needs to be processed and tabulated, another cryptographic tool known as the "digital signature algorithm" (DSA) is used. However, even in these particular cases, the data contained in the e-vote can still be tampered by an entity present inside or outside of an e-voting infrastructure; alternatively, the e-vote can still be misread or misinterpreted by the server(s) as it is being processed and tabulated.

For example, when an e-vote is transmitted across the network medium (and when the DSA is being used), the e-vote is actually further broken down into a pair of digitally signed subrecords. The first subrecord consists of the name of the candidate for whom the voter has voted, as well as the electronic "presence" of where the e-vote was actually cast (e.g., it could be IP address of the voter's computer or wireless device). The second subrecord simply tells the server (which is processing and tabulating the e-vote) how the candidate's name appears to the voter on their particular e-voting kiosk, computer, or wireless device (e.g., in a wireless device, different Web browsers can be used, thus rendering how a candidate's name looks like on an e-voting website to be different).

It should be noted that while this overall record might very well be encrypted and deemed to be secure, these subrecords, as just described, are not encrypted in any fashion. As a result, these subrecords are prone to cyber-based attacks and hacks, as well as other forms of tampering. Although the "shell" of the overall record might be encrypted, any alterations or damage done to these subrecords can also in turn adversely affect the overall record.

In effect, this can also lead to a vote for a particular candidate to be actually misrepresented as a vote for a different candidate (by simply rearranging the two subrecords of the overall record), thus possibly affecting the outcome of an election.

It is also important to keep in mind that an e-voting infrastructure is not a static piece of technology. Rather, it can also be considered as a "dynamic" piece of technology that needs to be upgraded over the course of time; moreover, the vendor of the e-voting technology upgrades its components and comes out with newer versions.

This upgrade process can also pose a serious security threat or risk to an e-voting infrastructure, especially from the standpoint of cryptography. For example, during any "firmware" upgrade process, the encryption keys (whether they are private keys, public keys, or even a combination thereof) need to be safely guarded and cannot be exposed to the external environment at any point of time during this process.

During this time, a cyber attacker can very easily impersonate any type of e-voting vendor, and even further produce and install e-voting infrastructure firmware that can appear to be very legitimate and authentic.

Although the use of cryptography-based tools and technology can greatly fortify the security environment of an e-voting infrastructure, as illustrated by these examples, it is still simply not enough. Therefore, the use of multimodal security solutions has come into play; these are instances where more than one type of security system can be used to protect the e-voting infrastructure.

Biometrics is one of the best forms of security technology that can be used in conjunction with cryptographic principles and tools. In this regard, this technology has already been initiated, especially facial

recognition, iris recognition, fingerprint recognition, and, most importantly, fingerprint recognition.

USE OF BIOMETRICS WITH E-VOTING

With the advent of the e-voting infrastructure around the world, many
technical issues are yet to be resolved regarding their use. Moreover,
citizens around the world should be assured that the e-votes casted will
be processed securely and confidentially, with, of course, their e-vote
actually being counted and not discarded in any shape.

To alleviate some of these technical issues, the use of cryptography
and its associated principles and concepts have been utilized, as it was
examined in detail in the previous section. However, with some of the
given illustrations, using this very sophisticated means of securing an
e-voting infrastructure still poses inherent weaknesses and threats.

Therefore, biometric technology has also been utilized in order to
provide an extra layer of security. Some e-voting technologies use various biometric modalities exclusively, but this is not the perfect security
solution to be utilized.

Rather, the use of biometric technology in an e-voting infrastructure
should be coupled with other layers of security, even with that of cryptography. Such security solutions are known as "multimodal biometric"
solutions, and this concept will be much further explored later in this
section.

In theory, at least, all of the biometric modalities that are used to
secure an e-voting infrastructure fall under two major categories: (1)
physical biometrics and (2) behavioral biometrics. These modalities can
be briefly summarized as follows:

- The physical biometric modalities include
  - Fingerprint recognition
  - Iris recognition
  - Facial recognition
  - Voice recognition
  - Hand geometry recognition
- The behavioral biometric modalities include
  - Keystroke recognition
  - Signature recognition

However, as it has been reviewed, not only in my previous book but
also in this book, not every above-listed biometric modality is in the
level of usage in terms of market applications. For example, the behavioral biometric modalities currently witness moderate usage, whereas

the physical biometric modalities are used much more heavily. In this regard, fingerprint recognition, iris recognition, facial recognition, and hand geometry recognition are still widely utilized, translating also into the e-voting infrastructure.

These specific biometric modalities can be used in all of the market applications that can blend into an e-voting infrastructure. These include the following:

- *Physical access entry*: This type of application ensures that only the legitimate government and election officials can have access to not only the polling stations but also to the servers that process and tabulate the e-votes and any other tangible assets that are involved with the e-voting infrastructure, including the most minute ones, such as the polling log books.
- *Time and attendance*: This type of biometric application can be used to ensure the proper clocking in and clocking out of all of the government and election officials who are employed to oversee the smooth functioning and processing capabilities of the e-voting infrastructure.
- *Single sign-on solutions*: Today, with the advent of the Internet, remote and wireless e-voting capabilities, extra efforts are required in order to ensure that only the legitimate and fully authenticated voters can cast their e-votes and have it processed and tabulated. This even has to take place at the e-voting kiosk itself, if the voter chooses to visit a physical polling place to cast their e-vote.

It should be noted that in the e-voting infrastructure of today, it is the e-voting infrastructure that is receiving wide attention and scrutinization in terms of e-voting infrastructure security: possessing the ability to, at least on the theoretical level, and guaranteeing the full verification and authentication of the voters before they cast their e-vote, whether being done remotely or at a polling station.

Thus, in this fashion, the two most widely used biometric modalities to confirm the identity of a voter are fingerprint recognition and hand geometry recognition. To a lesser extent, iris recognition and facial recognition are used also to confirm the identity of a voter.

As it has been reviewed in Chapter 3 regarding the e-passport infrastructure, there also exists a severe lack of a set of best practices and standards in terms of the development and deployment of e-voting infrastructure, at least from the standpoint of the biometric technology utilization. For instance, one particular country may use a much more sophisticated level of fingerprint recognition than another country (e.g., one government requires that all of its citizens enroll fingerprints of all 10 fingers, and the government of another country may require only one fingerprint).

Countries that have adopted their own e-voting infrastructure are now becoming cognizant of the fact that there is a lack of a set of best practices and common standards. Therefore, quite surprisingly, the governments which have adopted an e-voting infrastructure are now turning to the U.S. biometrics industry for guidance and direction to create certain standards. As a result, the policies and directives that are used in the United States are being adopted worldwide. Some of these policies include the following:

- *ISO/IEC 7816-11*: These are the standards that set forth how biometric technology may be utilized to confirm the identity of just one individual (e.g., an e-voter).
- *Common Biometric Exchange Format Framework*: These set of standards specifically stipulate how biometric templates and their corresponding information can be transmitted and sent across a network medium (e.g., in the case of an e-voting infrastructure, these sets of standards would relate as to how the biometric template should be transmitted from the voter's computer or wireless device to the servers that process and tabulate all of the e-votes).
- *XML Common Biometric Format*: This protocol specifies how biometric templates are to be transmitted from the point of origination to the point of destination over the Internet.
- *ANSI B10.8*: This standard sets forth how the unique features of fingerprints are to be extracted for one-to-one matching scenarios. (In the case of an e-voting infrastructure, this would relate to how the unique fingerprint features of a particular voter are to be extracted in order to confirm his or her identity before he or she is allowed to cast his or her e-vote.)
- *ANSI/NIST ITL 1-2000*: This protocol stipulates how both the fingerprint and facial recognition biometric templates are to be formatted.
- *ESIGN-K*: This mandate is used only in the European Union, for their respective e-voting infrastructure. In this regard, it deals specifically with how signature recognition is used when confirming the identity of a particular voter.
- *DIN V64400*: In countries with much more advanced e-voting infrastructure, smart card technology is utilized. For instance, it may not be necessary for an e-voter to have his or her fingerprint scanned in an optical sensor at the polling station; rather, the smart card that he or she possesses will contain the fingerprint recognition templates. All that needs to be done is to present the smart

card to a special type of card reader to process the fingerprint recognition templates, in order to confirm the identity of the voter.

- *BioAPI*: This is an actual grouping of biometric vendors in the United States. Collectively, they all have set forth individual practices and standards in an effort to help modernize the communication interfaces between the various biometric modalities and the applications they serve. In the case of an e-voting infrastructure, this would be the communication that takes place between the fingerprint recognition device and the e-voting kiosk, in order to fully confirm the identity of the e-voter before he or she is allowed to cast their particular ballot.
- *Biometric API (BAPI)*: Presently, in most e-voting infrastructure, Microsoft software is used in some fashion or another. This protocol merely specifies how the application protocol interface (API) should be best designed to suit an e-voting infrastructure.

Apart from the above-mentioned U.S.-based protocols and standards that are being adopted worldwide, the governments of other nations are also realizing that there are certain project management 1/N based variables (as they relate to specific use of the biometric modalities) that need to be taken into consideration before an e-voting infrastructure can be implemented and deployed once again in the next election.

Therefore, a separate initiative is also being undertaken for the governments all over the world to recognize the most common project management variables that need to be taken into consideration as they launch their respective e-voting infrastructure. Some of these variables include the following:

- *Cost of the biometric modality*: Although the cost of one biometric device is now considered to be very affordable, this cost can be greatly multiplied when it is implemented into an e-voting infrastructure. This is primarily because millions of voters will now have to be registered into various biometric databases in order to have their identity confirmed before they can be allowed to cast their e-vote. In this regard, the use of fingerprint recognition is a much more viable alternative financially to incorporate with an e-voting infrastructure as opposed to utilizing either iris recognition or facial recognition modalities.

  However, apart from the cost of the biometric modality in use, other costs and financial expenses also need to be taken into consideration, including the e-voting infrastructure being deployed. For example, there is the overall cost of the IT component as well, in particular, the servers that are being used to process and tabulate all the incoming e-votes. If an election is totally dependent upon e-voting, there will be significant other costs associated with extra memory and processing power, which will be required by these particular servers.

- *Metrics of the biometric modalities*: Since the e-voting infrastructure is an all-encompassing component to the government of any nation (primarily because the voting process needs to be conducted in the most efficient and smoothest way possible for all the citizens involved), very careful attention thus needs to be paid to the actual performance metrics of the particular modality (or modalities) in use. Thus, in this regard, the two most performing metrics to be looked at are the
  - *False reject rate*: This performance metric merely refers to where a true and legitimate e-voter's identity is falsely being denied by the biometric system that is used in the e-voting infrastructure. For example, this could be very well due to the external environmental conditions that are occurring at the polling station (such as different lighting environments if facial recognition is being used), or even the outside temperature could play a crucial impact upon the optical sensor of a fingerprint recognition device being used at the polling kiosk. Therefore, it is very critical that the chosen biometric modality to be used in an e-voting can tolerate the impacts from the external environment, which could in turn affect the voter to have his or her identity from properly being confirmed.
  - *False accept rate (FAR)*: This performance metric reflects the statistical probability that an identity of an impostor will actually be confirmed by the biometric system, and as a result, he or she will thus be able to cast their e-vote under false pretenses. In a way, this can be likened to voter fraud, but on a much higher and more sophisticated platform. Another situation where this could happen is when by mistake, a legitimately identified voter is confused with yet another legitimately identified voter. In these cases, one of the votes will be rejected, and if this keeps occurring throughout the election period, this could finally have a negative impact upon the outcome of a particular election. Therefore, a biometric modality with a sufficiently lower FAR metric needs to be implemented into the e-voting infrastructure.
- *Resiliency of the biometric system from identity theft attacks*: Given the sophistication level of today's hackers and cyber attackers, any technology or software are prone to security threats and vulnerabilities. This even pertains to the biometric modalities. Even though there are hardly any documented cases of identity theft occurring from using a specific biometric modality, scientific research has shown that any latent images left on an optical

sensor can actually be reconstructed in order to create the actual raw image, such as in the case of a fingerprint. On account of this, as well as other issues pertaining to direct contact biometric modalities (such as hygiene concerns), the use of non-contactless biometric modalities (such as iris recognition) should be given serious consideration in the use of an e-voting infrastructure.

- *Fail-safety component of the biometric system*: It is a universal fact that not every person can be enrolled into a biometric system. For instance, as it pertains to the e-voting infrastructure, a particular person may not be able to register his or her fingerprint at the e-voting kiosk of a polling station; alternatively, some voters may just totally deny and object from using a biometric system in order to have their identity confirmed. In this fashion, the government of a nation must have in place other alternative means in order to confirm the identity of a particular voter, even if it means using the traditional, manual methods, which have been utilized throughout several decades.

  In addition, the fail-safety component of a biometric system refers to its ability to literally bounce back from either a human-made disaster or a natural disaster. For example, if on an election day the e-voting infrastructure is hit by a cyber attack, the biometric system still must be able to be resilient enough to "bounce back" within minutes, so that the identification of the voters will appear to be a seamless process. Also, another very critical component of the e-voting infrastructure (as well as the biometric modality it uses) is the databases it possesses. If these databases are also hit by a cyber attack, they must be able to be restored and brought up to normal operations in just a matter of a short time, even if the backup and restoration processes have to occur at an offsite or a remote location.

As it has been reviewed extensively throughout this chapter, cryptographic principles and methodologies have been heavily utilized in order to protect an e-voting infrastructure, especially when the e-votes are initially transmitted and then sent to the central servers for processing and final tabulation. However, it was also pointed out that there are a number of critical flaws with just relying upon the principles of cryptography and encryption, and that other tools are needed as well, especially biometrics.

In this regard, the principles of biocryptography can be a prime tool for further fortifying the security of an e-voting infrastructure. In my previous book, an extensive chapter was devoted to examining this new area of cryptography.* Essentially, the idea here is to further protect a biometric

---

* R. Das. *Biometric Technology: Authentication, Biocryptography, and Cloud-Based Architecture*, CRC Press, Boca Raton, FL, pp. 329–354, 2014.

template by scrambling it at the client side (which in this case would be the voter's computer, wireless device, or even the e-voting kiosk at the polling station) and descrambling at the server side (which in this case would be the servers where the e-votes are being tabulated and processed).

The recent scientific study conducted by Ossai and colleagues in "Enhancing E-Voting Systems by Leveraging Biometric Key Generation"[*] further examined the use of biocryptography in an e-voting infrastructure. To simulate a particular e-voting environment, the simulation software known as "PROTEUS ISIS Version 7.6" was utilized. Unlike some other research studies that have examined the use of biometric technology in an e-voting infrastructure, this specific research study also employed the use of "virtual private networks" (VPNs) in order to add an extra layer of protection.

Essentially, a VPN is literally a private network that is encompassed into the overall, worldwide Internet infrastructure. The data packets that traverse across the VPN are actually encapsulated into another data packet, in order to provide for that extra layer of protection. This scientific study made use of a subset of the VPN known as the "OpenVPN." Rather than using closed source software to build the VPN architecture, open source software is utilized, as its name implies.

Specifically, the OpenVPN makes use of the virtual network interface (VNI) architecture as well. Essentially, this tool captures all incoming network traffic (which are data packets) before they are encrypted, and then sounds out the network traffic to the appropriate places of destination after the data packets have been decrypted.

In an e-voting infrastructure, the OpenVNI performs the following functions:

1. It receives the e-votes from all the voters who have casted their ballots electronically; after collection, the data packets that correspond to the e-votes are further compressed.
2. After the completion of the compression process, the data packets are encrypted (via the usage of the appropriate mathematical algorithms).
3. These compressed and encrypted data packets are then sent across the virtual private tunnel to the receiving end (servers).
4. At this receiving end, the OpenVPN tool then double-checks for the authenticity and the integrity by performing reverse cryptographic functions (this is dependent once again on the mathematical algorithms that are being used).
5. The data packets are then decompressed.

---

[*] V.C. Ossai. Enhancing e-voting systems by leveraging biometric key generation (Bkg). *American Journal of Engineering Research.* 2(10), pp. 180–190, 2013.

6. The data packets are then reconstructed into a readable and decipherable format to the end user (in the case of the e-voting infrastructure, it would be the election and government officials).

To utilize the principles of biocryptography into an e-voting infrastructure, the principles of biometric encryption have also been utilized in this scientific study. With this specific process, the biometric template of the voter is securely bound to a cryptographic key in such a fashion that neither the key nor the biometric template can be retrieved, except only in those cases where the voter's identity has been successfully confirmed in a verification (or 1:1) scenario.

To further elaborate upon this biometric encryption principle, as it has been proposed for use in an e-voting infrastructure, a separate biometric key is first generated for the voter when he or she is first enrolled into the biometric system at the e-voting kiosk. In addition, a separate digital cryptographic key is generated during this enrollment process and is later regenerated for the verification process (when the identity of the voter is being actually confirmed).

Using the appropriate mathematical hashing functions, the biometric template is then "hashed." This resultant hash then becomes the actual digital cryptographic key. This specific key is then correlated with the appropriate fingerprint, and is a private key. Subsequently, a public key is also generated (which is associated with the private key) utilizing the standard hashing algorithms. This then becomes the private/public key combination if a public key infrastructure is utilized in an e-voting infrastructure.

Therefore, when a voter casts his or her specific ballot, this e-vote is broken up into a series of data packets, and are then further encapsulated into other data packets (as it was mentioned earlier), and literally tunneled over a secured network. Then, at the receiving end (the servers in the e-voting infrastructure), these encapsulated data packets are then de-encapsulated via the AES 128 encryption algorithm. These e-votes can be now be tabulated, and the overall results can be presented to the citizens of a country (which in this study happens to be Nigeria, which has 36 independent provinces).

It should be noted that the biometric technology in this study is only used to confirm the identity of the voter before he or she casts e-vote; it is not used for any other purpose. In the hypothetical e-voting infrastructure developed by the researchers, two separate VPN setups are used and they are as follows:

1. A remote access VPN (this is used in the cases where the voters cast their e-vote from their own computer or wireless device)
2. An onsite VPN (this is used in the cases where the voters cast their ballot at an e-voting kiosk at a polling station)

In the situation where the voters cast their ballot at an e-voting kiosk, the following modules are present:

- Keypad function buttons (these are used to help navigate the voter through a series of nominees for a particular election)
- Visual display unit
- Optical fingerprint sensor
- Visual network interface

The PROTEUS ISIS version 7.6 was utilized to simulate the e-voting processes in an election held in Nigeria. The preliminary results have indicated that the use of fingerprint recognition technology (as well as the use of the biometric key generation technique) and VPNs provide a much more robust security environment than just strictly cryptographic-based e-voting infrastructure. In other words, by using two layers of security, the components making up an e-voting infrastructure can be furthermore secured, thus greatly mitigating any kinds of threats, both insider threats and cyber-based attacks.

Most e-voting infrastructure existing today primarily uses one biometric technology in order to confirm the identity of a particular voter. Although in theory any biometric modality can be used to accomplish this purpose, fingerprint recognition is widely used. There are a number of reasons for this. First, after hand geometry recognition, the fingerprint recognition has been in existence for a long time.

Therefore, it is very much a proven technology that can serve millions upon millions of people effectively in large market applications, such as that of e-voting. Second, since this biometric technology has been around for such a long time, it has been widely accepted and used by many countries.

Third, fingerprint recognition technology has become very miniature (strictly speaking in terms of hardware) and as a result, it can literally "weather" many of the changes in the external environment, especially if the polling stations are held outside as opposed to inside a specific building. Fourth, both enrollment and verification (and even identification) times have greatly increased in speed, in fact, less than one second.

On account of this type of technological breakthrough, once again, millions upon millions of citizens can be very quickly enrolled and further verified by an e-voting kiosk (or an e-voting website, if the voter is casting his or her ballot via a computer or any other wireless device).

This stands in stark comparison to the traditional voting methods, where voters could potentially stand in line for hours waiting to have their identity confirmed to cast their particular ballot.

Despite the fact that biometric technology can be used to greatly speed up the time it takes for a voter to have his or her identity confirmed and to have the ability to cast his or her vote, it is still not enough to truly secure and fortify an e-voting infrastructure in its entirety (but truthfully speaking, this type of infrastructure can never really be made 100% secure).

An e-voting infrastructure needs to have at least two layers of security: cryptography and biometric technology. Despite this multiple layer of security, various types of security issues and threats still persist. In fact, this problem is more prevalent in e-voting infrastructure that is located in developing nations (such as those in Asia and Africa than compared to those in the developed nations of North America and Europe).

To further substantiate this hypothesis, a scientific study was conducted by Olaniyan and colleagues, titled "A Proposed Multiple Scan-Based System for Electronic Voting,"* to see how the use of a unimodal biometric system (this is where just one biometric technology is used) in an e-voting infrastructure based in the sub-Saharan African nations would fare against mitigating the security threats and risks which are posed to it. The results have been astonishing. Despite using an established fingerprint recognition system from a very reputable biometrics vendor, the following security issues were still prevalent:

- *Physical violence*: The threats and actual use of physical violence still occur in many of the e-voting environments in these nations. For instance, the hijacking of elections, discounting e-votes, rigging of the IT assets of an e-voting infrastructure, as well as the physical destruction of e-voting components are still very much a commonplace occurrence, despite using biometric technology to make sure that only legitimate people can enter into a polling station and cast their respective ballots.

- *Voting by underage citizens*: This can also be referred to as simply "underaged voting." In these situations, children have been known to cast their own ballots, despite the fact that they supposedly had their identity confirmed by a fingerprint recognition system.

- *Multiple votes being cast by the same voter*: This was a problem very much prevalent when the traditional methods of voting were utilized. The concept of e-voting was created in order to help greatly mitigate this problem. Currently, this has worked in the developed nations, where more checks and balances are set forth in order to make sure that one e-vote is cast and processed for each voter. However, despite the fact of using a fingerprint recognition system, it was further discovered in this particular scientific study that multiple e-votes were still being cast by just one voter. Nevertheless, as it was also found out, this problem in the developing African nations does not stem because biometric

---

* O.M. Olaniyan, T. Mapayi, and S.A. Adejumo. A proposed multiple scan biometric-system for electronic voting. *African Journal of Computing & ICT*, 4, 2(1), pp. 9–16, 2011.

technology is being used. Rather, it comes from the corrupted politicians in those countries who otherwise encourage the citizens to register their identity at multiple polling stations.

- *An inflation in the total number of votes casted*: In these sub-Saharan African nations, apparently only 500 voters are allowed to cast their e-votes. In other words, the citizens of these countries are assigned to a polling station based upon their geographic location and are prohibited from visiting other polling stations to prevent the problem from multiple e-votes being cast by the same voter. However, this law is hardly enforced in these countries, and as a result, it has been claimed by both election and government officials that more than 1000 voters have been known to cast their e-vote at a particular polling station. Again, this security issue does not stem from the fingerprint recognition systems that are being used at these polling stations. Rather, it originates from the same voter being allowed to register at multiple polling stations. It should be further noted that the fingerprint recognition systems deployed at these polling stations are not cross-linked with each other. As a result, this acts as a catalyst that allows the same voter to register at the various polling stations. If these fingerprint recognition systems were in fact to be cross-linked with each other, the same voter would not be allowed to engage in multiple registration tactics.

On account of these security threats and risks, which still exist despite the fact that fingerprint recognition has been used to help greatly fortify the respective e-voting environments, a majority of the African citizens (in fact, two-thirds of them) do not have any faith in their own governments that their e-vote will be actually processed and counted.

In order to help further remedy these security threats and risks inherent in a unimodal biometric system, another scientific study was conducted by Abiodun and colleagues titled "Design of a Secured Electronic Voting System Using Multimodal Biometrics."*

This study also geared toward those African nations on the sub-Saharan portion of the continent. In their proposed multimodal biometric system, both fingerprint recognition and facial recognition were utilized.

In their proposed methodology, a voter is first presented with a graphical interface of the pictures of all of the political candidates for a particular election. The premise behind is that it will be much easier for the citizen to cast their e-vote and will also be afforded a certain degree of privacy.

---

* O. Abiodun and A. Tolulope. Design of a secured electronic voting system using multimodal biometrics. *International Journal of Innovative Research in Computer and Communication Engineering*, 2(12), 2014.

After the voter selects the candidate(s) of his or her choice, he or she will then be prompted to have his or her identity confirmed via the use of fingerprint recognition. This is deemed to be the first stage of authentication in the e-voting process.

In fact, it is only after the voter has been initially authenticated that he or she will be allowed to cast their e-vote and have it tabulated. After the voter has been authenticated by the fingerprint recognition system, his or her e-vote will then be processed; however, it will not be tabulated and counted yet by the servers of the e-voting infrastructure. In order for the processed e-vote to be actually counted in the election, the voter must have his or her identity confirmed a second time.

The biometric modality used here is that of facial recognition. It was not specified in this particular scientific study where the facial recognition system should be placed. It could be placed at a polling station in a number of key strategic locations, but the two most common places where the voters will have to have an image of their face taken is just immediately outside the e-voting kiosk or just inside of it.

It would obviously be much more prudent to place the facial recognition system just inside the e-voting kiosk, so that it would not be prone to the challenges associated with the external environment. In this regard, one of the most crucial variables that can affect a facial recognition system is that of changes of the lighting in the external environment.

It was concluded by the researchers of both scientific studies that the use of a multimodal biometric system, especially when facial recognition and fingerprint recognition are used in conjunction with one another, can greatly help in mitigating some of the threats and risks that are associated with an e-voting infrastructure. However, the researchers also cautioned that although this scenario is possible by using two or even more layers of biometric technology, security at an e-voting infrastructure can be only further enhanced by human vigilance and monitoring.

In other words, there cannot, and should not, be any kind of corruption among the election and government officials who oversee the effectiveness of an e-voting infrastructure. It was also noted that the use of such non-contactless biometric modalities would work well in the developing nations where the actual acceptance of biometric technology is high. For example, the use of facial recognition or even iris recognition would not work well in the developed nations such as the United States and in Europe, due to privacy rights claims and civil liberties violations.

In this regard, contact-based biometric technologies, such as hand geometry recognition and fingerprint recognition are still necessary to be used. The only other form of a non-contactless biometric technology that would otherwise work very well in an e-voting infrastructure is vein pattern recognition.

No matter what technologies or specific topologies are chosen and utilized to protect an e-voting infrastructure, there is one trend occurring that will remain a fact in the coming years and possibly even decades: The probability of voters actually visiting a polling station to actually cast their ballot is quickly diminishing.

As it has been enumerated many times throughout this chapter, casting an e-vote in an uncontrolled environment will be the way that a majority of voters will have their e-votes processed and tabulated. With the explosion of the Internet and wireless/mobile devices, voters can now cast their ballot from literally wherever they are on the planet, whether they are traveling or are in the comforts of their own home.

In this regard, the use of the cloud will become a key component in any kind of e-voting infrastructure, especially when biometric technology is being used to confirm the identity of the particular voter. In fact, the use of biometrics in a cloud-based environment was reviewed extensively in my previous book. Essentially, it was discussed that an entire biometrics platform (or infrastructure) can reside in an Internet service provider (ISP). This environment would consist of all the components that are required for any biometrics-based deployment.

This includes everything from the servers and the databases, which are needed to store all of the biometric templates and their associated data, as well as conducting the verification and/or identification transactions, and transmitting those results back to the place of business or organization. In the end, the ultimate goal of a business or organization is to merely acquire the biometric hardware they require, and sign up for a biometrics-based service account with an ISP who is willing to provide such services.

This is very analogous to actually signing for software as a service account with an ISP, but in this case, the appropriate terminology would be "biometrics as a service" (BaaS). The BaaS structure can also be extrapolated to that of an e-voting infrastructure. This means that it is quite possible for the polling stations to eventually disappear one day, and the entire infrastructure could be outsourced to an ISP, very much in the same way that software as a service tools exist today.

However, of course, this will be quite some time off in the future, and it will not appear all at once. Rather, a phased-in approach will more than likely be used until an e-voting infrastructure can literally be placed, or outsourced to the cloud.

For purposes of this chapter, the e-voting infrastructure will still be considered to be at a centralized location, such as that of an election headquarters building. This location consists of all the servers, software applications, and databases, which are required to process and tabulate all of the e-votes. However, similar to a client server network–based topology, just under the election headquarters would be all of the various onsite polling stations in the various state and local precincts, where the voters come to cast their ballot.

These various polling stations would consist of their own e-voting kiosks in which the voter would have their identity confirmed by an already-existing biometric device. After the vote is cast, these e-votes would then be transmitted to the servers of the election headquarters in order to be processed and tabulated.

Presently, in these cases the only circumstances where a BaaS would have to be required is when the voter is casting his or her e-vote in an uncontrolled environment (such as a personal computer or wireless device), and their identity is going to be confirmed via the use of biometric technology.

By placing this type of authentication service with an outsourced party such as an ISP, the government and election officials can be almost 100% assured that the verification and/or identification transactions will occur very quickly, and that the stored biometric templates will be under some of the most secure environments possible.

By utilizing such an approach, both the technical and social risks associated with using biometric technology in an e-voting infrastructure will be placed solely in the hands of the ISP, thus alleviating both the government and election officials of this burden. The biggest advantage of this, of course, is that more attention and resources can be provided, ensuring that an e-voting infrastructure is running to the smoothest and most efficient levels possible.

The only instances where government and election officials would have to consider using biometric technology in an e-voting infrastructure is if these modalities are actually utilized at the e-voting kiosks themselves. In order to use the biometric technology in a cloud-based environment (and in a very specific application such as securing the e-voting process), the National Institute of Standards and Technology has recently invented a new network protocol, known as the "Web Services Biometric Devices" (WS-BD).

The use of this specific type of protocol allows for the standardized communications between a voter's computer and/or wireless device (from which the e-vote will be cast) and the servers at the election headquarters, which will count and tabulate these particular votes. However, apart from this primary advantage, the use of this protocol also brings in other advantages to an e-voting infrastructure in those cases where the votes are cast remotely, in an uncontrolled environment. These include the following:

- Both increased time and cost savings as larger amounts of network bandwidth will be needed to process all of the incoming e-votes to the central servers.
- Since it is quite possible that there could be millions upon millions of citizens in a particular country, who will cast their votes

in an uncontrolled environment, the use of the WS-BD protocol will allow for massive amounts of biometric templates to be stored into the servers and the databases of the ISP who will be providing the authentication services.

- As it has been discussed in this chapter, it is primarily fingerprint recognition that is used to confirm the voter identities as they cast their ballot. However, with the adoption and use of the WS-BD protocol, many other biometric modalities can also be used in order to confirm the identity of a particular voter. Some of these modalities include iris recognition, facial recognition, and even voice recognition.

In a recent scientific study conducted by Chakraborti ("E-Voting Security System through Biometric Cloud Computing Integration with Virtual Server Application")[*], the implementation of the WS-BD protocol specifically into a particular e-voting infrastructure was further examined. At this point, it should be noted that a general, cloud-based environment consists of the following three platforms:

1. Infrastructure as a service
2. Platform as a service
3. Software as a service

All of these specific cloud-based platforms were also reviewed extensively in my previous book. However, as it was discovered in specific research study, in order to provide biometric-based authentication services to an e-voting infrastructure, which is housed in a cloud environment, three more distinct and unique platforms will have to be created as well, which includes the following:

- Cloud computing with biometrics as a service
- Identity as a service
- Biometric authentication for the cloud

Under the first newly configured platform, this would consist of the major components that would allow for the verification and/or identification. For example, this platform would consist of the raw image capture, the matching component (which essentially would be used to create one composite of the numerous raw images that would be captured), as well as the mechanisms that are needed to complete the

---

[*] B. Chakraborti. E-voting security system through biometric cloud computing integration with virtual server application. *European Journal of Academic Essays*, 2(1), pp. 6–9, 2015.

enrollment process on part of the voter. (The enrollment process is where the voter presents his or her unique physiological and behavioral traits for the first time to a biometric system. An enrollment template is then created, and this is what gets stored into the database of a biometric system.) This new platform would also consist of a functionality that would allow the voter to be authenticated and registered into an e-voting infrastructure whenever convenient (this is also known as the "on-demand" function of a cloud computing environment); in addition, it allows for scalability (which would permit the management of multiple kinds of biometric modalities and technologies to be used).

The identity as a service platform can be considered to be very similar to the cloud computing with biometrics as a service platform, but it allows for a much more comprehensive set of identity-based services to be incorporated into an e-voting infrastructure, as well as the management of the entire biometric templates of the voters who are casting their ballots remotely and in an uncontrolled environment.

Finally, the biometric authentication for the cloud platform consists of all the encryption-based protocols, methodologies, and tools needed to help further fortify and secure the biometric templates as well as all of the verification and/or identification transactions occurring at the server level of the ISP.

This highly specialized platform will also take into consideration any kind of further security designs that are needed, the metadata of which is contained in the various biometric templates (this can also be referred to as the "data about the data" that is associated with the biometric template), APIs, any needed bulk and parallel processing subcomponents, as well as a means for establishing redundant communication lines between the voter's computer/wireless device, and the overall BaaS infrastructure located with the ISP.

In order to fully accommodate the provisioning of these new platforms into an overall BaaS within an e-voting infrastructure, the already existing "infrastructure as a service" (IaaS) platform will also need to undergo some major restructuring. For instance, this includes reconfiguration and redeployment of the virtual servers, the operating systems that reside on it (for a BaaS scheme, it is anticipated that both Windows and Linux will be utilized), as well as the virtualized database servers.

According to this research study, the methodology by which a voter would cast his or her ballot utilizing the BaaS scheme includes the following steps:

- *Registration*: This is the overall process in which a potential voter will be granted his or her right to vote in the specific geographic location where they reside.

- *Data collection*: This is where the voter's physiological and/or behavioral data is captured and unique features are extracted from.
- *Database template phase*: At this point in the process, the unique features captured in the previous step are mathematically converted over to the respective enrollment template and permanently stored into the database for later comparison with the verification template.
- *Matcher*: This is where the enrollment template and the verification template are compared to against one another in order to determine and ascertain the level of similarity (or dissimilarity) between the two.
- *Legitimation*: This is the process by which the voter is identified and authenticated, so that he or she will be able to cast their vote in an uncontrolled environment via the BaaS.
- *Casting of the votes*: In this component, the secure website upon which the voter can cast their e-vote is presented to him or her.
- *Collection of the votes*: This refers to the transmission of the e-votes to the centralized server at election headquarters for subsequent processing and final tabulation.
- *Cloud database*: This is considered to be the final phase of the BaaS component of an e-voting infrastructure, as all verification and/or identification transactions of the voters are stored here for subsequent analysis and/or auditing.

A CASE STUDY OF E-VOTING WITH BIOMETRICS

This chapter has reviewed exhaustively the concept of voting from way back to the early 1800s to the modern day e-voting infrastructure. These types of systems have been deployed worldwide, but interestingly enough, the use of an e-voting infrastructure primarily exists more so in the developing nations than in the developed nations. The primary reason for this is not so much of a technical one, but rather it is a social one, as we have seen with biometric technology in general.

In the developing nations, such as those primarily found in Africa and Asia, the fundamental right to vote and being counted as a citizen in the eyes of citizen's own government is a freedom, which is now being greatly cherished.

Thus, the adoption and embracement of an e-voting infrastructure is very high in these geographic regions. However, in the developed nations, such as those found in Europe and particularly the United States, the right to vote and other forms of freedom (which have been endowed to us by our Constitution) are liberties that we have enjoyed for quite a long time, and therefore, taken for granted. As a result, there is almost 100% deployment rate of e-voting infrastructure in these particular geographic regions.

This is so because to some degree or other, we know that as U.S. citizens, we will be recognized in the eyes of our government, and at least on a theoretical perspective, we do have some assurance that our vote will be counted and tabulated in the final results for the respective candidates.

Therefore, as a result, the need for 100% adoption of an e-voting infrastructure is not there. This is not to say that e-voting does not exist in the United States, it does; however, it is widely dispersed across the geographic regions. In other words, there is still a strong blend of the traditional methods being used as well as e-voting.

To conclude this chapter, we look at a case study that examines the deployment of an e-voting infrastructure in Mozambique. This system was deployed in full by Innovatrics, SRO (Bratislava, Slovak Republic), a leading Slovakian-based biometrics vendor.*

INNOVATRICS AND THE REPUBLIC OF MOZAMBIQUE

Need

In June 2007, the Secretariado Tecnico da Administracao Eleitoral, a division of the Mozambique National Electoral Commission, recognized the need to enroll the country's citizens using a unified and electronic procedure. In their elections, the country has suffered from a tremendously high rate of voter fraud. Since the nation's population is greatly spread out, and even difficult to locate because of the daunting terrain, other requirements have persisted in revamping their current voting processes. Some of these are as follows:

- The use of 3500 mobile devices that could enroll Mozambique citizens who are located in the desolate, rough terrain.
- Technical support would be needed throughout all of the capitals of the nation's 11 provinces.
- Have the ability to print out a voter list at the local polling stations.
- The implementation of a centralized, national database that would contain the records of all the voting citizens.
- The overall need to deploy an e-voting infrastructure that would greatly reduce the cases of voter fraud and submission of multiple votes at different polling stations. This would call for the separate implementation of an end-to-end biometric analysis and capture system (also referred to an "AFIS-based infrastructure").

---

* Innovatrics. *Elections and Voters' Registration Mozambique*, http://www.innovatrics. com/references/civil-identification, (n.d.). Accessed May 2015.

Solution

Although the government of Mozambique chose to partner with a local company to deploy the biometrics in their soon-to-be implemented e-voting infrastructure, Innovatrics was called upon to provide the actual biometrics-based solution. This primarily involved the usage of their "ExpressID AFIS" biometrics solution; there were other components involved as well, and they included the following:

- An "IDKit PC" software development kit to provide for both the registration and authentication functionality in the country's new e-voting infrastructure.
- The actual biometric hardware, which were the 320LC fingerprint recognition scanners provided by Cross Match Technologies.
- The mobile registration units consisted of USB scanners as well as miniature fingerprint recognition systems.
- Other computer-related hardware included the usage of Hewlett-Packard-based servers as well as the Oracle 11g database (this is used to store all of the biometric templates and conduct duplication checks among the citizens).
- The use of ASP.NET to further develop software applications that would be used to help the citizens have their fingerprints enrolled into the fingerprint recognition systems and subsequently be stored into the database.

Results

On account of the implementation of this biometric system into the e-voting infrastructure of Mozambique, over ten million citizens were registered to vote over an extremely short period of time, and an electronic-based voter roll was also created for use in the future elections. The use of this particular biometric system ensured that every voter is unique in the system, thus greatly curtailing voter fraud and the submission of multiple votes by a particular citizen.

How the Adoption and Usage Rates Can Be Increased in the United States

CHAPTER 5

Strategies for Increasing the Adoption Rate of Biometrics in the United States

In summary, this book can be viewed as a continuation of my previous book, *Biometric Technology: Authentication, Biocryptography, and Cloud Based Architecture.*[*] Chapter 1 of this book, as well as the preface and further reading, has outlined in more detail the exact content topics of the previous book.

Generally speaking, this book was very technically oriented, and geared toward the C-level executives (such as chief information officer, chief executive officer, or even the chief financial officer) who are interested in procuring a security tool, such as biometric technology, and implementing it at their place of business or organization.

This book was designed and written in such a way that it would be more related to project management, which would guide the C-level executive through every step of procurement, acquisition, deployment, and implementation of a particular biometric system.

As discussed in detail in this book, biometric technology is one of those security tools that not just impacts people in terms of providing a greater level of protection, but it also impacts people at both an interpersonal and macro social level. In this book, the various biometric modalities were compared to other security-based technologies. These other tools could be a router, a firewall, a network intrusion device, and so on.

When this comparison was made, it was discovered that it was biometric technology that had the most impact upon not just end users, but the public at large, and society as a whole. Why is this so?

---

[*] R. Das. *Biometric Technology: Authentication, Biocryptography, and Cloud-Based Architecture*, CRC Press, Boca Raton, FL, pp. 329–354, 2014.

One of the primary reasons is that when a particular biometric technology (such as fingerprint recognition or facial recognition) is being utilized to confirm the identity of an individual, it is a piece of our physiological/biological selves or even psychological mannerisms that is being captured. In this regard, each individual possesses a set of unique and distinct features that makes one different from other individuals.

It is these kinds of features that all of the biometric modalities utilize to confirm the identity of a particular individual. Although this entire process may sound complex, in reality, it has become quite simplified, and just takes a short period of time to accomplish and complete.

It should be noted that some of the biometric modalities that are being used have more impact upon society than other specific modalities. There are many reasons for this (discussed in detail in Chapter 1 of this book), but some of the biometric technologies in this realm include facial recognition, the potential of DNA recognition, retinal recognition, and even to a certain degree fingerprint recognition (primarily because of its direct contact nature—there are fears among societies, especially in the United States, that people can contract serious ailments and/or sicknesses from using it).

This book focuses upon the social implications that biometric technology utilization brings to the world. Very few books have examined biometric technology in this regard, and we firmly believe that this book will bring to the table more insight concerning the social impacts that biometric technology has upon the society as a whole.

However, it should be noted that the way people perceive the impact of biometric technology varies greatly from country to country, as well as from the many geographic regions located throughout the world. For example, Asia and Africa where the economic regions are considered to be much lower as opposed to the United States or Europe, in general, the acceptance rate of biometric technology tends to be much higher.

Of course, many specific reasons can be cited for this trend, but the overall finding among social scholars is that in these areas of the world, the citizens are not recognized as unique individuals by their own governments. On account of this lack of recognition, these groups (and even classes) of citizens are not able to immediately receive entitlements, which they deserve, as dictated by the laws of their respective countries. Even if these citizens do receive any benefits, it may not be exactly what they are entitled to. For instance, through corruption and bribery in many of these geographic locations, the allocations of these entitlements can vary greatly, often favoring those citizens who are recognized by their governments.

However, by adopting a biometrics-based infrastructure, citizens of these disparate regions can now be counted and officially recognized by their respective governments. For example, by having their fingerprint or iris or even their face enrolled and contained into a biometrics database, there is now both concrete and irrefutable proof of their existence, which is something that their government cannot deny from possessing.

As a result, the appropriate amount of entitlements can now be calculated very easily, quickly, and, above all, accurately, and allocated to every citizen without much interference by government officials. Also in many of these geographic regions, the fundamental principles of democracy are not endowed or adopted.

Although underdeveloped countries do not have a communistic form of government, the exact type of law being followed cannot be ascertained easily because of the level of corruption and bribery present. One of the biggest consequences of this is that the citizens of these countries do not afford the right to vote. While elections may be held in the theoretical sense, there is no uniformity or a clear set of guidelines regarding the proper voting procedures and the counting and tabulation of the votes.

This was clearly exemplified in Chapter 4, which examined the use of e-voting infrastructure around the world. For instance, in the sub-Saharan region, many countries still use the traditional methods of voting and attempt to switch over to an e-voting infrastructure. But once again, because of rampant corruption, the citizens of these countries cannot be confident enough that their rights as a voter will be respected at the respective polling station or, for that matter, that their votes will be even counted at all.

However, with the various biometric modalities (in particular, fingerprint recognition and iris recognition, and even to a certain degree facial recognition), the citizens of these particular countries can now be registered in the appropriate election biometrics database. The advantages of using biometric technology in an e-voting infrastructure are enormous. For example, not only a quick, efficient, and highly accurate method of confirming the identity of a citizen is provided but also the issue of multiple votes being cast by the same voter is now almost eliminated.

Moreover, by making use of biometric technology in an e-voting infrastructure, the citizens of these countries in the sub-Saharan region can now be assured with a much higher degree of confidence that their votes will actually be processed and tabulated into the final results. More importantly, an audit trail has also been created that serves as irrefutable proof that votes have been cast and processed. This fact will be especially useful whenever an audit of the voting process is required, or whenever a third party is called upon to confirm the validity of the tabulation process.

In these specific geographic regions, the adoption and use of the e-passport infrastructure has started to escalate. As it was discussed quite extensively in Chapter 3, for a long period, traditional paper passport has been utilized in order for a citizen of a given country to travel overseas into a different point of destination. Over time, these traditional paper passports have evolved into what are known as "machine readable passports."

This simply means that the photo of the passport bearer is now digitized, and other pieces of information are in a scrambled format, which can be scanned and easily read by a passport reader. On account of many security issues with this, e-passport started to evolve.

Essentially, the e-passport is also another type of paper passport, but instead of a paper, it contains a special memory chip or even a smart card, which contains the biometric templates of the passport bearer. For instance, when a voter applies for his or her e-passport at the local government office, the raw images of his or her physiological beings are taken and converted over into the appropriate biometric templates (in these specific types of applications, fingerprint recognition, iris recognition, and facial recognition are primarily used).

These templates are then transmitted into the memory chip or smart card of the e-passport; as the citizen travels abroad, these biometric templates are scanned by an e-passport reader, and the identity of the foreign traveler is confirmed. Just like the e-voting infrastructure, there are numerous advantages to this as well.

For instance, the foreign traveler does not have to spend hours waiting to be processed at both immigration and customs; within seconds, he or she can enter into the country of destination (assuming that his or her identity has been positively confirmed), and many of the security vulnerabilities, which were prevalent in the traditional paper passport, are now eliminated through the use of biometric technology in the e-passport infrastructure.

However, apart from providing a means to travel abroad, the e-passport is now being used in many of the developing regions around the world as a means of proving one's identity for domestic reasons. For example, the citizens in these nations can present their e-passport as a means to confirm their identity if the traditional methods of voting are still used (in other words, if there is no e-voting infrastructure present), or it can also be used to claim medical insurance.

Above all, the possession of an e-passport in these particular regions of the world also gives the citizens an added sense of confidence that they are actually being counted as citizens in the eyes of their own government by giving them something personal that they can hold onto for a long period.

However, in stark as well as sharp contrast, it can be seen that the adoption rate of biometric technology is much lower in geographic regions of the economically developed countries. Now, this is not true for all nations in this category (e.g., in Europe, the adoption rate of biometrics is still fairly strong in nations such as the United Kingdom), but is especially true for the United States.

Given the size and the huge and complex diversity of people who make up this country, the specific reasons why the adoption rate of biometric technology is so much lower (as opposed to the adoption rate of biometric technology in the developing nations) are quite complex and numerous.

Probably the most easily understood and accepted reasons among the social scholars is that the U.S. citizens are provided many rights, liberties, and freedom by the constitution, unlike citizens of other countries (even the developed ones of Europe). As a result, we often take for granted that we will be counted as individuals in the eyes of our own federal government, and that we will receive the entitlements we deserve.

Moreover, as citizens, we often take for granted our right to vote and the abilities that we possess to travel quickly and readily overseas, as well as our legal system, which also guarantees our rights to be presumed innocent until proven guilty, until we are judged by a group of peers in an established court of law.

If for some reason or another, we are denied our "inalienable rights" as guaranteed to us by the constitution, we are also afforded certain courses of action (or recourses), which will give us back those deprived rights or freedom. In addition, many other citizens around the world are not even given this vehicle either. In other words, the bottom line is that we have the fundamental right and freedom to say "yes" or "no" to many situations that we, as U.S. citizens, face every day in life.

Biometric technology is an area where this decision can be quickly implemented. While we may view the different biometric modalities with wonderment, if the American public is asked to use a particular biometric technology, the answer is often "no." In this regard, we often claim that the use of biometric technology is a sheer infringement of our fundamental rights to privacy and civil liberties.

The topic of the low acceptance rate of biometric technology has been very controversial for quite a long time. The only time when the acceptance of biometric technology greatly escalated was right after the tragic events of 9/11. However, shortly after that, its acceptance by the American public has, and continues to, greatly declined. The most basic reason for this trend, which has been cited, is that the American public simply does understand what biometric technology is all about.

In this regard, the American public has often viewed biometric technology as a "black box" phenomenon. This simply means that because of the lack of fundamental understanding of what a particular biometric modality can do, there is very often fear and misjudgment about using it, which thus results in its total rejection. On account of this, there have been many calls in the biometrics industry for the vendors to teach not only their customers but also the American public as a whole as to how biometric technology works, and the advantages it brings in terms of security.

Another area that causes a strong apprehension of biometric technology is how the federal government uses and stores the biometric templates of U.S. citizens. On account of this lack of understanding, the fear of "Big Brother" watching is also very strong and prevalent.

Consequently, there have also been cries in the biometrics industry for the federal government to disclose how the biometric templates are utilized and stored. However, of course, a fine line needs to be drawn so that U.S. security is not compromised in this regard. If these macro steps are taken, the adoption rate of biometric technology is expected to increase in the United States.

Despite this, when compared to other nations around the world, the adoption rate of biometric technology in the United States will take longer time than expected, given the large gap that continues to exist. However, there are "pockets" of growth of both the usage and the acceptance rate of biometric technology in the United States.

It is heavily anticipated by the biometrics industry that as specific pockets of growth evolve, this will be the next major catalyst that will help to "spike up" the adoption rate of biometric technology in the United States. In other words, the fundamental belief is that as the American public (both the corporate and non-profit sectors) sees how successfully biometric technology is being used in specific applications, it will greatly help increase the believability of the various biometric modalities, and subsequently the overall adoption rate in the United States.

Therefore, the remainder of this chapter will be devoted to examining some of these pocket areas of biometric technology growth, and they can be used to increase its overall acceptance rate in the United States, focusing upon these specific market applications:

- Single sign-on solutions
- Time and attendance
- Wireless devices

In the world of security, the use of the username and password combination has long been the traditional means of securing information technology (IT) assets and granting individuals in businesses and organizations the ability to access proprietary and confidential information, which is needed to accomplish their everyday job tasks. In fact, the specific use of this security mechanism has been around for 20 years and it has worked in successfully thwarting off both hackers and attackers in gaining unauthorized access.

However, with the advent of the Internet and wireless devices, as well as the sophistication level of the cyber attacker, the username and password combination has now proved itself to be in fact one of the worst security tools to use in fortifying the IT infrastructure of any business. For example, with what is known as a "dictionary attack," a cyber attacker can very easily launch an attack against a corporate server, which houses the database of usernames and passwords. With this tool, the passwords can be guessed and figured out literally, in a couple of hours.

Otherwise, the cyber attacker might launch a piece of malware over the Internet (such as a Trojan horse), which can install itself on every computer or wireless device that accesses the network medium. Through this, as the end user types in his or her respective username and password, the innocent looking (to the end user), yet very malicious piece of malware can covertly record them and transmit to the cyber attacker for later access.

In response to this, both businesses and organizations have implemented into their security policies new requirements that mandate the creation and use of much more stringent passwords. For instance, rather than creating a password that is literally "password," the end user must now create a password that contains a mixture of upper and lower case letters, punctuation marks, and even numbers.

In response to this, the end user may very well be just tempted to create his or her password to be "Pa$$word1." Although this may technically meet the requirements for the security policies put into place, businesses and organizations are now requiring their employees to make the creation of a password to be much more complex. So in this example, the newly created password would now look something like this: "Pas$WoRd1.0."

On account of this new level of complexity in the actual creation of a password, many employees now write their newly created login information on a "post-it note" and attach to their workstation monitor screen. This trend has become to be known as the "post-it syndrome," which thus totally defeats the purpose of creating a very complex and secure password in the first place.

There have been more cyber-based attacks on Corporate America because of this reason. Subsequently, the IT support teams across the business and organizations have had to constantly reset passwords. Although this is a very simple task to accomplish, the costs in the end can be very daunting. For example, it can cost as much as $300 per employee for every password reset.

In response to the increased rate of cyber attacks against the username and password combination, as well as the staggering administrative costs of having to reset them every time it has been compromised, business and organizations in the United States are now looking toward the use of biometric technology as a means to totally replace the password. In this regard, the use of both fingerprint recognition and iris recognition are starting to gain traction in this new market segment called "single sign-on solutions." In this case, with one swipe of a finger, or through one simple scan of an iris, an end user or an employee can login into his or her workstation or even access confidential and proprietary information in just a matter of few seconds. The advantages of using biometric technology in this type of market application are actually quite enormous.

For example, there exists a means through which an end user can have their identity confirmed to a level of almost 100% (which is much greater than that of a username and password combination). In this case, the financial overhead is quite low (e.g., there are no longer any more administrative costs associated with having to reset a password—if a biometric template has to be reset, the existing one can be deleted quickly from the database, and the end user can complete the enrollment process in just a matter of seconds), the biometric modalities are very easy to implement and deploy (for instance, the actual biometric technology now physically resides in the computer or wireless device or comes as a USB device), and the actual cost of acquiring such biometric devices is also quite low. Finally, the so-called post-it syndrome is also totally eliminated.

In fact, now the leading developers of operating systems, particularly Microsoft, have implemented the use of biometric technology as a single sign-on solution into their platforms. For Windows 7 and subsequent operating systems, a component known as the "windows biometric framework" has now been incorporated. With this new technology, businesses and organizations can now even create their own specific single sign-on solution software applications in order to best meet their unique security requirements.

For the single sign-on market application, fingerprint recognition is still being extensively used; however, iris recognition is also starting to make serious headway. The adoption rate for the use of biometric technology in this specific sector has been actually pretty high among the American public, as the perceived advantages of using such modalities far exceed the benefits offered by the username and password combination. In the end, this market segment could very well help spike up the overall adoption and usage rates of biometric technology in the United States.

In the United States, a bulk of the economy as well as the gross domestic product is made up of activity conducted by the small-to-medium-sized businesses (SMBs). Many of these entities have a small workforce and, of course, an extremely limited budget, as they are first starting out into the enterprises of their respective industries. On account of this fact, many of these SMBs still use the traditional methods to keep track of the time their employees have worked.

For example, many of these business entities still use the old-fashioned time card system. That is, as an employee shows up to their respective place of employment, he or she takes an attendance card and slides into a time clock to record what time he or she started his or her shift. The method is also true when the designated work shift comes to a close and for any breaks taken during the shift.

Although this type of "time and attendance" system may have proven its worth during the past few decades, it has also proven its strong disadvantages. For example, it is an enormous expense for these SMBs to manually enter all of the clock-in and clock-out times of their employees into a spreadsheet, as well as the paperwork, which is required to accurately compute payroll and to maintain an appropriate trail.

However, another problem also persisted: "buddy punching," a phenomenon that costs these SMBs an enormous amount of expenses. This phenomenon occurs when, for example, an employee calls off sick from work and has his or her friend still punch his or her attendance card into the time clock so that he or she still gets paid, even though he or she has not physically appeared at the place of employment to conduct his or her daily job tasks.

Now, if a business is very small, this problem can be caught early on. However, if it is medium sized with a reasonable sized workforce, this could very well go unnoticed for a long period, and as a result, the employee will still keep getting paid for the work he or she has not accomplished or completed. In order to help remedy this staggering problem, Corporate America has also turned to the use of biometric technology, with much better results than expected.

For this specific market application, hand geometry recognition has been used most extensively, as well as for the longest period. However, recently, other biometric modalities have made their way into this particular market segment such as fingerprint recognition, vein pattern recognition, iris recognition, and even facial recognition. The benefits of using biometric technology have proven to have many advantages in this market application, which include the following:

- *A very low training curve*: By using biometric technology, the time and effort required to teach employees how to properly enroll and be verified into a particular modality is very low.
- *An irrefutable audit trail is created*: With the utilization of biometric technology, an audit trail is automatically kept and stored into the database for however long it is deemed to be necessary. Therefore, if a particular issue ever arises as to how many hours an employee has worked, it can be quickly and easily resolved as opposed to having manually sort through all of the time cards.

- *Payroll is automatically calculated*: Gone are the days, through the use of biometric technology, when payroll has to be calculated by entering the clock-in and clock-out times into a spreadsheet. For example, the biometric modalities of today now include software packages with their respective hardware that has this payroll calculation functionality. Also, various application protocol interfaces are now available for any business or organization to develop their own customized payroll calculation interface to meet their exact needs. In the end, the hours it took to compute payroll with a spreadsheet have now come down to just a matter of seconds using biometric technology.

- *There is no need for an administrative staff*: With the use of the modern biometric modalities and the associated software packages, which come with it, an SMB in the United States (or for that matter anywhere else in the world) does not have to hire a staff of individuals devoted to accomplish the tasks of entering hours worked or calculate payroll—the biometric modality does it all. Also, since everything is now virtually electronic based, there is no further need to have to store an enormous amount of payroll-related paperwork—it is now all stored and the database of the biometric modality that is being used is very easily accessible.

- *Buddy punching problem is eliminated*: Since each and every employee of an SMB now has to use his or her own unique, physiological/biological-based properties to clock in and clock out, the issue of punching in and out, respectively, for another employee when he or she is not present at the workplace is now 100% eliminated. For an SMB, this means that in this regard, there is no extra financial resource being spent in paying an employee when he or she has not worked. If the employees are hourly based, then using a biometric-based time and attendance system, he or she is paid for the amount he or she has worked, no more and no less.

On account of these pronounced benefits of using biometric technology over the traditional clock-in and clock-out methods, SMBs in the United States are being much more receptive toward the adoption and usage of the various biometric modalities for this market application. However, it is even more interesting to note that the utilization of vein pattern recognition has started to greatly increase. This is primarily due to the fact that this particular modality is much easier to install and deploy than hand geometry scanners, and the issue of hygiene in the workplace is also to a certain degree overcome by the use of this non-contactless technology (e.g., the use of hand geometry recognition for this market application still requires direct contact, and it could still be a serious issue of employees in an SMB).

In the end, if the success stories and the benefits of biometric technology for time and attendance applications were made more known to the American public, it is quite possible that the overall acceptance rate of biometric technology in the United States could greatly increase as well.

At present in the United States, probably the biggest market driver for increasing the adoption rate of biometric technology is that of the wireless devices, especially the smartphone market. In today's U.S. society, smartphone has literally become an extension of both our personal and professional lives.

In our personal lives, we use our devices to not only maintain ties with family and friends but also even shop online and have the respective products and/or services delivered straight to our doorsteps.

Professionally, the advent of the smartphone (as well as other types and kinds of wireless devices) has literally allowed the American workers to conduct their daily job tasks in a remote and virtual environment. Soon will be gone the days that an employee will have to travel to a physical office location in order to conduct and deliver his or her everyday job tasks.

As a result of this particular phenomenon, many mission-critical corporate files are now being stored on employee's smartphones and wireless devices. Thus, the need to secure such pieces of technology is now becoming even more paramount.

For example, as it has been discussed earlier in this chapter, the username and password combination has been the primary tool used to secure smartphones and related wireless devices, at least from the perspective of logical access entry.

In terms of the actual physical security of these technologies, specialized locks and cables have been used to secure them, wherever an employee chooses to conduct his or her everyday work activities. But even here, these tools have reached their limits.

In order to combat the latest security threats and risks posed by the cyber attacker, many of the wireless vendors are now requiring their customers to implement even more stringent passwords (in an effort so it cannot be guessed or figured out) on their smartphones. For example, in addition to using a standard PIN number to secure their wireless device, customers are now further required to implement some sort of password with a high level of entropy attached to it as a means of creating a two-level (or multimodal) security layer.

However, as it was also discussed, trying to actually enforce such a complex password policy is almost a fruitless effort, as many smartphone customers will try to find a way to circumvent it. As a result, wireless vendors have even adopted other types and kinds of security measures, such as instituting the use of a "remote wipe" functionality. With this mechanism, if the employee of a business or an organization actually loses his or her smartphone or wireless device, the network or security administrator can then issue a command from his or her workstation to actually delete all of the corporate information that resides upon it, so it does not fall into the hands of a malicious third party.

However, even this security mechanism has its flaws. For example, there will often be a lag time from when the employee realizes his or her smartphone or wireless device is lost or stolen to when the "remote wipe" command can actually be issued.

It is during this critical lag time that a cyber attacker can do the most damage by stealing very quickly the corporate information that resides on the smartphone or the wireless device.

So, recently, a majority of both the wireless carriers and computer manufacturers (such as vendors who actually produce and distribute tablets, notebooks, etc.) have now implemented the use of biometric technology to further secure their various product lines.

In this regard, fingerprint recognition has been used widely. For instance, on many wireless devices, there will be a very small optical scanner, which is used to enroll and subsequently confirm the identity of the owner of a wireless device.

The same type of biometric technology even exists on smartphones today. The true pioneer in this area has been the Apple Corporation, Cupertino, California, when they first implemented the use of fingerprint recognition technology into their iPhone product line (the actual smartphone model that carried this biometric modality was the iPhone 5 series).

In order to have a competitive advantage in this security marketplace, Apple actually outright purchased another biometrics vendor, AuthenTec Corporation, which was based in Melbourne, Florida. At the time, this business entity was the leader in manufacturing fingerprint sensors for all types of wireless devices. As a result, other major vendors such as Samsung, Microsoft, and even Google have followed suit as well.

Apart from fingerprint recognition being used, other biometric modalities are also being examined to secure wireless devices. These include the likes of iris recognition, facial recognition, and even voice recognition. In this regard, the usage of these non-contactless biometric technologies is actually gaining a much larger than anticipated positive reception among the American public. The primary reason for this is that ease of use is much greater with these non-contactless forms of biometric modalities versus the direct contact modalities of fingerprint recognition.

For example, although the actual process of confirmation of the identity of the actual owner of a particular wireless device takes only 1 second or so, the time required on part of the end user to get acclimated to where the optical sensor is on iPhone can take quite some time to get fully used to.

However, if iris recognition or facial recognition was to be utilized instead, all that an end user has to do is literally just take a picture of his or her eye or face with the camera present on the smartphone. If voice recognition was to be used, the end user has to merely speak into the receiver component of his or her smartphone, and within a few seconds, his or her identity will be automatically confirmed.

These are primary examples of how biometric technology can be used to protect the actual smartphone or the wireless device itself. There is another new type of application that is stemming off of the use of smartphones, known as "virtual payments." With this, an end user can actually download an application into his or her smartphone, which will store his or her credit card information.

Through the use of a wireless communications protocol known as "near field communication" (NFC), an end user can just merely tap his or her smartphone onto a point of sale (POS) terminal to pay for his or her products or services, and the total amount is then deducted from the application which has stored his or her credit card information. This method of payment obviously offers a lot of convenience, such as a quick and effective means of payment.

The use of virtual payments has taken off in other parts of the world and has just started to gain momentum in the United States. However, this payment methodology suffers from a serious flaw: its total lack of security. This is primarily because the use of NFC protocol is not encrypted in any way whatsoever.

Thus, the use of biometric technology has been called upon once again, not only to secure the lines of wireless communications between the smartphone and the NFC reader (which actually collects the credit card information from the virtual payment application on the smartphone) but also to positively confirm the identity of the end user who is making the virtual payment. The American public has become aware of this and actually feels quite comfortable and positive about using the various biometric modalities, to not only secure their identities but also further protect their credit card information, which is used in making virtual payments.

In conclusion, the adoption rate of biometric technology in the United States is at very low levels, and as a society, we lag far behind the rest of the world in terms of the usage of the various biometric modalities available today. This book has cited and explored in quite detail the various reasons why this is so. No doubt there are many of them, probably the biggest reason for this is that we, as a society, are afforded many rights, freedom, and liberties when compared to other citizens around the world.

It is because of this that we possess the right to exercise our choice to say "yes" or "no" to many of the situations we face in life every day, including whether we choose to use a particular biometric modality or not.

The freedom and liberties that we enjoy today will never be taken from us, but it is also a fact that biometric technology will become the upcoming security tool, which will be used to not only protect our personal identities but also secure our borders. Now, this is not to say that biometric technology is the ultimate security tool in use.

Just like anything else in life, biometric technology has both advantages and disadvantages, as well as its set of strengths and weaknesses. Truthfully speaking, it works best when it is used in conjunction with other non-biometric security technologies.

The U.S. society has to recognize this fact and also consider that the existing ways of fortifying our borders, IT infrastructure, the way we conduct business, and protecting our own selves will soon become outdated. Other security methodologies will have to be adopted and quickly deployed into place, one of them being biometric technology.

The adoption rate of biometric technology will take a very long time indeed to increase. However, with proper disclosure, transparency, and communicating the benefits it brings to the table, as well as showcasing the market applications it has been successful in, it is quite possible that the U.S. society as a whole could be much more accepting and embrace the use of biometric technology in their everyday lives much quicker than expected.

Further Reading

Many of the principles I covered in Chapter 1 were derived from my first book, *Biometric Technology: Authentication, Biocryptography, and Cloud-Based Architecture.*[*]

Specifically, the first book is divided into five chapters:

1. *An Introduction to Biometrics*
2. *A Review of the Present and Future Biometric Technologies*
3. *For the C-Level Executive: A Biometrics Project Management Guide*
4. *An Introduction to Biocryptography*
5. *An Introduction to Biometrics in the Cloud*

Chapter 1 provides an introduction to biometric technology and its major components. It covers the following topics:

- An overview of both physical- and behavioral-based biometric technologies
- A formal definition of biometrics
- The science of recognition and its granular components
- Defining what a biometric template exactly is
- What a biometric template consists of—the mathematical templates
- Breaking down some of the myths and social phobias surrounding the use of biometric technologies
- Understanding the differences between verification and enrollment templates
- An overview of the entire biometric process
- An examination of the most important biometric metrics as well as the various key performance indicators
- The biometric testing standards established by the U.S. federal government

---

[*] R. Das. *Biometric Technology: Authentication, Biocryptography, and Cloud-Based Architecture*, CRC Press, Boca Raton, FL, pp. 329–354, 2014.

- Defining what a biometric sensor is and its role in both the physical- and behavioral-based biometric technologies
- A review into the typical biometric market segments (which include primarily logical access control, physical access control, time and attendance, law enforcement, and surveillance)

Chapter 2 examines the characteristics, distinctions, advantages, and disadvantages of both physical- and behavioral-based biometric technologies. Specifically, the following subject matters are covered:

- An introduction to both the physical- and behavioral-based biometric technologies
- The main differences that are present between the physical- and behavioral-based biometric technologies
- A step-by-step guide as to whether to use a physical- or behavioral-based biometric technology
- A close examination of both the physical- and behavioral-based biometrics, which include the following:
  - The physical biometrics
    - Fingerprint recognition
    - Hand geometry recognition
    - Vein pattern recognition
    - Palm print recognition
    - Facial recognition
    - The eye: iris and the retina
    - Voice recognition
  - The behavioral biometrics
    - Signature recognition
    - Keystroke recognition
  - The biometric technologies of the future
    - DNA recognition
    - Earlobe recognition
    - Gait recognition

Chapter 3 provides a comprehensive project management guide for the C-level executive considering implementing a biometric technology. The topics covered include the following:

- Biometric technology system architecture
- The sensing and data acquisition components
- Signal and image processing
- Data storage
- Biometric template matching
- Threshold decision making

- Administrative decision making
- The biometrics project management life cycle

Chapter 4 examines the new and unique field of biocryptography, which combines both the science and the technology of biometrics and cryptography. The subject matter covered in this chapter includes the following:

- A separate review of cryptography and biocryptography
- An introduction to cryptography, surveying the following topics:
  - An examination of cryptography
    - Encryption/decryption
    - Ciphertexts
    - Symmetric and assymetric key systems
    - Types and kinds of cryptographic attacks
    - Block ciphers
    - Initialization vectors
    - The key distribution center
    - The hashing function
    - Public and private keys
    - The science behind public key infrastructure
    - The use of digital certificates
    - How public key infrastructure works
    - A review of the lightweight directory access protocol
    - Cryptographic standards and best practices
    - How to secure both public and private keys
    - The security vulnerabilities associated with hashing algorithms
    - A review into virtual private networks (VPNs)
    - An examination of Internet protocol tunneling
    - The potential of mobile VPNs
    - The components of a VPN
    - How to build and implement a VPN
  - An examination of biocryptography
    - The cipher biometric template
    - Biocryptography keys
    - Biocryptography in a single biometric system
    - Biocryptography in a client–server biometric system
    - Biocryptography in a hosted biometric environment
    - How biocryptography can be used with both VPNs and Internet Protocol Security

Chapter 5 examines and reviews the possibilities of deploying biometric technology as a full-blown, cloud-based offering. In this regard, this is known as "biometrics as a service." The topics in this chapter include the following:

- An introduction to cloud computing
- The concepts of cloud computing
- The unique features of the cloud, which consist of the following:
  - Scalability
  - IT asset scaling
  - Fixed and proportional costs
  - Availability and reliability
  - Service-level agreements
  - On-demand usage
  - Resource pooling
  - Elasticity
- The cloud computing delivery models
  - Infrastructure as a service
  - Platform as a service
  - Software as a service
- The cloud computing deployment models
  - The public cloud
  - The community cloud
  - The private cloud
  - The hybrid cloud
- Various security threats and risks that are posed to cloud computing
- Mechanisms involved with cloud computing
  - Load balancers
  - Pay-per-use monitoring
  - Failover systems
  - The hypervisor
  - Resource clustering
- Cloud computing cost and service quality metrics
  - Network usage
  - Server usage
  - Cloud storage device usage
- A review of biometrics in the cloud
  - Virtual servers
  - Storage
  - Network
- A business case study as to how biometrics in the cloud would look like and function
- A review into the advantages and disadvantages of biometrics in the cloud

Index

For Product Safety Concerns and Information please contact our EU
representative GPSR@taylorandfrancis.com Taylor & Francis Verlag GmbH,
Kaufingerstraße 24, 80331 München, Germany

Printed and bound by CPI Group (UK) Ltd, Croydon, CR0 4YY

01/05/2025

01858449-0001